Schriften des Stadtarchivs Wiesbaden
Band 9

Schriften des Stadtarchivs Wiesbaden

Herausgegeben vom Magistrat der
Landeshauptstadt Wiesbaden – Stadtarchiv

Band 9

Wiesbaden 2004

Anni Baker

Wiesbaden and the Americans

1945 – 2003

The Social, Economic, and Political Impact of the U.S. Forces in Wiesbaden

Wiesbaden 2004

ISSN 0940-8037
ISBN 3-9808702-1-9

© Magistrat der Landeshauptstadt Wiesbaden,
Kulturamt - Stadtarchiv

Umschlag (Front Cover): Fahnenzeremonie im Camp Lindsey,
März 1973 / Ceremonial lower of the Stars and Stripes at Lindsey
Air Station, March 1973; © Wolfgang Eckhardt

Druck und Herstellung: Druckerei Zeidler, Mainz-Kastel
Printed in Germany

TABLE OF CONTENTS

Foreword   I

Preface   9

Introduction   13

The Americans Arrive   21

    The Americans Capture Wiesbaden 21
    First Directives 24
    Displaced Persons 27
    Reestablishing Order 29
    Denazification 32
    Reeducation and German Youth Activities (GYA) 36
    American Organizations in Wiesbaden 40
    USAFE 41

Little America   45

    Morale and Discipline of U.S. Troops 45
    American Family Members Arrive in Wiesbaden 52
    Requisitioning 55
    Shortages 61
    Establishment of a Permanent Military Community 64
    Continued Housing Shortages 67
    American Housing Complexes 72
    Growing Resentment of the American Presence 77

German-American Friendship   83

    German-American Marriages and Families 83
    Efforts to Improve German-American Relations 86
    German-American Clubs 88
    German-American Friendship Week 90
    Other German-American Interaction 92
    African-Americans in Wiesbaden 94
    German-American Activities in the 1960s 95

Economic Relations   105

    The Americans as Employers 106
    The Black Market 108
    Currency Reform and its Effects 111
    The Economic Miracle and German Employees 112
    The Labor Shortage 113
    The Gold Flow 116
    Base Support Services 118
    Increasing Economic Challenges 120
    Financial Difficulties for American Personnel 122

Vietnam and the 1960s   127

    Changes in Base Life 128
    Declining Morale 131
    Drug Use 134

Crime 136
Racial Tension 139
The Student Movement, Protest, and the GIs 140
German-American Activities 142

USAFE Leaves Wiesbaden 153

USAFE Moves from Wiesbaden 154
Brigade 76 157
American Ghettoization 161
Hostages Released and Taken to Wiesbaden 164

Modernization and Opposition 167

Environmental Damage 167
Stationing Aircraft at Wiesbaden Air Base 170
City and State Reaction 172
BI (Bürgerinitiative) „Keine Reaktivierung des Flugplatzes Erbenheim" 174
Concrete Plans Announced 176
The BI court case 178
American Life in Wiesbaden 179
Oberbürgermeister Achim Exner 183
Erbenheim Reactivation as a National Issue 188

After the Cold War 199

Illustration Sources 208

Acronyms 209

Citation Abbreviations 211

Bibliography 213

Foreword

In the past six decades German-American relations have undergone a fundamental transformation. Initially Germany and the U.S. were bitter wartime enemies. Then, after the military defeat of the terrorist regime of National Socialism in our country, an occupying power was established under American hegemony in the Western zones. The solid bond of a common partnership between the U.S. and Germany – and not least a military alliance in the framework of NATO – has existed for quite some time now.

When the U.S. troops conquered German cities, towns and villages, they posted "Proclamation No. 1" by the Supreme Commander of the Allied Forces, General Dwight D. Eisenhower, up and down the country. In this document General Eisenhower – who was later to become U.S. president – stated that they had arrived "as conquerors but not as oppressors". Their explicit aim was to "obliterate National Socialism and German militarism". For this purpose, the NSDAP (Nazi Party) and all its sections had to be dissolved. The previously "cruel, harsh and unjust" statutory orders had to be repealed, "all German law courts, educative and training institutions" had to be closed and everyone suspected of "having committed crimes and cruelties" had to be prosecuted.

Yet soon after the first official newspaper licenses were issued, the reorganization or reconstitution of political parties and labor unions was allowed, and the functioning of schools and the judiciary resumed. Elections were held as early as 1946, first on a local level and then in the Länder (states). At the same time, measures of systematic denazification were implemented. In all these measures the U.S. authorities closely cooperated with the small minority of Germans who had courageously withstood the pressures of National Socialism, or at least had proven to be immune to Nazi indoctrination.

For many different reasons we owe lasting thanks to our American liberators who became our allies. We owe them thanks for their gentle but determined way of leading the Germans along the road of democracy. We owe them thanks for their sustained economic assistance which was granted even before the introduction of the Marshall Plan. We owe them thanks for the Berlin Airlift during the blockade of 1948-49 which, incidentally, was coordinated and organized from Wiesbaden. We owe them thanks for their assistance during the whole "Cold War" period which began in 1947. As soon as four years after the end of the war, they approved the founding of the Federal Republic. In 1955 they approved the end of the occupation regime, and finally, in 1990, they approved the reunification of East and West Germany.

Of course, the presence of the U.S. military in Germany after the end of the occupation was not free from its irritations, conflicts and tensions. Even the America Houses, the German-American friendship societies, study visits to the U.S. for young and talented political leaders, and American cultural initiatives failed to provide a counterweight. Measures such as the initial banning of fraternization, the seizure of living space, the strict segregation and separation of American and German residential areas and shopping centers as well as the rather brief stationing periods of military staff served to work against a solid co-existence and mutual understanding.

Nevertheless, the overwhelming majority of Germans gradually came to regard and respect the U.S. as a reliable guarantor of our freedom. Thus, many cultural innovations and influences from the USA – such as Hollywood films, jazz and rock music, Minimal Art and Pop Art – as well as relaxed clothing styles and "cool" manners were so eagerly absorbed in this country that German society brought up a younger generation whose lifestyle and thoughts were in sharp contrast to those of the previous generation.

It is true that there have been different studies of a general character on the history of Americans in Germany since 1945. Yet this subject has rarely been analyzed and presented from the point of view of local history. That is why I am all the more pleased that quite some time ago our city archive succeeded in engaging Anni Baker, an historian who is both competent and committed in equal measure, to work on a brief survey of this aspect of our city history. She lived and worked in Wiesbaden for a number of years and then completed a PhD at Boston College in 1997 with her dissertation *Unsere amerikanischen Freunde? Wiesbaden and the U.S. Air Force during the Vietnam Era*. At present she is an assistant professor of history at Wheaton College in Norton, Massachusetts. As an expert in European history as well as in military and women's history, she gives regular lectures in her own country in which she includes the situation in Wiesbaden, the Hessian state capital. This is why she is now regarded as "Wiesbaden's ambassador to the U.S.".

For her latest study, Anni Baker has not only utilized all the relevant American and German archives, but has also consulted with many contemporaries. These include Heidemarie Wieczorek-Zeul, a local member of parliament and Federal Minister for Economic Cooperation and Development, the two former Wiesbaden lord mayors Rudi Schmitt and Achim Exner, the present lord mayor Hildebrand Diehl as well as activists from the local peace movement. She looks upon temporary German-American misunderstandings and differences of opinion in the context of the seizure of land in urban and rural areas by the U.S. military. This was often regarded as excessive and unnecessary and led to subsequent noise pollution and environmental damage. Her theses have contributed to a substantial reconsideration of the U.S. military presence in Germany amongst the American intellectual community.

Anni Baker, as she herself points out, will always remember her years in Wiesbaden "with warm-heartedness and thankfulness" since our city has been her second home for a long time. Equally, Baker notes that her fellow Americans who also spent part of their lives in Wiesbaden – or are still living here – "are proud of being a part of Wiesbaden's history". This truly critical book cannot deny its author's American point of view.

As agreed with Anni Baker, this book is published in English in order to reach as many fellow-citizens and guests of American and other nationalities as possible. Let us regard this Anglo-American publication as an expression of our friendship and solidarity with our American friends.

Rita Thies
Head of the Department of Culture, City of Wiesbaden

PREFACE

With the fall of the Berlin Wall and the demise of communism in the last decade of the twentieth century, the world seemed to stand on the brink of a new, more peaceful era. Many thoughtful observers hoped for a "peace dividend", expecting that the massive numbers of U.S. troops stationed around the globe would finally return home.

But events in the 1990s showed that a new, peaceful world would not emerge from the ashes of the Cold War quite so easily. Famine in Somalia, civil wars in Haiti and in the disintegrating Yugoslavia, attempted genocide in Rwanda, and drug trafficking in South America and Central Asia were just some of the serious problems bedeviling the human community in the aftermath of the Cold War.

On 11 September 2001, Islamic radicals crashed civilian aircraft into the World Trade Center in New York City and the Pentagon in Washington D.C., the most deadly attack (thus far) of a campaign waged since the 1991 Gulf War by the terrorist group Al Qaeda. The group's major aims included the removal of U.S. military forces deployed in Saudi Arabia – and indeed, many Saudis not otherwise supportive of the terrorists sympathized with this goal. The presence of large numbers of U.S. troops in foreign nations, a presence which generated controversy at various points during the Cold War, has continued to elicit the strongest reactions from both friend and foe.

The impact of the American presence has not always been so cataclysmic. Germany, for example, has hosted a huge number of U.S. forces since 1945, which for the most part has been accepted by the civilian population with relative equanimity. This book examines the decades-long presence of U.S. forces in one German city. The story related here is not a tale of forcible occupation and civilian resentment, as some would have it – rather it is the complex history of an ever-changing relationship, affected as much by local perceptions and policies as by larger geopolitical developments.

There is much to learn in the story of the United States Army and Air Force presence in Wiesbaden, particularly how two former enemies, finding themselves in a vast economic and political imbalance, nevertheless overcame the past and moved on as equals. Equality does not imply continual consensus – the Germans and Americans in Wiesbaden had their share of disagreements over the years. However, they developed strategies through which they mediated conflict and deepened the friendly ties between the two communities. Of course, the lessons from Wiesbaden cannot be applied universally to every instance where U.S. forces live among a civilian population. But perhaps the example might stand as a model for American forces deployed outside the United States, grappling with the challenges of the twenty-first century.

All authors accumulate large numbers of people to whom they owe most sincere gratitude for aid in the long and often frustrating effort of research and writing. In this case, the period in which these debts were accumulated extends back over a decade, to the late 1980s, when I lived in Wiesbaden and worked for the University of Maryland at Lindsey Air Station. I would like to acknowledge the friendship and support of all my friends and colleagues of that interesting time, especially Sue Connors, Marci Lattuca, Jean Mandola, George Neblitt, Doug Lemmon, Al Lau, and Jayne Traendly, whose history of the USAF Regional Medical Center in Wiesbaden was essential to my work. In addition to my friends in Wiesbaden, I would like to thank Robert Grathwol and Donita Moorhus, colleagues and dear friends whose enthusiasm for the study of the U.S. forces overseas inspired my scholarly work.

Those responsible for the maintenance of good German-American relations in Wiesbaden provided invaluable help for this project. Former Oberbürgermeisters Achim Exner and Rudi Schmitt, as well as current Oberbürgermeister Hildebrand Diehl, generously made time in their busy schedules to answer my questions and discuss their experiences. Heidemarie Wieczorek-Zeul, currently Federal Minister for Cooperation and Economic Development, also offered her thoughts and perceptions; for her contributions I am extremely grateful. General (ret.) David C. Jones, former commander of the United States Air Forces in Europe (USAFE), spoke with me about his time in Wiesbaden. Very important as well were U.S. Forces Liaison Viktor Herrfurth and former Public Affairs Officer Klaus Müller, professionals whose recollections and expertise proved invaluable. The

Public Affairs Office in Wiesbaden allowed me full access to their archive of the Wiesbaden Post community newspaper, and most recently, Paul Nelson, the current Public Affairs Officer at the Wiesbaden Army Airfield, discussed with me the present state of German-American relations in Wiesbaden.

I would like to thank a number of others who spoke with me about their involvement in German-American affairs in Wiesbaden, including Horst Domes, Frank Beucker, and Jürgen Zettlitz, all of whom shared fascinating and thought-provoking experiences for this book. Others involved in the German-American community include Ronald and Inge Hirst, who have given generously of their time and wisdom over many years, and whose friendship I cherish.

Archival research stands at the heart of any historical study. In the United States, Walton Moody and the librarians at the Center for Air Force History, formerly at Bolling Air Force Base provided me with much of the essential archival material for my doctoral dissertation and for this book. The staff at the Center for Military History in Washington, D.C., and at the Military History Institute in Carlisle, Pennsylvania, aided me in collecting information on the U.S. Army presence in Wiesbaden. The staff at the National Archives in College Park, Maryland, assisted me in finding much valuable information relating to Wiesbaden during the postwar occupation of Hesse, the state (Land) of which Wiesbaden was and is the capital. Stephen P. Gehring and Dr. Bruce Saunders at the U.S. Army, Europe (USAREUR) Historian's office in Heidelberg were very helpful, as were the staff at the United Nations archives in New York City. Most centrally, the Stadtarchiv Wiesbaden has been my home base, my refuge, and my inspiration for all the years I have been researching the history of the U.S. forces in Wiesbaden. My gratitude goes to all the archivists there, especially Jochen Dollwet, who worked long and hard on the final preparations for this book.

The photos in this book have been provided by a number of generous sources, including the archives listed above as well as Thomas Brasser, Ronald Hirst, Mrs. June Scholl and L.T. Brezan. I am grateful for the cheerful and unstinting help all have given me.

Several colleagues have read, commented, criticized; Laura J. Hilton, of Muskingum College, provided valuable advice on the section on Displaced Persons; Thomas Leuerer shared his knowledge gained from his project on the U.S. military community in Würzburg; Philipp Gassert commented on research on the reactivation controversy in the 1980s. Ronald Hirst read a final draft of the manuscript and made careful notes which improved the accuracy of the text immeasurably. Fran Weldon of Wheaton College cheerfully accepted any and every task relating to the final preparation of this book, for which I thank her. Of course, all errors in the book are my responsibility alone.

A few special acknowledgements are in order. First of all, Dr. William O. Kerr of Wiesbaden, whose unique brand of friendship I have come to depend on, in good times and bad.

Secondly, I could not have begun, let alone completed, this work without the help and support of Axel Ulrich of the Wiesbaden archive office, who advised, encouraged, organized and cheered me on unfailingly throughout the many phases of this project. He and his wife Gilla shared their gift of friendship with me and others, for which I am eternally grateful. I have never met more generous and giving people in my life; I am truly blessed to have known such friends.

Finally, my husband, Michael, my son, also Michael, and my daughter Therese, a Wiesbaden native, have shared the trials and tribulations of the creation of this book. I hope it makes them proud.

INTRODUCTION

Wiesbaden has long cultivated a reputation as a vacation spot, a place where people from all over Germany, Europe, and the world come to rest and relax. During the summers of 1814 and 1815, for example, the German poet Johann Wolfgang von Goethe vacationed in Wiesbaden.[1] The Russian novelist Feodor Dostoyevsky gambled, and lost, in the city's casino. In the late nineteenth and early twentieth centuries, Kaiser Wilhelm II favored Wiesbaden for its spas and concerts, as did many other royal personages (and those who aspired to royalty). In the postwar era, however, Wiesbaden has broadened its importance, as capital of the state of Hesse, as a center for such industries as publishing, film, banking and insurance, and, interestingly, as a hub for the American armed forces in Germany.

Since 1945, Wiesbaden has been home to hundreds of thousands of American military personnel and civilians. Many well-known figures of American culture, from tennis star John McEnroe to author James Carroll to the 1970s pop group "America", have spent parts of their youth in Wiesbaden as "military brats", or children of military personnel. Thousands of American babies have been born in the USAF Regional Medical Center on Konrad-Adenauer-Ring. U.S. presidents from John F. Kennedy to Jimmy Carter have visited the city and its military installations.

In spite of this shared history, spanning over fifty years, American personnel and Wiesbadeners know relatively little about each other, and particularly little of past decades, when circumstances were very different from those of the present. When questioned about the history of the U.S. forces in Wiesbaden, individuals will often project their personal experiences of the American community in Wiesbaden onto the past. Some will say that the German-American relationship has always been excellent; others will claim the opposite. The reality, of course, is much more complex than any single generalization can embrace; during any given period, problems and tensions coexist with cordiality and appreciation.

This book is an analysis of the relations between the German and American communities living side by side in Wiesbaden, from the inception of the relationship at the end of the Second World War to the present time. It aims to be more than a recitation of facts; in order to reach beyond individual impressions, so often colored by nostalgia or good manners, the historian must examine the many factors influencing the wealth, morale, and power of the military community to form a clear picture of its unusual character. The size, prosperity, and public face of American military communities in Wiesbaden and throughout the world are shaped by outside events and policies, especially by decisions made in the U.S. Congress, to a much greater degree than in "normal" civilian communities. The overall health and status of the American presence, in turn, affects its relations with – and reputation in – the host city.

Not surprisingly, military and geopolitical concerns, originating at the highest levels of national leadership, have had a decisive influence on military communities. A prime example of this influence is the evolution of German-American relations in the early years of the occupation. In 1945, military policy banned all interaction – fraternization – between Americans and Germans. The ban was widely flouted, but it did set the tone for relations in the first weeks and months of occupation as distant and punitive, not unexpected in the aftermath of a fierce war. Soon after, U.S. policy changed from non-fraternization to reeducation and democratization of the German populace. This new approach emphasized closer relations between Americans and Germans, but in the model of a teacher to a student – an attitude many Germans found patronizing. As the Cold War grew more frigid, American policy changed yet again, and Americans were instructed to view the Germans not as students, but as democratic allies, partners against the threat of the Soviet Union. This is but one example of the way that evolving policy – usually in response to geopolitical concerns far removed from Wiesbaden or central Germany – refocused the direction of the German-American relationship.

Another factor of great importance to German-American relations, and to the morale and status of the Americans in Wiesbaden, was the financial health of the military community. Not surprisingly, in the 1940s and 1950s, the Americans enjoyed a high standard of living relative to the German civilians around them. They were both admired and resented for this, but in any case they were viewed as powerful and important. As the German economy gained ground, however, its very success began to chip away at the financial health of the military bases, which depended, in a sense, on a fixed income – the funding authorized them by Congress. The American community could not compete with private businesses for local employees, who naturally preferred to work for the higher wages competitive German firms offered. On military bases, cost-cutting measures became ubiquitous as the "gold flow" – currency exchange imbalances – alarmed economists and financial experts. Vietnam further hurt the economic status of the Americans in Wiesbaden, draining funds desperately needed for installation maintenance, personnel services, and public relations. The annual Open House at Wiesbaden Air Base, for example, a long and popular social tradition, gave way under financial pressures in the early 1970s. President Richard Nixon's decision to take the United States off the gold standard, while a necessary step to revive the flagging economy of the nation, severely hurt Americans in Wiesbaden by throwing the dollar-Deutschmark exchange rate into turmoil.

A cursory glance at these and other examples might suggest that the American military community was entirely dependent on decisions made in Washington, D.C., Bonn, or even Moscow. But the Americans in Wiesbaden exerted control over their own destiny as well. Both military and civilian officials in Wiesbaden have always cultivated cordial relations with one another, solving problems quickly before they poison the atmosphere. Throughout the years, official relations were bolstered by less formal contact between individuals and social groups, such as German-American friendship clubs. The U.S. community was fortunate to have an extremely effective public relations officer in Klaus Müller, a German who perfected his English while in a POW camp in the United States, and who strongly supported the American presence in Germany. For several decades he and others of the wartime generation labored to create a web of formal and informal ties between their native and adopted cultures.

The American military community is not a "normal" society, if indeed there is such a thing. Several characteristics make American military communities, whether in the United States, Germany, or other parts of the world, demographically unusual, with attendant strengths as well as weaknesses. First of all, membership in the American military community is based solely on occupation – virtually everyone attached to the military community works for the U.S. forces in some capacity or is a family member of an employee. Most obviously, active duty military personnel stationed in Germany serve in the U.S. Army or Air Force, or, less commonly, in the U.S. Navy or Marines. Family members and others might work as civilian employees of the armed forces, as employees of private companies contracting with the military, or as "non-appropriated funds" employees – civilians paid with funds that the military community earns through various services, such as restaurants and clubs, for example. Civilian employees can be American, German, or other nationalities, but they all hold identification cards which allow them access to the base. The ID card separates the military community – civilian or active duty, American or German, employee or family member – from the outside society.

A second characteristic of the military community is its transience. This pertains both to the individuals making up the community, and the physical area itself. Military personnel are rotated from Germany to the United States every few years, and officers often spend even less time in one place. Moreover, no one chooses to come to Wiesbaden, or any other military base; rather, personnel request an assignment in Germany or Europe. In almost all cases, it is true, personnel consider themselves fortunate to be sent to Wiesbaden, but they have no choice in the matter. On the other hand, there is an element of continuity in the U.S. civilian employees of the military community. Many have lived and worked in Wiesbaden for decades, and retire in the area, continuing to socialize within the community. Enlisted personnel, too, can request an extension of their tours in the city, although this request is not always granted.

The military bases themselves come and go at what seems to be a dizzying rate. Beginning with widespread requisitioning and confiscation in 1945–1946, the Americans have held a huge amount of German property in their control. They released most of the requisitioned homes and offices by the late 1950s, but retained former Wehrmacht and Luftwaffe bases, as well as assorted fields, storage depots and other miscellaneous property. In the 1950s and early 1960s, housing areas and barracks were built for the use of the U.S. forces, sometimes involving further requisitioning of property. Hainerberg Housing Area is a case in point; the sixty-seven hectare parcel was originally on the outskirts of Wiesbaden, an area dotted with small farms and forests. Land was purchased or requisitioned by the Germans for American use. Today it is the largest U.S. housing area in Wiesbaden. As a result of cost-cutting measures in the 1970s, however, some of the smaller properties, or those considered luxuries – the Steuben Hotel in downtown Wiesbaden, for example – were released to their owners, usually the federal or state government. Today, at the beginning of a new century, many of the properties once considered integral to the Wiesbaden American military community are no longer held by the U.S. forces – Lindsey Air Station (LAS) and Camp Pieri have become German housing areas, and the USAF Regional Medical Center is closed and shuttered. Of course, these changes are minor compared to those in the many military communities that have folded up completely in the years since the Cold War, including major installations in Frankfurt and Berlin. The nonpermanent nature of both personnel and bases was sometimes lost sight of during the Cold War, but this factor shaped relations between the Americans and Germans nonetheless.

Thirdly, military communities do not generally include the same demographic profile that civilian cities and towns do. For one thing, military communities are "younger" than their civilian counterparts. Military personnel can enlist as early as age seventeen, and until recently were eligible for full retirement benefits after twenty years of service. The largest numbers of personnel in the armed forces are between the ages of twenty and twenty-three.[2] Moreover, relative financial stability, combined with the loneliness of being away from home and friends, often spurs young soldiers to marry and start families at a young age. The military also has a much higher percentage of men than women, even as increasing numbers of women serve in the armed forces. Currently, women constitute about fourteen percent of the U.S. active duty population.[3] There are, of course, large numbers of military wives and female civilian employees in and around the bases. And the military community is much more racially integrated than virtually any American town or city. On average, about thirty-five percent of the armed forces are nonwhite. Enlisted forces are more black, and the officer corps is more white,[4] but except for differences among ranks, personnel of all races live as neighbors, attend schools together, work together. Segregation occurs informally, in terms of social choices. But even here, interracial friendships and marriages are more common in military life than in civilian communities in the United States.

The combination of external factors such as changes in governmental policy and easing of geopolitical tensions, and the extreme transience of personnel and installations, can alter the character of a military community, its relations with its civilian neighbors, and the experience of individuals living in the community over a period of just a few years. Therefore, an examination of the history of a military community, such as this study of Wiesbaden, will reveal many transformations over the decades, as well as levels of continuity.

It must be emphasized that the experience of the Americans in Wiesbaden cannot be taken as representative of military communities throughout Germany. Wiesbaden was different from other installations in several significant ways. First is the fortunate characteristic, already mentioned above, of a longtime commitment to good German-American relations, and as time went on, a pride in that cordial relationship. Some other military communities worked as diligently to achieve similar results, but some did not.

Second, for many years the American community in Wiesbaden had an especially elite reputation. Wiesbaden was the seat of the Hessian military government during the postwar occupation of Germany, as well as the headquarters for many civilian and military organizations operative during that era. More significantly, Wiesbaden was chosen as headquarters for USAFE in 1945, and served this purpose until 1973, when the headquarters was transferred to Ramstein. The USAF Regional Medical Center, the largest American military hospital outside the continental United States, also brought Wiesbaden status and attention, as, for example, when the fifty-two Americans held hostage in Iran in 1979–1980 were flown to Wiesbaden for medical care after their release.

USAFE headquarters and the medical center ensured that Wiesbaden's American population included a higher percentage of officers, especially field grade officers – major and above – than the typical military community. In the 1960s, for example, there were 102 colonels and twelve generals assigned to Wiesbaden, a very high number for the twenty thousand strong community. And finally, studies have suggested that throughout the Cold War years the Air Force itself was considered to be "higher status" than other branches of service,[5] a perception shared by many Americans and Germans. Wiesbadeners who were at all involved in German-American relations liked to cite the fact that Wiesbaden was one of the premier military installations in Germany, a claim that was, until the 1970s, entirely true.

This is not to say that relations between the German host community and the American installation have always been problem-free. The most serious challenges have been externally generated, stemming from policy decisions made far from the city, or from larger societal tensions in western post-industrial societies. During the late 1960s and early 1970s, Wiesbaden's American community wrestled with the same turbulence and conflict that plagued other military installations, colleges and universities, and society in general. Drug abuse, increasing crime, and racial tension between white and black soldiers damaged the good reputation of the Americans in the city, resulting in a decline in trust, widespread perceptions that American soldiers preyed on German civilians, and a corresponding belief among Americans that they were not welcome in the city.

In the mid-1970s, when USAFE left Wiesbaden and the U.S. Army tank unit known informally as Brigade 76 arrived, German interest in and enthusiasm for the American military waned, although members of both communities tried to maintain the contact they had enjoyed before the move. In the 1980s, good relations were further put to the test with USAREUR's plan to station a total of 181 aircraft at Wiesbaden Air Base (WAB), in the face of intense opposition from neighboring communities.

Discussions of the rules, regulations, and even of unofficial habits of the American population – or, for that matter, of the German civilian community – also occurred with regularity. To characterize these discussions as disagreements would be, perhaps, too strong. German and American officials met regularly through the years to ensure that problems would be solved before they became serious. Such issues included the air pollution produced by a smoky generator in the early

1960s, oil runoff from Brigade 76's tanks into Käsbach Creek, and noise and traffic concerns. In some cases, the pollution from the generator, for example, the ultimate cause of the problem was external; American military installations throughout the world were required by Congress to use lower-grade American coal in generators designed for higher-grade fuel, leading to the smoke and soot that irritated neighbors and begrimed the air. Regardless of the ultimate origins of problems, however, the two communities worked together to solve them as quickly and cordially as possible.

A military community, by its nature, is self-enclosed, mission-oriented, and nonpermanent. In spite of these limitations, the Americans and Germans in Wiesbaden have managed to create a common history in the decades after the Second World War. Today, untold numbers of Americans cherish vivid memories of their lives in Wiesbaden, while German residents can relate stories – good and bad – of their interaction with their American neighbors. The history of Wiesbaden is not complete without a chapter on the Americans; likewise, the history of the U.S. armed forces requires a look at the people and culture surrounding them as they carry out their duties. This is a study of the American community in Wiesbaden, its glory days and dark ages, its unique subculture and its interaction with its host community.

---

1 Albert Schaefer, *Goethe in Wiesbaden. 1814 und 1815* (Herausgegeben von der Landeshauptstadt Wiesbaden, 1965).

2 www.defenselink.mil/pubs/almanac/almanac/people/how_old.html. Department of Defense, „How Old They Are", Defense Almanac, statistics compiled by the American Forces Information Service, May 1999.

3 www.defenselink.mil/pubs/almanac/almanac/people/women.html. Department of Defense, „Women in Uniform", Defense Almanac, statistics compiled by the American Forces Information Service, 9 May 2000.

4 www.defenselink.mil/pubs/almanac/almanac/people/minorities.html. Department of Defense, „Minorities in Uniform", Defense Almanac, statistics compiled by the American Forces Information Service, 9 May 2000.

5 Charles C. Moskos, *The American Enlisted Man: The Rank and File in Today's Military* (New York: Russell Sage Foundation, 1970).

THE AMERICANS ARRIVE

As the Americans moved through western Germany in late 1944 and early 1945, they were faced with physical chaos, a disintegrating economic system, countless victims of National Socialist brutality from across Europe, and, in many areas, a political vacuum – all this while the war dragged on. The U.S. armed forces, like armies everywhere, were trained to fight wars, but in Germany they did more than conquer militarily; at war's end, the Americans assumed responsibility for a zone of occupation in the south, encompassing the West German states of Bavaria, Hesse, and part of Baden-Württemberg. In this role, they had contact with Germans on many levels, not simply as enemies in combat.

But U.S. policy toward defeated Germany was unclear and even contradictory. From the very first days of the Occupation, German-American relations were guided and influenced by policy directives from Washington. Guidelines for occupation policy were spelled out in a document known as JCS1067, which mandated harsh treatment of the German civilian population rather than an approach based on relief and reconstruction. While the directive was eventually superseded by the more conciliatory JCS1779, the official emphasis on containment and punishment could be seen in the initial interaction between the Americans and Germans.

The Americans Capture Wiesbaden

Wiesbaden was just one of hundreds of cities, towns and villages captured by forces of the 80th Infantry Division of the XX Corps, U.S. Third Army, in their slow and methodical sweep across southern Germany in the spring of 1945. Unlike other central German cities which were centers of industry or military activity, Wiesbaden was not an especially significant target of the advancing armies, and its occupation, on 28/29 March 1945, took place without resistance or fanfare. Most citizens continued their daily activities in spite of the impending change. Inge Hirst, a high school student in 1945, recalled her family's first encounter with the invading forces:

> We didn't realize the Americans were that close on the Rhine. We were happy-go-lucky girls, not paying

attention. No one was really afraid. My sister was on the Biebricher Allee, she was coming home from her friend's house on a bicycle, and she saw two rows of soldiers marching. She was only 16 or so. She rang the little bell because she wanted them to let her through, and they did. After she was through the line, she thought, oh my God, what was that.[1]

Teenagers, even in wartime, it would seem, had their own pressing concerns; most adult residents awaited the American approach to Wiesbaden with a mixture of hope and trepidation. Some regarded the Americans as liberators, and optimistic rumors spread like wildfire. One tale suggested that no buildings would be requisitioned because the Americans brought their own housing facilities with them. Others were more fearful; gossips claimed that the Americans were forcing all captured German airmen to enlist in the U.S. Army. An American intelligence operative noted that "the town is (...) full of rumours [sic] and some of them are really fantastic".[2] The only point of consensus was that the Americans – as liberators, oppressors, or in some unknown capacity – would arrive eventually.

A few far-sighted and responsible city officials helped to make the transition from German civilian authority to American military rule a relatively smooth one. They accepted the inevitability of U.S. military occupation, and they struggled in the last days to avert a state of anarchy. Stadtkämmerer Dr. Gustav Heß, Verwaltungsrat Fritz Reeg, Stadtwerke director Christian Bücher, and others led the way in opposing Hitler's "scorched earth" policy, endorsed by Nazi functionaries in Wiesbaden. After Bürgermeister Felix Piékarski, by all accounts a committed Nazi, had abandoned his post and fled the city, Heß and Reeg cancelled a potentially disastrous evacuation decree and formed an emergency government to await the arrival of Allied troops.[3]

The advance on the Rhine-Main region began on 16 March, as the 80th Infantry Division moved toward the area from the southwest. U.S. troops of the 317th Infantry Regiment captured Mainz on 22 March, but the bridges over the Rhine River had been destroyed by retreating Wehrmacht troops, which resulted in a six-day delay in the capture of Wiesbaden. Finally, on 28 March, the 2nd Battalion of the 317th traversed the great river in assault boats, arriving at Kastel and Kostheim where, according to after-action reports, "strong resistance met the assaulting troops" in the form of small arms fire and anti-aircraft guns.[4] These areas were heavily shelled in response – in the last days of the war the U.S. forces did not risk American casualties, but rather responded to the feeblest resistance with overwhelming firepower.

The men of the 80th Infantry Division, 3rd U.S. Army load their vehicles and materiel into landing craft, in preparation for crossing the Rhine River at Mainz.

Wiesbaden avoided such a fate, although a few Nazi holdouts made plans to defend Wiesbaden to the end. Local Nazi leader Philipp Brest organized a Volkssturm defense unit and dispatched it to the Biebricher Allee, along which the Americans were likely to enter the city. The unit, made up of six elderly men and six adolescent members of the Hitler

Youth, had at its disposal a few World War I era weapons and a barricade of felled trees – not likely to keep the Americans at bay for long. The leader of the tiny troop, seventeen-year-old Erich Diefenbacher, wisely dispersed his men, the adults with fictitious written orders to collect food and blankets, the Hitler Youth with instructions to bring supplies from their homes, where, Diefenbacher correctly presumed, their mothers would force them to stay.[5] This strategy undoubtedly averted a great deal of pointless damage and destruction, not only to the members of the troop but to the city itself.

As a result, the 1st Battalion of the 317th, having crossed the Rhine on a temporary pontoon bridge, marched quietly past the abandoned barricade on the Biebricher Allee toward Wiesbaden. Residents of Biebrich, the first to encounter American troops, placed white bed sheets or table linen in their windows as a sign of nonresistance.

The 3rd Battalion also crossed the river, moved to the north, and captured Erbenheim and Bierstadt. At 5:45 on the morning of 28 March, Heß ordered that a white flag be raised outside the city museum on Wilhelmstraße, and within a few hours Americans from the 1st Battalion had arrived in the heart of the city. According to Wiesbaden historian Herbert Müller-Werth, one Major Chatnay appeared at the Rathaus on 29 March at eight o'clock in the morning to accept the official transfer of authority.

First Directives

The first imperative for the American occupiers of Wiesbaden was to ensure the safety of the U.S. troops in the city. The underground resistance movement known as Operation Werewolf, while grossly overestimated by U.S. military intelligence, had in fact successfully carried out acts of violence in other occupied towns. American officers wished to protect their men from even isolated acts of revenge. To this end, Chatnay decreed a general curfew for civilians, except during the hours from seven to nine in the morning and from three to six in the afternoon, and ordered that all weapons, from military machine guns to privately-owned antique pistols, be surrendered. This strict curfew, similar to those in other towns, remained in effect until the unconditional surrender of Germany on 8 May.

American soldiers then posted General Eisenhower's famous

Proclamation Number One, introducing the U.S. Occupation to the civilian population, on advertising columns and walls of buildings. "We come as conquerors, not as oppressors", the decree announced. The Proclamation stated that the Americans possessed absolute authority and that "[e]veryone in the occupied area must obey the orders and publications of the military government immediately and without opposition". While Proclamation Number One did not address specific aspects of the U.S. Occupation, its stern language dimmed the hopes of those who expected a more friendly "liberation" presence.

Chatnay's next concern was to provide billeting for the weary troops. Contrary to earlier rumors, the Americans did not bring their own housing facilities, but instead requisitioned buildings in the center of Wiesbaden to be used for housing and offices. The Hotel Rose became the headquarters for the 80th Infantry Division,[6] "where the German managers treated the troops as though they were visiting royalty", according to one American account.[7] The entire area was cordoned off with barbed wire, which "ran from Luisenstrasse to Taunusstrasse and down about 300 yards, enclosing the Nassauer Hof and back to Luisenstrasse (…) the only way to get in was with a pass", recalled an American pilot stationed in Wiesbaden in 1946.[8] In the next weeks and months, officials requisitioned many other properties outside the enclosed center in the downtown area as well, to accommodate the growing number of American personnel in the city.

The combat troops of the 317th were not to remain in Wiesbaden for long. They rested for two days, and on 31 March they resumed their push toward the strategically more significant target of Kassel, in the north. Before leaving, the 317th transferred authority over Stadtkreis (SK) Wiesbaden to Military Government (MG) Detachment F1D2. Det. F1D2, headquartered in Wiesbaden, was also placed in charge of a larger area known as Regierungsbezirk (RB) Wiesbaden, which encompassed the towns and villages in the region, extending as far as the Taunus Mountains. In July, an MG unit known as E1A2 took over administration of the RB. From the first days of the U.S. Occupation, then, Wiesbaden emerged as an administrative center for the American forces.

In April 1945, Det. F1D2 consisted of twelve officers and twenty men, under the command of Lt. Colonel Leroy Cowart. The unit requisitioned a large office building at Bierstadter Straße 7,[9] in one of the most beautiful and elegant sections of the city, and began the task of governing Wiesbaden and the surrounding area. In addition to the orders issued by the 317th, F1D2 gave further instructions to the civilian populace, which were posted on walls and advertising pillars and announced over mobile loudspeakers confiscated from the Wehrmacht. F1D2 directives limited travel to no more than six kilometers from home, and required MG permits for vehicles. Nazi paraphernalia was prohibited, as were assemblies of almost all kinds. A dusk-to-dawn blackout, which had been in effect throughout the war years, continued under the Americans until the end of the war in May. All post, telephone and telegraph offices were closed and placed under guard, and civilian communication services halted, not to be resumed in the U.S. Zone until October 1945.[10] Cowart ordered the confiscation of all cameras, binoculars – even opera glasses – and communications devices, including carrier pigeons, which were to be "either killed or [have] their wings clipped".[11] Det. F1D2 also confiscated all property belonging to the Wehrmacht or to any organ of the Nazi Party. These included the airfield in Erbenheim known as Y-80, which had been captured by the 1st Battalion of the 317th; the recently completed military hospital on Wielandstraße; and the adjacent Ochamps, Oranien, and Gersdorff Kasernes on Schiersteiner Straße.

As soon as Det. F1D2 had addressed immediate security and logistical problems, it turned to tasks that would challenge even the most resourceful government. The difficulties facing the occupiers stemmed from Nazi policies and the devastation resulting from the criminality of the regime. Unfortunately, however, Occupation authorities had little to go on but JCS 1067, the directive issued by the Joint Chiefs of Staff, which was harsh and punitive but provided little concrete detail. Of immediate concern were, first, the shelter and rehabilitation of large numbers of refugees and displaced persons in Germany, and second, the denazification and reeducation of German society.

Displaced Persons

The broadest definition of "Displaced Persons", or DPs, would include all civilians displaced by the war. However, in postwar Europe there were two categories of DPs – United Nations DPs, who were eligible for UN rations and shelter in a UN-run camp, and ex-enemy DPs, who were not eligible for UN assistance.[12] Occupation authorities established two major centers for UN DPs in Wiesbaden. The first was the former Gersdorff Kaserne on Schiersteiner Straße. This installation had a long and proud history as a barracks for troops of the Duke of Nassau, and later for elite Prussian units.[13] It was occupied during the 1920s by French and British troops, and then became a Wehrmacht post. In later years a popular rumor among the American forces said that the Gestapo had used the installation, but this tale, like so many others, was untrue. In April 1945, Gersdorff became Schiersteiner Kaserne Displaced Persons' Camp No. 563. The second housing area for DPs was Camp 712, established in December, on the former Wehrmacht installation in Kastel known as Von Goltz Kaserne.

Both camps were administered by trained personnel of the United Nations Relief and Rehabilitation Administration (UNRRA), mostly civilians from Western Europe – France, Belgium, the Netherlands, and Great Britain.[14] Camp 563 housed thousands of laborers who had been brought, usually forcibly, from German-occupied regions throughout Europe to work in Germany, in local factories, farms, or in the service of the Wehrmacht. The majority of residents at 563 were of Eastern European extraction. Precise numbers fluctuated, but throughout 1945 the camp's population hovered at around 7,500, of which approximately 6,000 were from Poland or the Baltic nations of Latvia, Estonia, and Lithuania. The remainder of the DPs at 563 represented a wide range of nationalities, including most of the ethnic groups of Western Europe. Camp 712 housed mostly Ukrainians as well as forced laborers who many years earlier had had their citizenship taken away, and were registered as stateless persons.

UNRRA personnel faced a difficult balancing act in providing food, medical care and a suitable living environment for the DPs. Because of their status as victims of the Nazi regime, DPs were entitled to extra rations unavailable to German civilians. Germans were authorized about 1,300 calories per day, while DPs could receive up to 2,500. This system, while well-intended and understandable, created tension between the German population, the Occupation authorities, and the DPs.[15] As food shortages became more severe, the MG received numerous reports that DPs were selling food and medicine on the black market. Security officials were hard-pressed to prevent abuses of the system by people accustomed to a harsh and lawless existence.

Ethnic antagonism was a serious problem that had emerged even before the establishment of the camps. Especially in Camp 563, where several Eastern European groups resided together, nationalist tensions created a dangerous atmosphere, and fighting frequently broke out. UNRRA personnel, following the example of the Allied forces as they moved eastward in the fall of 1944, separated the various nationalities into distinct "neighborhoods" with their own governing bodies. Relief workers also dealt with violence in the camps by repatriating Western European DPs as quickly as possible. They reasoned that, in view of the extreme overcrowding in the camps, it was illogical to detain them when their homes were less than a day's journey away. The fate of the Ukrainian DPs in Camp 712 was more tragic. They feared Soviet retaliation, or did not wish to return to life under Soviet rule, and they steadfastly refused UNRRA offers of transportation home. Similar concerns affected Russian prisoners of war, who, with the promise of better treatment by their captors, had volunteered for duty under the Nazis. The Yalta agreement had allowed for forced reparation of Soviet citizens, but neither Ukrainians nor Russian collaborators evinced any desire to return home. After much resistance, these DPs were unceremoniously transported to the Soviet Zone of Occupation, where, according to witnesses, they were shot by Soviet military authorities.

When the Americans occupied Wiesbaden and the DPs liberated from local labor camps, they not unnaturally took revenge on their captors, sometimes violently. One of the few rumors that, according to an Intelligence Division report, "seems to have some foundation in fact, is the one about Poles and Russians going out and shooting people at night and breaking into houses".¹⁶ The same report noted that German civilians wondered at the Americans' inability to discipline the DPs. After twelve years of Nazi methods, the civilian population may well have viewed any attempt to control DPs while adhering to principles of law as weak and ineffectual.

Angry and vengeful DPs, desocialized by years of Nazi brutality, presented a security threat to American forces as well as to German civilians. To make matters worse, former members of the SS and other Nazi organizations from the Ukraine or the Baltic countries often attempted to register as DPs, at once shedding their former identities and qualifying for generous rations. There were even cases of German Nazis attempting to change identities and register as DPs. Of course, former Nazis and collaborators were expelled from the camps when they were discovered, but the necessary investigations, conducted by the Army, took valuable time and resources from other urgent tasks.

UNRRA personnel in Wiesbaden not only managed the local camps, but, as representatives of one of the three UNRRA headquarters in Germany, they also oversaw camp operations throughout the north central zone, designated as District 2. As administrators of District 2, they worked closely with the MG, and were dependent on it for supplies, security, and even office space. Not surprisingly, considering the chaotic conditions at the time, MG received its share of criticism from the UN workers. "The relief programme", one UNRRA report noted, "has been carried through. [But] apart from furnishing the essentials of subsistence, the Military [sic] have no understanding for other but restrictive measures of discipline."¹⁷ On one hand, the MG came under fire from German civilians for being too lax in combating DP crime, while on the other it was criticized by UNRRA personnel for being overly concerned with punitive discipline. Such was the lot of the MG in those disordered early days.

Reestablishing Order

Considering the chaotic situation at war's end, crime in Wiesbaden was not as bad as it might have been. "[Even] in the light of conditions, a defeated people, shattered cities, a scarcity of food, clothing and shelter, a disorganized, demoralized police force, inexperienced and unarmed, the situation has never been alarming",[18] concluded the MG Public Safety Division optimistically. The dusk-to-dawn curfew put into effect by Det. F1D2 doubtless helped control criminal behavior, but even when the curfew was lifted on 30 May 1946, a predicted increase in crime did not materialize. Most offenses, before and after the lifting of the curfew, were minor and nonviolent ones involving theft, black marketeering, unauthorized possession of U.S. property, entering unauthorized areas, moral offenses, and crossing borders. In fact, many of these were only classified as crimes in the peculiar circumstances of Occupation Germany. The perpetrators, of course, included not only DPs, but German civilians and American military personnel.

American personnel were most likely to be arrested for public drunkenness or disturbing the peace, crimes related to their relative freedom from restraint in Germany. DPs, on the other hand, were often blamed for theft and looting. In a report in 1946, for example, the Provost Marshall of the 3rd Infantry Division estimated that fifty percent of the crime in Wiesbaden was committed by DPs,[19] including DPs employed by the MG. "I caught two Polish guards going through the vacated houses looking for loot", reported a soldier assigned to patrol

Penalty for Looting	Verbot der Plünderung
All persons are warned that **Plundering, Pillage and Looting,** is a violation of Military Government Proclamation Ordinance 1, Article 1, Section 16 and is a capital offense, punishable by death.	Alle Personen werden darauf aufmerksam gemacht, daß **Plünderung, Raub und Diebstahl,** eine Verletzung der Military Government Proklamation, Befehl Nr. 1, Artikel Nr 1, Sektion 16 darstellen und als schwere Verbrechen mit dem Tode bestraft werden können.

A placard warns that the punishment for looting is death – a punishment that was never enforced.

American housing areas. "I ordered the[m] back to their posts and gave them a severe reprimand for leaving their posts and looting."[20] In this case, as in many others, the punishment was less than draconian – stealing was so common that the jails would have overflowed if every petty theft were punished by incarceration.

Closer examination suggests that blame for criminality should have been much more broadly assigned, and that DP crime rates were exaggerated in MG reports. German civilians were at least as likely to be culprits in looting or stealing incidents. "[Upon returning from a trip] we found three German boys and a middle-aged man and the owner of the house and his wife in our billets [on Lahnstraße]", reported one member of the 3rd Infantry Regiment:

> *The sign on the door saying the room was 'off limits as soldiers were living there until Monday evening' was torn from the door, and the other door connecting our room with an adjoining room was broken open. The Germans were supposed to be cleaning up any papers that were left behind in the homes but their main object was looting, as all PX rations for the week were stolen including cigarettes, candy, plus toilet articles (...). We searched the Germans whose duty it was to clean rooms. We found 2 flashlights, soap, cigarettes (...).*[21]

A soldier from the same unit recalled that "after the convoy had cleared the area the German civilians began swarming through the vacated buildings removing furniture etc., despite the presence of Polish guards and German policemen".[22] Police sometimes participated in looting themselves: "(...) we noticed German police taking articles of household goods and passing them over the fence to German women",[23] reported one soldier. Stolen goods could be traded on the black market, a substitute economy in which virtually all Germans, DPs and Occupation personnel of various types participated (see chp. "Economic Relations").

A more important problem for the police involved re-legitimizing their role as upholders of the law – after twelve years of state terror it was difficult for Germans and DPs to trust any type of security forces. MG's

Public Safety Division began the process. Nazis were removed from their positions, American instructors provided training in "democratic police methods", and German police worked alongside American law enforcement units. According to a Public Safety report, "[t]his system of joint patrols greatly enhances the prestige of the German Police in the eyes of the public and affords them a better opportunity to accomplish their police mission".[24] As the Occupation went on, the Americans increasingly relied on Germans to provide security for the civilian population.

For those unlucky enough to be charged with crimes, the MG established a system of Summary, Intermediate and General courts. The courts tried U.S. military personnel and civilians, Allied nationals, Germans, and DPs – anyone charged with a crime in the U.S. Zone. In theory, any qualified Allied national could serve on the MG courts, but in practice all court personnel were American, with the exception of translators, clerks and other lower-level employees. The German court system had not disappeared, but it was severely compromised by its support or tolerance of the Nazis. The Americans found it difficult to reform the justice system because of the scarcity of trained lawyers and judges free of the National Socialist taint. Only slowly did the Americans locate sufficient numbers of qualified individuals to serve in German courts.

Denazification

Denazification, or the purging of German society of all vestiges of Nazism, was another imperative of the MG in Wiesbaden and elsewhere. Even before Germany had surrendered on 8 May 1945, American authorities viewed denazification as one of their principal responsibilities. F1D2 began its first denazification procedures immediately, when it removed from office all civilian government officials who had maintained any ties to the Nazi Party or government. Dr. Heß, the leader of the emergency government, although competent and well respected by the Americans, was thus deemed ineligible to remain in the government because of his former position as city treasurer under the Nazi regime. In spite of their disqualification, Cowart ordered Heß and other city officials to remain at their posts until replacements could be found. On 21 April,

Georg Krücke, who had served as Wiesbaden's Oberbürgermeister until his removal by the Nazis in 1933, was elevated to his former position. Krücke established a new city government within the next few weeks, appointing civilian officials with experience and ability, but the final authority rested with the MG.

Unfortunately denazification proved to be a much more difficult task than this early example would suggest. Even within the city government, an intelligence report noted, "[e]verybody says that there are still Nazis in the city administration but they expect that they will be fired soon. They realize that it is impossible to dismiss all the Nazis at once".[25] Under the rigorous criteria used by the Americans, a forbiddingly large number of local officials would be characterized as Nazis.

Because early, informal denazification was done unsystematically, irregularities and hypocrisy were rampant. The Americans needed knowledgeable German help so desperately in the early months that licenses or operation permits, functioning as certificates of denazification, were given out with little oversight "by everyone from the corporal of the first squad that entered a town to functional officers of Military Government",[26] complained one report. In July, U.S. Forces, European Theater (USFET), the newly created umbrella entity in charge of all U.S. forces in Europe,[27] issued directives aimed at standardizing denazification in the U.S. Zone. USFET officials circulated a list of previous affiliations that would be grounds for removal and punishment, and detailed the methods that would be used to investigate employees. The MG created a separate division, known somewhat mysteriously as the Special Branch, to conduct denazification investigations.

At first denazification procedures were to apply only to individuals in the German government and public service, but in August 1945 USFET expanded denazification to apply to leaders in private enterprise and the professions. Finally, Law No. 8, the most sweeping denazification decree, was passed on 26 September. It stated that members of the Nazi Party or Nazi organizations were prohibited from working in any capacity other than that of common laborer. According to yet another rumor, Lt. General Lucius D. Clay, then deputy Military Governor of the U.S.

Zone, passed this law in anger when he discovered that his barber had been a member of the Nazi Party. This law affected virtually all adults in the U.S. Zone, and the Special Branch soon found itself overwhelmed with Fragebögen, the notorious questionnaires required of German adults.

As the effects of Law No. 8 began to be felt by large numbers of Germans, denazification became one of the most unpopular policies of the MG. Most Germans agreed that Nazi bigwigs should be removed from positions of leadership, but when the program began to punish anyone who had been a member of the party at any time, it lost a great deal of support. It did not appear to take into account the fact that many people had joined the party only in order to keep their jobs or for other tactical reasons, rather than out of sincere enthusiasm for Nazi aims. Perhaps more significantly, the denazification program of the Americans did not punish fervent supporters of Nazism who had never belonged to any official Nazi organization but who were guilty of committing crimes in the name of the party.

The whole system reached gridlock rapidly because of the large volume of cases to be examined and the small number of American personnel available to handle all the work. On 5 March 1946, the American denazification program was turned over to the German Ministry for Political Liberation, under German Law No. 104 for Liberation from National Socialism and Militarism. Rather than being administered by the Special Branch, denazification was carried out by tribunals run by Germans, of which there were 104 in Hesse.

Although this eased the burden for the Americans somewhat, several major problems with the German tribunals emerged. First, most of the personnel were lay people who needed training before they could make fair judgements about the complicated matter. Second, there was an overall lack of space for housing, offices and equipment, and the tribunals were forced to vie for space with other organizations, a struggle they often lost, especially if competing with American MG units. Third, as time went on, the tribunals became targets of criticism, from both German and American circles, that the punishments meted out were overly lax. In order to ensure that denazification as conducted by the German tribunals was sufficiently rigorous, the MG created the Denazification Division, to replace the Special Branch. This new division spot checked cases and reviewed decisions. Oversight, however, did not halt widespread criticism nor did it make the process any less cumbersome.

All in all, the denazification program was unpopular with Americans and Germans alike, mostly because it was at once too harsh on individuals who had only reluctantly been part of the Nazi system, and at the same time seemed to let more serious offenders off the hook. For many Americans in the Occupation forces, denazification must have appeared to be somewhat bewildering. While Americans were aware, of course, of Nazi crimes, and initially viewed the Germans as enemies in war, interaction with German individuals softened these perceptions. Americans found it difficult to punish local officials and businessmen who took pains to be friendly and helpful to the Occupation forces – but who, perhaps, had been as friendly and accommodating to Nazi officials in earlier years. Moreover, Americans had not themselves suffered from occupation by the Nazis. They had relatively little direct experience of the cruelty of the regime, in the way the French or Russians did. In numerous individual cases, then, Americans bent the rules for their new friends.

Some continued to object to the sloppiness of denazification. Investigator Erwin Benkoe with the MG's Information Control Division filed harshly critical reports detailing the ease with which former and unrepentant Nazis still operated in the city:

> *A NSDAP Blockleiter continued to cash in membership fees of Nazis in the NSDAP after the Americans arrived (…). Wehrmacht officers have secret meetings regularly in Friedenstrasse (…). Nazi Party meetings take place regularly, for instance in Parkstrasse 67 (…) a Nazi activist, who had terrorised his surroundings (Blockleiter Koerner, Augusta Str 5, Wiesbaden) is now Procurist in Zellstoff Fabrik Waldhoff and is as fresh and proud as ever; a NS Frauenschaftsleiterin (Feikert, grocery am Markt, Wiesbaden) tells her friends "(…) just wait till my friends from the SS come back (…)", a Nazi activist, who*

> *had fled when the Americans arrived, now returned and dragged the Jew who was put into his apartment by the housing office into court to have him evicted, because he (the Nazi) needs his place to live in, (the case Katz Wiesbaden Courthouse, September 8th); in these and countless other cases the Nazis are anything but subjugated, demure or beaten. They keep friends with each other, [and] instigate with fellow Nazis against others, trying to reassert themselves.*[28]

In the same report, Benkoe charged that Nazis who had been ordered to clean the streets twelve hours a week rarely showed up for duty, and when they did, they "did not work too hard". He claimed that Mayor Krücke reluctantly ordered the Nazis to work only after the MG insisted, and fabricated excuses to delay the work:

> *Oberbuergermeister Kruecke was in no rush to have his friends, the Nazis, clean the streets. After the first week passed, Kruecke sent word back to Military Government, there was not enough gasoline, not enough trucks, to haul the debris. He was told to get pushcarts. After another week Kruecke sent word back, not enough shovels and pickets etc. Three weeks passed by before the first small contingency of Nazis appeared for work, taking it more easy than the WPA ever did.*[29]

It is difficult to know what to make of these reports. In another report, Benkoe alleged that widespread and continuing discrimination against Jews in Wiesbaden was a growing problem, but as Benkoe's source noted, "[there are] many things that one really knows are true, but which one cannot show proof. The fair Americans demand only facts – no rumors".[30] Benkoe's reports often contained few facts, but numerous passionate allegations of wrongdoing and injustice.

Reeducation and German Youth Activities (GYA)

A second level of effort to eliminate vestiges of Nazism involved "reeducation" of the German population. As early as June 1945, the State

Department issued guidelines on German reeducation, but for the next two years, denazification was ascendant, in keeping with punitive regulations. In July 1947, however, new directives emphasized reconstruction and rehabilitation rather than punishment in occupied Germany. Moreover, by 1947, fear of communism effectively counterbalanced the urge to punish the Germans, and food and fuel shortages compelled the Occupation government to interact with the Germans in a relief or charitable capacity. These factors resulted in a shift toward reeducation efforts.

Reeducation of young people had been a concern of the Americans from the first. Many young Germans had endured years of Nazi indoctrination and forced participation in the Hitler Youth or Bund Deutscher Mädel, the Nazi youth organization for girls. German elementary education had been severely compromised, with many teachers enthusiastic Nazis and textbooks reflecting the racist values of the National Socialist regime. Schools were closed as soon as U.S. troops occupied Wiesbaden, and remained closed until teachers were denazified. Overall, fifty-two percent of the teachers in Hesse lost their jobs because of their Nazi affiliations, which left a huge shortage of trained teachers to fill those positions.[31] To make matters worse, school buildings throughout the city were requisitioned for use by the Occupation forces, and returned only months later.

Elementary and secondary schools began to open in the autumn of 1945, but textbooks were in short supply. This was a difficult problem to overcome because of the shortage of printing supplies throughout Germany. Eventually, the Occupation forces managed to collect a barely sufficient supply of textbooks from Switzerland, and in October the first new denazified books began to be distributed.

The schools were run by German teachers and administrators, albeit with American oversight. The Americans did, however, organize their own, less formal attempts at youth education, known as German Youth Activities (GYA). At first GYA activities were unorganized and probably somewhat spontaneous – individual soldiers organizing baseball games or giving out candy. "The American soldier is like a big child and has a good heart", said one man interviewed by Intelligence, and his view was shared by many who remarked on American kindnesses to children.[32] USFET encouraged such contacts between American soldiers and German youth – both for the reeducation of the youth and to keep the soldiers away from German women. The MG, however, had other views. It wished to have some oversight and coordination with respect to youth activities, to be sure that the values of democracy and demilitarization were being emphasized. "In some Kreise in Land Greater Hesse troop commanders were known to have organized German boy scout groups dangerously bordering on paramilitary lines", warned the Education and Religious Affairs Division of the MG. As the Division correctly noted, uncoordinated youth activities would allow "the indiscriminate organization of uncontrolled youth groups by non-military Government personnel and yet to hold Military Government responsible for their actions", and given the frequent criticism of the MG, they understandably wanted to minimize problems connected with GYA activities.[33] By October 1945 USFET came around to the MG's point of view, sending out a regulation requiring USFET GYA activities to be in accordance with the MG framework. Still, a "rather confused situation continued to exist in youth activities", noted a Division report.[34]

In April 1946 a unified GYA program swung into full gear. USFET ordered Army commanders to appoint full-time officers as liaisons with the MG to coordinate GYA programs. By 1948, GYA reported that there were 386 groups in all of Hesse. Wiesbaden GYA activities were directed by one officer in charge, eight officer volunteers and nine enlisted volunteers. The first report of the program noted that it included eight separate youth groups, and counted over 550 young people involved in the program. Two years later, an article in the military community newspaper claimed an astonishing rate of success for the GYA: "out of 86,000 young people between the ages of 10 and 25", the paper said, "50,000 have received GYA help".[35] The GYA program in Wiesbaden received a building at 14 Friedrichstraße as a youth center, where classes and groups could meet. This facility was used by thousands of children.

The GYA program throughout the city, however, enjoyed a popularity perhaps somewhat less than it appeared from official reports. The success of individual youth groups depended on committed and competent adult leaders, which, unfortunately, were all too few. One unusually successful GYA group came from the 686th AAF Band and was run by a private named Harry Choy, who organized a group of about forty boys. "I have taught them the principles of a democratic club (...). They have already elected a president, vice president, and secretary", reported Choy.[36] The club offered sporting activities, parties, and regular meetings, which were described in detail in Choy's monthly reports. When he left Wiesbaden, however, the program languished. Wiesbaden's Women in the Air Force (WAF) unit, Squadron D, also conducted many GYA activities for German girls. But other units lacked qualified and interested personnel. There were instances of soldiers assigned to run GYA activities who merely lent sports equipment to the youth and then went off to relax on their own.

More commonly, units organized special events, like holiday parties and summer picnics, which involved a certain amount of one-time effort but no sustained commitment. In this sense, the Christmas season of 1947 was the high point of GYA activity. Not only did individual units sponsor Christmas parties, but 300 American wives organized a series of parties for about 2,400 children. This winter was the harshest of the postwar period, and the candy, cookies and presents distributed through GYA – including unsaleable clothing from the Post Exchange (PX) – were probably the only gifts most children received.

In any case, the German youth, too, seemed less interested in lessons about democracy than in refreshments and entertainment. Young people participated in GYA because of the "food, gum, and Cokes",[37] as one child explained. In the cold winter, the spacious Youth Center provided warmth and light, including quiet rooms where children could do homework or read a few of the several thousand books in the library. Other popular GYA entertainment activities included camping and hiking, indoor and outdoor sports and hobbies. Until the last days of the program, however, GYA personnel were begging for more participation from a wider variety of units. "There is a constant need for more individual units to conduct German Youth Activity groups (...) [so] that the pressure of the work at the Center may be relieved by having groups meet out in other places", a GYA officer wrote forlornly.[38] But as far as it went, the GYA probably was enjoyable for German and American participants who made the effort, and at its best GYA set the pattern for American sponsorship of activities in later years.

American Organizations in Wiesbaden

In August 1945 the designations of the MG were simplified somewhat. MG Det. F1D2 became F-15, and MG Det. E1A2 became E-5. A USFET unit for "military administration", known as the 2nd MG Battalion, also operated in Wiesbaden, performing "housekeeping duties" for the Americans in Wiesbaden – issuing travel orders, pay, ration cards and the like. Colonel James R. Newman commanded this unit as well as E-5. Still, the organization of the MG was cumbersome and perplexing. As Newman rightly pointed out to General Clay in Berlin, "there is constant confusion because the present system combines separate functional and military administration operations under the same commander".[39] The problem persisted in spite of later reorganizations and streamlining.

E-5/F-15 and the 2nd MG Bn were far from the only American organizations in Wiesbaden. On 19 September the Americans established the state of Greater Hesse (later shortened to Hesse), with Wiesbaden as its capital. In the following months, numerous military and civilian organizations arrived to establish headquarters in the city. The American Red Cross (ARC) set up its U.S. Zone headquarters on Taunusstraße, and the District 2 headquarters of UNRRA occupied offices in the Paulinenstraße building known as the White House, for its resemblance to the residence at 1600 Pennsylvania Avenue. The headquarters for the European Exchange Service (EES) moved to Wiesbaden, as did one of three Central Collection Centers (CCC), where looted art was assembled, catalogued and returned, when possible, to its owners. Other residents included the War Crimes Commission (WCC), the European Air Transport System (EATS), the 1st Constabulary Brigade headquarters, and most significantly, the headquarters of USAFE.

These organizations came to Wiesbaden not only because the city was the state capital but because the MG, or, as it was officially titled, the Office of Military Government – Greater Hesse (OMG-(G)H) itself was

James R. Newman (standing) headed the military government in Wiesbaden, first as a colonel, then as a civilian.

headquartered in the city. OMG-(G)H grew to be a large and complex government responsible for overseeing the reconstruction of the entire state. It was activated on 29 May 1946, taking personnel and duties from the defunct E-5, and was headed by Newman, who resigned his Army commission and took the job as a civilian. OMG-(G)H consisted of over a dozen divisions replicating the organization of the Office of Military Government, United States (OMGUS) in Berlin, headed by General Clay. OMG-(G)H employed at its peak thousands of German civilians and American military personnel, and occupied five floors of the Landeshaus on Ring 1.

USAFE

In September 1945, the headquarters of USAFE, an organization which would have decades-long ties to Wiesbaden, moved to the city from its temporary location in St. Germain-en-Laye, France.[40] USAFE was not yet part of a separate United States Air Force – the division of U.S. Army and U.S. Air Force took place only in 1947.[41] By that time, USAFE had become the primary "tenant organization" in Wiesbaden, taking over from USFET's 2nd MG Bn most of the responsibilities for administration and support of the American population. USAFE handled a variety of tasks in areas like finance, military police, billeting, and medical services.[42] Interestingly, USAFE ran the officers' clubs, while USFET administered clubs for enlisted men and women – an indication of the relatively high percentage of officers in USAFE, in contrast to the enlisted soldiers comprising the vast majority of USFET personnel. In May 1946, all USFET organizations were transferred to USAFE, which became the central military unit in Wiesbaden for the next three decades.[43]

On 21 November 1945 Wiesbaden Air Force Station became the official appellation of the American military community in the area, which included Army and civilian organizations as well as USAFE.[44] The official name of the community changed several times over the years – in 1947 it was called the Wiesbaden Military Post (WMP), and later it was known by the unfortunate acronym WARCOM before becoming the 7101st Air Base Wing (ABW). Whatever its title, the military community as a whole remained the organizational foundation for Wiesbaden's U.S. forces until the 1990s. While the proportion of Army and Air Force units in the Wiesbaden area fluctuated over the years, German authorities and U.S. military leadership regarded the military community as a single entity throughout the decades of American presence in the city.

---

1   Inge Hirst, interview by author, tape recording, Wiesbaden, Germany, 9 March 1996.
2   PIR 1: Intelligence Report compiled by T/Sgt. George K. Schueller, 6871st District Information Services Control Command (DISCC), 6 June 1945.
3   On 19 March, as the Allies approached various points along the Rhine, Hitler ordered that all military, communications, transportation, industry and supply plant be destroyed so that the enemy could not use it. Moreover, on 24 March Gauleiter Jakob Sprenger ordered a complete evacuation of all civilians from the Mainz, Wiesbaden, Frankfurt and Darmstadt areas. Had these orders been carried out, unimaginable suffering and death would have resulted. For an account of the opposition to the Nazi scorched earth orders in Wiesbaden, see Herbert Müller-Werth, „Schicksalstage Wiesbadens am Ende des Zweiten Weltkrieges", *Nassauische Annalen* 67 (1956): 204–7; also Heike Glaser, *Demokratischer Neubeginn in Wiesbaden: Aspekte des sozialen, wirtschaftlichen und politischen Wiederaufbaus nach 1945* (Wiesbaden: Schriften des Stadtarchivs Wiesbaden, Band 4, 1995), 33–35.
4   AGO: "Headquarters 80th Infantry Division, After Action Report", G-3 Section, March 1945.
5   Erich Diefenbacher, „Vom Flakhelfer zur amerikanischen Militärregierung: Vier schicksalhafte Jahre 1945–1949, zur Zeit der Ministerpräsidenten Geiler und Stock. Vergessen, – das geht nicht", in *Republik, Diktatur und Wiederaufbau, Hessische Persönlichkeiten des 20. Jahrhunderts*, vol. 4 in Kleine Schriftenreihe zur hessischen Landeskunde.

6 The XX Army Corps replaced the 80th, and subsequently left when USAFE headquarters moved in. Müller-Werth, "Schicksalstage Wiesbadens", 212. It is important to note that these troops were part of the U.S. Forces, European Theater (USFET), not the separate organization of the Military Government (MG).
7 *Wiesbaden Post (WP)*, 11 March 1949.
8 Ronald M.A. Hirst, interview by author, tape recording, Wiesbaden, Germany, 9 March 1996.
9 Glaser, 41.
10 HESS 1: "Communications (Post, Telephones, Telegraph)", 165.
11 Wolf-Arno Kropat, *Hessen in der Stunde Null, 1945/1947: Politik, Wirtschaft und Bildungswesen in Dokumenten* (Wiesbaden: Selbstverlag der Historischen Kommission für Nassau, 1979), 13,17.
12 Laura Hilton, Muskingum College, letter to author, 14 January 2001.
13 See the three-volume history of Gersdorff Kaserne (Camp Lindsey) by R.M.A. Hirst, "How to Goldplate an Antique OR Ninety Years at Lindsey", unpublished manuscript, 1987.
14 HESS 1: Memo, "Responsibility for Displaced Persons Assembly Centers" from OMG-(G)H, 27 December 1945, Wiesbaden, Appendix 1.
15 Hilton, letter to author.
16 PIR 1: Intelligence Report compiled by T/Sgt. George K. Schueller.
17 UNRRA 1: Monthly Team Report, 15 June 1946.
18 HESS 1: "Public Safety", 15.
19 UNRRA 2: Monthly Report, 30 April 1946.
20 IOT: Hqs and Hqs Company 3rd Infantry, Statement of Robert J. Weber to Warner L. Bruner, 3rd Inf. Investigating Officer, 7 March 1946.
21 IOT: Hqs and Hqs Company 3rd Infantry, Statement of Millard K. Lesher and Melvin V. Cooper to Warner L. Bruner, 3rd Inf. Investigating Officer, 7 March 1946.
22 IOT: Hqs and Hqs Company 3rd Infantry, Statement of 1st Lt. Robert D. Gilmore to Warner L. Bruner, 3rd Inf. Investigating Officer, 8 March 1946.
23 IOT: Hqs and Hqs Company 3rd Infantry, Statement of George Plummer to Warner L. Bruner, 3rd Inf. Investigating Officer, 8 March 1946.
24 HESS 1: "Public Safety", 15.
25 PIR 1: Intelligence Report compiled by T/Sgt. George K. Schueller.
26 HESS 1: Section 4, "Internal Affairs and Communications, Special Branch", 7.
27 On 1 July 1945 ETOUSA, the organization for administration and supply of troops, became USFET. The other organization for fighting the war, SHAEF, was deactivated two weeks later. On 15 March 1947 USFET became the U.S. European Command (EUCOM), which exists to the present day. See Bryan T. van Sweringen, "A Short History of the U.S. European Command: 1945–1997", *United States European Command*, http://www.eucom.mil/history/shorhist.htm [sic], (25 August 2000).

28 PIR 1: Intelligence Report compiled by T/4 Investigator Erwin Benkoe, 6871st District Information Services Control Command (DISCC), 22 September 1945, 1.
29 Ibid., 2.
30 PIR 1: "Development and Present State of the Jewish Question in Wiesbaden", Intelligence Report compiled by T/4 Investigator Erwin Benkoe, 6871st District Information Services Control Command (DISCC), 16 September 1945, 10.
31 HESS 1: "Education and Religious Affairs", 65.
32 PIR 1: "Reactions on Conduct of American Soldiers and House Requisitioning", 11 May 1946.
33 HESS 1: "Education and Religious Affairs", 133.
34 HESS 1: "Education and Religious Affairs", 134, quoted in text – Letter, "Youth Activities", 10 December 1945.
35 *WP*, April 1948.
36 USAFE: "Report of Assistance to German Youth", December 1946, 12.
37 Edward Peterson, *The American Occupation of Germany: Retreat to Victory* (Detroit: Wayne State University Press, 1977), 158.
38 USAFE: "Report of Assistance to German Youth", January 1949, 5.
39 HESS 1: Letter from James E. Newman, OMG-(G)H, to Lt. Gen. Lucius Clay, Deputy Military Governor, U.S. Zone, OMGUS Berlin, "Proposed Reorganization of Land Greater Hesse and Mil Govt Detachments", 11 February 1946.
40 For a brief time, officials used "USAFIE" as the acronym for the United States Air Forces in Europe.
41 Patricia Parrish, *Forty-Five Years of Vigilance for Freedom: United States Air Forces in Europe, 1942-1987* (Ramstein Air Base, Germany: Office of History, Headquarters, United States Air Forces in Europe, 1987), 9.
42 ETOUSA: Policy Administration of Wiesbaden Area 1945-1946; Memorandum from Brig. Gen. R.Q. Brown, Headquarters Commandant, Hq Comd, USFET, to Hq Comd, USAFIE, 22 August 1945.
43 ETOUSA: Powers and Duties of Organizations and Units 1945–1946; Letter from Brig. Gen. J. DeF Barker, Chief of Staff, USA, to Commanding Officers, Wiesbaden Air Force Station, 30 April 1946.
44 USAFE: "HQ Command Narrative", November 1946, 2.

LITTLE AMERICA

As soon as the war ended, the discipline and morale of the U.S. forces began to plummet. Combat had served to focus the energy of the men on fighting and winning, but this main goal having been met, millions of servicemen found themselves at loose ends, weary of army life and impatient to go home. Soldiers also quickly learned that they wielded immense power and wealth relative to the German population. It was an explosive combination.

In 1946, the Army began implementing a partial solution to the problem of soldier indiscipline when it resettled wives and children of military personnel into the U.S. Zone. The arrival of American family members and the creation of "Little Americas" – self-contained American communities with housing, shopping, schools, recreation and worship facilities – emerged as an attempt to improve life for the Americans stationed in Germany and minimize the types of interaction that led to tensions between the two populations.

From the very first days, American military communities in Germany had a distinct character and identity, different from the Germans but also separate from Americans who lived in Germany in other capacities, such as students, businessmen, diplomats, or members of religious groups. The military community was a deliberate creation of the U.S. government, and its standard of living, morale, and discipline were to a large extent dependent on policy determined by Pentagon officials and by Congress. Esprit de corps and quality of life in the military community, in turn, affected German-American relations, and shaped the reputation of the troops in the eyes of the German public.

Morale and Discipline of U.S. Troops

Within weeks of their arrival in Wiesbaden, the American soldiers developed a reputation for enthusiastic "fraternizing". Broadly speaking, fraternization meant any unnecessary contact with Germans, including sharing meals, attending worship services together, and playing with or giving food and candy to children. In the first months of the Occupation, fraternization was illegal under Army regulations; U.S. and British leaders had decided on a non-fraternization policy toward the Germans in early 1944, and prohibitions had been in effect from the initial penetration of the German border by Allied troops.[1] The fraternization ban prevented MG officials from becoming friendly with German civilian officials they worked with, and briefly delayed the implementation of GYA activities, although by June 1945 the ban exempted contact with children.[2]

"Fraternization", however, soon came to refer to sexual relations between American men and German women. These were officially forbidden, but authorities acknowledged that contact was widespread. Commanders attempted to stem the tide of promiscuous behavior by emphasizing the legal dangers of flouting the ban, and through various moral exhortations: "[The soldier who fraternizes] will develop promiscuous habits that will be difficult to break when he returns to his wife or sweetheart; he will develop the habit of selfish sex satisfaction (...)",[3] ran one letter to commanders of units in USFET. Commanders also tried to distract their troops with sports, education and military training. These efforts, not surprisingly, were ineffective, and in October 1945 enforcement of the ban was quietly dropped.[4]

One serious consequence of promiscuity was venereal disease (VD), most commonly gonorrhea but also the more dangerous syphilis. Syphilis rates were unusually high in Wiesbaden – about twenty percent of all VD cases[5] in the city – and penicillin was not yet in widespread use. GIs were instructed to use "V-Packette" prophylactic kits and other protective measures, and venereal disease control officers made aggressive efforts to locate and treat sexual contacts. The VD rate, while high, did drop considerably between 1946 and 1948. In the summer of 1946, over fifteen percent of GIs in Wiesbaden were infected, but by the beginning of 1947 the rate had dropped to ten percent, and by the end of that year was down to just under seven percent.[6] By 1948, most units in Wiesbaden met USAFE's goal – an infection rate of five percent or less.

Drinking to excess was another popular pastime, and, like promiscuity, did not reflect well on the U.S. forces. Drunkenness frequently led to fights, harassment of women, vandalism, and generally "disturbing the peace". Americans became as notorious for their rowdiness as for their

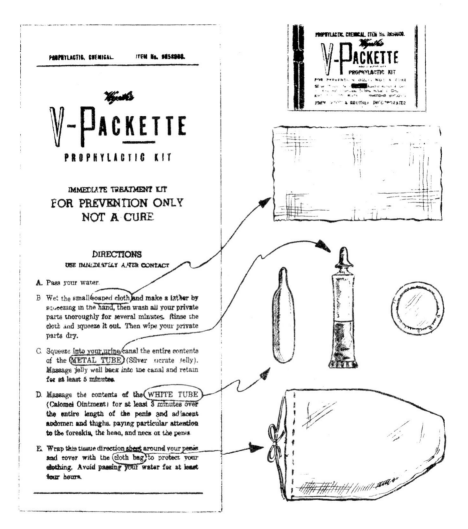

Attempts to stem the VD epidemic included warning messages and distribution of the „V-Packette", a chemical prophylactic procedure.

sexual behavior: "Der Ami ist prima, solange er nicht betrunken ist, denn dann schlaegt er sich mit Jedem, der ihm in den Weg kommt, aus Spass an Schlaegereien" (The Ami is great, as long as he isn't drunk, because then he fights with anyone who gets in his way, just for the fun of fighting), noted a young German worker in Wiesbaden.[7] While VD was a public health problem, drunken rowdiness became a public safety concern, and was perhaps more deleterious to the American image in Germany due to the public nature of the behavior and the likelihood of damage to property and violence to persons.

Commanders and other members of the U.S. military community worried about the collapse of discipline. At a meeting of unit commanders in February 1946, participants bemoaned "the high venereal disease, accident and AWOL [absent without leave] rates, the general unsatisfactory personal appearance of the troops and the carelessness in saluting and military courtesy".[8] In a November editorial in the *Wiesbaden Post*, a weekly newspaper published by the command, the problem was laid out in stark terms. The author cited a recent example of rowdiness in which two drunk soldiers had been arrested in a German bar for throwing chairs and harassing Germans, and rhetorically questioned whether such behavior was worthy of the sacrifices of so many American soldiers lying in the graveyards of Europe. The article concluded:

> *The eyes of the world are upon us. Your speech, your actions and your thoughts are a reflection of 135 million Americans. The Germans are especially watchful – they observed the actions of two Joes the other evening. Is their attitude toward you going to be one of admiration and respect or scorn and contempt?* [9]

In the same issue, the *Post* also reprinted an article from *Collier's Magazine* entitled "Heels among the Heroes", whose leader read: "American GIs in Germany have a heavy responsibility, yet some of them behave like Peck's Bad Boy. The pay-off will intensify our foreign problems." The article was reprinted in the newspaper to remind readers of the problems existing in the Wiesbaden military community.[10]

By 1948, foci of delinquency in Wiesbaden were well established. One was the 89th Enlisted Men's Club at Schwalbacher Straße 52, which had been singled out as early as 1946 for special condemnation. The Venereal Disease Control Board determined that "evidence at present does not indicate that this club is contributing to the venereal disease problem", but the very fact that the club was under investigation suggested ongoing concern. Problems also centered around the Walhalla Theater in downtown Wiesbaden. "[The] location of the Walhalla Theater was considered undesirable", noted the control board primly – not only was the theater itself a problem area but the neighborhood had become known as a meeting place. When a new American theater on Camp Lindsey opened in June 1948, and the Walhalla returned to its German owners, VD control officers breathed a sigh of relief.[11] "The opening of 'Commander Theater' within Camp Lindsey", the *Post* wrote, "is another of the many completed installations which are rapidly divorcing troops from the city of Wiesbaden proper. Especially pleased are both General Smith and the local Burgomeister [sic]"[12] – not only because requisitioned property was being returned, but the soldiers would be under tighter control.

In addition to the creation of recreation opportunities on the military bases, the MG attempted to control American access to German establishments. Although bars and restaurants throughout the city had been requisitioned for the exclusive use of GIs, many still frequented German clubs, where military police exercised less authority. In the fall of 1947 MG considered a proposal to place "all restaurants, Beer Halls, Hotels, etc, OFF LIMITS". The measure was rejected and, the Air Police noted unhappily, "no recommendations or suggestions were made in lieu of the disapproved policy, thus the Command remains [void] of any policy for the control of Americans or Allied personnel while patronizing such German establishments".[13] In early 1949 the decision was reconsidered, and in February the MG issued an off-limits order: "All German cafes, restaurants, bars and hotels not authorized by Military Government or HQ EUCOM[1] were declared off limits to EUCOM personnel, military and civilian, effective immediately."[14] This edict was perhaps not as harsh as it might have appeared at first. General Clay, now the commander of

---

1 EUCOM: European Command.

EUCOM, reminded American personnel that "one is not supposed to be able to get food in German restaurants or hotels without ration coupons, which EUCOM personnel do not have".[15] In theory, then, there appeared to be no need to place German establishments off-limits.

The antics of American soldiers became legendary among the German populace, and often found their way into popular culture. A German vaudeville show at the Capitol Theater, according to a USAFE report, was "outstanding for its bad taste and attacks on Occupation forces and activities", in particular a sketch called "On the Wilhelmstrasse for the sake of a Lucky Strike", a spoof on prostitution and the use of American cigarettes as currency. Occupation authorities were not amused, and the show did not receive a renewal of its license.[16] Germans could do little else, however, than laugh at the problem, because the desperate state of the German population with regard to food, fuel and other necessities of life exacerbated the growth of amateur and professional solicitation. German women suspected of prostitution were regularly "rounded up" and brought in for venereal disease checks, but prostitution as such was not punished. In the strange, desperate world of postwar Germany, conventional morality was an unaffordable luxury for most people.

American criminality reached its peak in 1947. GIs were implicated in black marketing rings, theft, and violent crime with disturbing frequency, as well as military crimes, such as being absent without leave (AWOL) or out of uniform. In response to the crisis, EUCOM established the U.S. Constabulary, a special police unit operating throughout the U.S. Zone, which curtailed American criminality and indiscipline dramatically. Wiesbaden and Frankfurt, as USAFE and EUCOM headquarters, respectively, had their own military police squadrons and did not fall under the jurisdiction of the Constabulary, although the headquarters of the Constabulary Brigade occupied the Henkell sekt factory on the Biebricher Allee, and Constabulary troops were billeted at Camp Pieri. In rare cases the Constabulary police might be called in to assist the Air Police, but generally the 7122nd Air Force Police Squadron handled incidents with the help of the restructured German police forces.[17] By 1948, criminal behavior in Wiesbaden had decreased by fifty percent, largely due to the efforts of the squadron.

In the late 1940s, the Henkell sekt building on Biebricher Allee became the headquarters for the 1st Constabulary Brigade.

American Family Members Arrive in Wiesbaden

The collapse of morale and discipline in the U.S. forces after the end of the war was not only a public health and safety menace, but also exacerbated the exploitative atmosphere of the Occupation era and delayed Germany's recovery. In order to limit or even reverse the damage done by this problem, USFET decided in late 1945 to allow American soldiers to bring their families to Germany. Not only would this move "normalize" the harsh barracks existence of the GIs, official thinking went, but the presence of American women and children would send a clear signal to all Europeans that the United States viewed the postwar situation optimistically. It also sent a subtle message to the Soviets, with whom official relations were rapidly deteriorating, that the United States had committed itself to a policy of involvement in European affairs and would not retreat into its traditional isolationist stance.

The first American family members left the United States on 18 April, 1946, sailing on the U.S. Navy ship *Thomas Barry*. The women and children arrived at Bremerhaven on 28 April, en route to military communities all over Germany and Austria. For the majority, however, Berlin or Frankfurt would be "home". Among the group were seventeen wives and seven children heading for Wiesbaden.[18] In the second contingent, arriving on 19 May, twenty-five adult family members and twenty-two children were reunited with their fathers and husbands in Wiesbaden. The number of American family members in Wiesbaden increased dramatically in the following months. A year after the arrival of the first seventeen wives, 929 American families with 1,606 dependents lived in the city.[19]

The change in MG policy that allowed large numbers of women and children to join their husbands and fathers in Germany turned out to be a decisive point in the history of German-American relations in Wiesbaden. With the integration of spouses and children, the Wiesbaden Air Force Station began to resemble more closely a natural society, a "changeover from the B.O.Q. tradition overseas to one of more or less permanent domesticity",[20] as a report on military families put it. As of January 1947, twenty-seven American babies were expected to come into the world in Wiesbaden and an American elementary school on Lahnstraße had opened. Shopping facilities reserved for Americans expanded: a relatively large American commissary opened in the Opel Haus across from the Wiesbaden Hauptbahnhof – although, as one American wife noted, canned food like mayonnaise tended to come only in institutional-style gallon jars. The PX in the Kaufhaus scrambled to order toilet articles, toys, household goods and furnishings, and something other than military apparel for its new customers. As a USAFE report noted: "There is a noticeable increase in general sanitation and cleanliness in the Community (...) a definite improvement in morale of troops (...) [a] lowering of venereal disease and a lessening of intemporate [sic] living."[21]

In many ways the presence of dependents had the anticipated beneficial effect on American personnel: "(...) already the dependents have made themselves a strong and respected part of the Wiesbaden Military Community (...) [they have] supplied co-operation, self-rule and a good degree of social self-sufficiency. Certainly the creation of this dependent community is one of the examples of the democratic way we seek to offer",[22] concluded one report. Most of the new arrivals, however, were the wives and children of officers – in January 1947 the military community included 507 officers' families but only 161 enlisted and 67 civilian families.[23] As the majority of active duty personnel were enlisted, the beneficial effect of wives and children on young enlisted men – the segment of the population most likely to engage in excessive fraternization and drinking – was certainly less than it appeared at first.

Some units, in fact, reported unexpected negative consequences of the arrival of family members. A frustrated unit historian of the 184th and 186th Medical Dispensaries, for example, bitterly described the challenge of providing medical care to dependents. Every family member in Wiesbaden, he wrote, required as much medical care as three soldiers, so the burden on the health providers was three times as great as the numbers would indicate. Much of this extra attention was, he suggested, unnecessary:

> *A psychiatric problem presents itself in the lack of suitable activities for dependents resulting in neurotic complaints of all kinds. This may only be true in Wiesbaden, but there is a great lack of anything to do among the wives and the teen-agers. Many live in hotels and have no occupation, they sleep late, dress up in the afternoon to sit with a few others and discuss troubles concerning housing and commissary difficulties. It is not a healthy mental atmosphere.*[24]

Overworked doctors were forced to listen to all sorts of complaints: "(…) such minor things as fatigue while standing in line three hours at the commissary, crowded conditions at the local theaters and gathering places, problems of inability to make the necessary social adjustments, husbands worrying over their dependents, and other difficulties encountered in the routine necessities of living in an enemy country."[25] In their professional capacity, doctors and other medical personnel were especially likely to hear the complaints of family members.

The billeting office, responsible for family housing, became another target of complaints. An exasperated billeting officer decried the lack of stamina and initiative of the newly arrived dependents:

> *It is surprising the time that is wasted by more or less insignificant complaints such as, which maid in the apartment will clean which walk, which family in an apartment can have the best room for their maid or which family in an apartment can have the biggest garage. Most of these complainants would probably not complain if they would only stop and realize that they are thousands of miles from the United States in a war torn county and it is not always possible to be provided with the clean, efficient, roomy quarters which they would normally occupy back home.*[26]

The resentment in the above reports might have stemmed from a certain amount of rank-related tension, as the wives of officers made what seemed like unreasonable demands on overworked enlisted personnel. However, it is probably true that in the early days of the Occupation, many American family members of all ranks had difficulty adjusting to the peculiar combination of luxury and hardship which was their lot in postwar Wiesbaden.

Requisitioning

Provision of adequate housing was one of the central difficulties with which MG officials wrestled as family members arrived. Entire neighborhoods were requisitioned for use as family housing areas, a measure causing no little hardship on the German population. Long after the tide of denazification procedures had diminished to insignificance, the problem of requisitioned housing became the biggest source of irritation and conflict in Wiesbaden, until the last owners of requisitioned buildings moved back into their homes in 1956.

In the earliest days, during the "wild phase", requisitioning was done with little formality and fanfare, and with virtually no consideration or sympathy for the German occupants. In April 1945 the first commander in Wiesbaden, Major Chatnay, simply presented acting mayor Gustav Heß with a list of hotels and homes to be taken over by the U.S. forces. In other cases, American soldiers approached the owners of a building and told them to leave. Inventories of household property were often neglected in the early phase of requisitioning. Moreover, because of the constant movement in and out of Wiesbaden, many units remained in the city for only a short time, and their members saw little reason to be thoughtful to their former enemies. One soldier recalled that requisitioning was a disaster for the homeowner:

> *Soldiers come and requisition a house, give the people one hour to move out, then the soldiers stay in the house for a few days and move on again. When the people come back to their house they usually find it in a sorry state. Some of the furniture has been destroyed by the soldiers and some of it has been looted by DPs in the interval, between the soldiers moving out and the owners moving back.*[27]

The number of office buildings, shops, and homes requisitioned by the Americans in Wiesbaden, even before the arrival of family members, was truly astronomical. Approximately one-third of the buildings in Wiesbaden had been destroyed by bombing in the war, mostly by a bomb attack occurring on the night of 2/3 February 1945; but this percentage was not as high as in many nearby cities, and some of the most beautiful structures in Wiesbaden were still useable. The Opera House and the Kurhaus, for example, were requisitioned and used as the ARC-administered Eagle Club, and an officers' club. At times it appeared as though the Americans requisitioned recklessly, impressed with the elegance and beauty of Wiesbaden and desiring it all for themselves. To make the situation even more serious, various units maintained their own clubs and recreation areas, duplicating those of other organizations. And of course, separate facilities existed for enlisted personnel and officers. There were officers' tennis courts, for example, on Parkstraße, while enlisted personnel used courts in Nerotal.

Under American occupation, Wiesbaden's famous Kurhaus became a club run by the Red Cross.

Besides the tennis courts, the Americans requisitioned numerous sports facilities, in large part an attempt by the command to offer an alternative to drinking and fraternizing. A map guide to the American community in Wiesbaden published in February 1947 indicated a wide range of recreation options: a field house with basketball and volleyball courts on

Liebenau- and Bingertstraße, a gymnasium at Unter den Eichen with similar facilities, a "work-out room" in the Eagle Club with weight lifting equipment and boxing rings, a nine-hole golf course on the outskirts of the city, a stadium for football and track, the Opelbad outdoor swimming pool, an indoor swimming pool, a baseball park, and a ski lodge in Bad Schwalbach.[28] For those who preferred more sedentary forms of recreation, as many as twenty-five clubs and bars for officers, civilians, and enlisted personnel provided spaces where Americans could drink fairly safely (and where female guests were carefully screened). Germans were not allowed into American facilities except as employees, or holders of special passes.

The Americans requisitioned a large number of hotels for use as officers' quarters or enlisted men's barracks. The number of facilities indicated in the 1947 map guide as reserved for officers and civilians suggests the extent of requisitioning in the city. The Albany, Bellevue, Silvania, Union, Regina, National, Einhorn, and Continental, for example, were used by company grade officers, while field grade officers lived in the Rose and Palast hotels. The Schwarzer Bock was reserved for VIPs. The Bären, Brüsseler Hof, Essener Hof, Goldener Brunnen, Goldenes Ross, Luisenhof, and Weißes Ross hotels were designated for civilian females;

„Social passes" were issued to specially screened German guests, generally young women, enabling them to visit the military clubs.

UNRRA personnel lived in the Dahlheim; and members of the Women's Army Corps (WAC) lived in the Metropole. Quarters for enlisted personnel were even more numerous. Most of these hotels were in the barbed wire compound in the center of the city, and thus convenient to offices and shopping. But from the German point of view, the extensive requisitioning throughout the downtown area made Wiesbaden, for a short time, an "American" city.

The arrival of family members increased the already heavy pressure on scarce German housing stock. USAFE established separate housing areas for families, the four main ones being Lahnstraße, Gustav-Freytag-Straße, Nassauer Straße in Biebrich, and in the suburb of Hofheim.[29] Other family housing areas were located in Bad Schwalbach, Eltville, and Schlangenbad. By the spring of 1946, when the first family members arrived, the "wild phase" was long over. MG reviewed requisition requests, checking for need and appropriateness; ideally, those who had been persecuted by the Nazis were relatively immune from requisitioning, while homes of Nazis were to the first to be taken, although this policy proved difficult to enforce. Housing officials took detailed inventories of the contents of the home, to be used, if necessary, for damage or loss claims when the owners returned. But the order to vacate was still immutable, and the inhabitants had only three hours to leave.

American personnel living without their families in hotels did not concern themselves with building maintenance and utilities. They ate at unit mess halls, often in their residences, and they usually had maid and laundry service. Family members in private homes benefited from extensive service staff as well. The first waves of families in Wiesbaden hired maids, gardeners, and maintenance men to operate the unfamiliar coal heaters in their homes, all of whose salaries, in the early days, came from Occupation funds paid by the Germans.

The residential centers were surrounded by barbed wire, with former forced laborers from Poland guarding the entrances, but in spite of preventative measures, crime quickly became a problem in the housing areas. Most of these crimes were break-ins and thefts, with the thieves stealing, according to one report, "cigarettes, candy, liquor, radios, watches and other similar items", which were bartered on the black market for food and clothing.[30] Moreover, the restricted housing areas themselves provoked resentment, according to the OMG(G)H Intelligence Branch. In a September 1946 review of German opinions toward the occupiers, an agent wrote that

> *German antipathy against the Americans is being fostered by the use of Polish Guards for military establishments. It is pointed out that the public finds this a particularly bitter pill to swallow since "Germans consider the Poles just as despicable as the Americans do the Germans". The use of barbed wire fences around American-occupied sections of the City is also described as the wrong psychological approach. Thoughtful Germans are thereby reminded that they are considered "as wild beasts, against whose thieving and assaults one cannot otherwise protect one's self* [sic]".[31]

In April 1947 the housing areas were no longer restricted; although Polish guards continued to patrol, they did not guard the entrances of American neighborhoods.[32]

Throughout the Occupation years, the U.S. forces in Wiesbaden maintained hundreds of requisitioned buildings even as they attempted to consolidate operations onto military installations. In some cases, the Americans allowed Germans the use of buildings, while not actually releasing them back to their owners. In early 1947, for example, the Americans lent the requisitioned Thallia Theater to the Germans "for the showing of motion pictures". The Opera House, while still remaining in American hands, reverted to the Germans for certain performances, attended by music fans from both nations.

German property owners and leaders of local government were certainly thankful when MG returned buildings to their owners, but they often complained of the slow pace of derequisitioning, and even more annoying, the apparent waste of space by the Americans. While Germans lived two or three to a room, in some cases the Americans kept entire buildings empty in case they were suddenly needed by a new unit transferring to the city. While this made sense from the perspective of the military, suffering civilians could not sympathize. The billeting office commented on a particular difficulty Wiesbaden faced:

> *[There are] reports of friction between Military Government and the local German authorities over Army failure to use fully all quarters or billets requisitioned from the local economy, and to derequisition such houses and apartments not being utilized. This point of difference is especially keen in Wiesbaden, since in normal times much of the local economy is dependent on the influx of visitors to enjoy the many mineral baths and springs. Some 12,000 applications by potential visitors are on file in the Oberburgomeister's [sic] office – but no tourist accommodations are available.*[33]

Extensive requisitioning – with no clear end in sight – meant that there was virtually no chance that Wiesbaden could rebuild its traditional tourist industry, or reshape itself into the "Kur- und Kongress-Stadt" envisioned by city leaders.

Shortages

The early years of Occupation were in some ways as luxurious for the Americans as they were hard and pinching for the Germans. But beginning in the winter of 1946/47, the Americans and Germans grappled together with a number of shortages of basic commodities.

The first of these shortages developed in the winter, as coal for heating grew scarce. While both communities took steps to conserve fuel, the situation highlighted the difference in living standards between the wealthy, victorious American community and the impoverished, defeated German population in Wiesbaden. For the Americans, the fuel shortage caused inconvenience and discomfort: "all offices, billets and other facilities would be required to maintain a maximum temperature of sixty-five degrees" because of the lack of fuel, according to a USAFE report.[34] Offices closed early when temperatures dropped to unbearable levels, although which temperatures were unbearable was not clear. The

Americans did not often question their own standards of comfort. The 317th Station Hospital, for example, reported without any comment that the German buildings on Wielandstraße needed to be retooled to suit American needs:

> *The heating equipment found here was required to run longer hours because of the difference in normal room temperature (...). The German temperature averaged around 55 degrees Farenheit [while] the normal temperature required by American standards approximated 70 degrees Farenheit* [sic].[35]

While the shortage of coal made life somewhat uncomfortable for Americans, it posed a serious danger to the health and lives of Germans. Many German civilians could not afford any coal at all; underfed and underclothed, they shivered the winter away in unheated, overcrowded rooms. Conditions were so bad that in February of 1947, several Germans came down with smallpox. Medical authorities feared an epidemic and immunized everyone, German and American, and the danger was averted. Still, public health officials were kept busy with cases of diphtheria, tuberculosis, whooping cough, and other infectious diseases.

As the winter of 1947 turned into spring, residents of Wiesbaden rejoiced at the arrival of temperate weather. Their happiness was short-lived, however, because with the warm spring and summer came a serious water shortage. Crops withered in the fields, reducing food supplies for the next winter, and the level of the Rhine River fell steadily. The problem was evident by April, and Americans were instructed by the base commander to minimize water use. But, according to the Air Installations Officer in charge of utilities and maintenance on U.S. bases and in requisitioned buildings, Americans continued to use a disproportionate amount of water. "While the American population was only 5 % of the city's total, its proportionate use of the water supply available was 20 % (...). Americans were forbidden, after failure of pleas for voluntary conservation, to water lawns, hose their cars, and even bathe too often."[36] The drought threatened to ruin the harvest and bring widespread hunger in the next winter, and hindered the fire department's ability to put out fires. Moreover, as desperate people used untreated surface water for drinking and washing, the danger of epidemics increased. The Chief Surgeon of EUCOM reported that forty-nine percent of the German population in the U.S. Zone were worm-infected, a result of eating unwashed vegetables.[37]

Air Installations continued its attempts to convince the American population to use less water, threatening fines and disciplinary measures. They appeared to have little effect: "use of water by the Occupation forces in Wiesbaden remained out of proportion with their numerical strength as compared with the German population, which is more used to the need for saving water", reported the unit historian.[38] However, the Americans themselves were not wholly responsible for their profligate use of water; investigators discovered that German maids and gardeners employed by American families believed that the shortage did not affect the Americans, and thus made no attempt to conserve while they were at work.[39]

In June, Air Installations noted for the first time that some of the German population were ignoring restrictions in their own residences. When American officials looked into the matter, Oberbürgermeister Redlhammer admitted that he had been forced to rescind water conservation regulations because of pressure from the German Ministry of Home Affairs. Air Installations tried to persuade Military Government to intervene and force the Germans to accept conservation rules, but without success. "It is ludicrous", the Americans protested, "for the Army authorities to initiate action to punish Army personnel who violate conservation procedure while [the] German populace can continue without effective restriction to use water which is acutely short". Suggestions for easing the crisis included placing limits on water usage by home gardeners – not, perhaps, a particularly wise policy, as the gardeners produced food for German consumption.[40]

The appeal to MG was unsuccessful. Interestingly, the mayor's inability to promulgate binding water conservation rules stemmed from a MG ruling that he could not "in his additional duty as Chief of Police (…) impose punitive measures upon the civilian population".[41] This rule, like many other MG rulings, was designed to decentralize power and reform the Nazi governmental structure, but in this case it had the unintended consequence of preventing necessary rules from being enacted.

The water shortage ended in the fall, but once again a fuel shortage loomed. The *Post* explained that fuel rations for the Wiesbaden Military Post would be adequate if conservation was strictly practiced: inhabited quarters and offices were to be kept at a maximum of seventy-two degrees Fahrenheit (twenty-two Celsius), and sixty degrees Fahrenheit (fifteen Celsius) when not occupied – hardly stringent measures.[42]

Establishment of a Permanent Military Community

As early as June 1946, USAFE began to consider ways to decrease overcrowding in Wiesbaden. One tactic was to move civilian organizations to other areas. The headquarters of the War Crimes Commission, UNRRA and ARC were among the first to go. In November 1946, the WCC moved to Augsburg, and the latter two moved to Bad Wildungen, albeit with considerable resistance from UNRRA. In September, as the move grew closer, one UNRRA supply officer quit in frustration, saying that "the functional center of the District for the Supply Department must necessarily be close to USFET, ARMY and MILITARY GOVERNMENT".[43] In spite of their pleading, MG shifted civilian organizations out of the city as quickly as possible. The move of UNRRA and ARC out of Wiesbaden did not help the overcrowding situation noticeably, because another major unit, Air Transport Command (ATC), moved from Paris to Wiesbaden, taking over the Taunusstraße offices that the two relief organizations had vacated.

The main gate of Camp Lindsey in 1947.

Much more efficacious was the gradual move by various units from downtown offices onto specified military bases in the Wiesbaden area. Chief among these was Gersdorff Kaserne / Camp 563, which MG promised to turn over to USAFE when the last of its residents had been resettled. By 1947, most of the DPs had moved to permanent homes elsewhere, and Camp 563's second set of occupants, approximately 600 German prisoners of war (PWs) assigned to the 2005 Labor Supervision Company, were being released from captivity.[44] The installation, renamed Camp Lindsey[45] – later Lindsey Air Station (LAS) – in honor of Captain Darrell R. Lindsey, an American B-26 pilot who had died in a raid over France, was gradually

The main gate of Camp Lindsey in the 1980s.

renovated as buildings became empty. The use of renovated buildings on Camp Lindsey, it was thought, would go far to ease the billeting crunch for enlisted personnel, as well as remove them from housing which was often less than satisfactory, according to the Billeting Office. "Lack of adequate sanitary facilities, overcrowding, and failure to maintain proper housekeeping standards" were chief among the problems of requisitioned enlisted residences.[46]

The first units moved into Camp Lindsey in 1947, and the consolidation of U.S. units on the installation proceeded rapidly in the following months. In May 1948, the biggest move of the year took place, with USAFE HQ Command, the support unit for the Americans in Wiesbaden, transferring to Camp Lindsey from its temporary location on 14 Wilhelmstraße.[47] It would be several years before the entire USAFE headquarters moved from downtown to the impressive building on Camp Lindsey; this final move would not occur until December 1953.

Another former Wehrmacht installation renovated for use by the Americans was Wiesbaden Air Base (WAB), in Erbenheim. Renovation at WAB moved forward more rapidly than the work at Camp Lindsey because WAB had not been used as a DP camp. Instead, the WAB airfield was put into use by EATS, the military "airline", which flew between the major cities of Europe, including Wiesbaden. Both Camp Lindsey and WAB provided office space as well as housing, which allowed requisitioned property to be returned to its owners.

By the end of 1947, USAFE reports reflected a significant transformation in the Wiesbaden Military Post, due in part to the presence of dependents, as the community became more stable and permanent. There was still a great deal of movement – units continued to transfer in and out of the city, and buildings were requisitioned and released. An increasing percentage of the Americans in Wiesbaden, however, worked in some support capacity for the U.S. community, rather than as part of a combat unit of USFET or as administrators of the German population through the MG. Besides the already mentioned Air Installations and the Information Office, American organizations in Wiesbaden included Billeting, Family Housing, Chaplains, Troop Information and Education, Supply, Engineering, Provost Marshall, Department of Defense Dependent Schools (DoDDS), EES and many others, all of which provided services and support for the American military community. To be sure, many of these units had existed even in wartime, but as the American population in Wiesbaden grew, so did the extent and complexity of support functions.

One of the most important organizations providing support for the American community was the USAF Medical Center on what is today Konrad-Adenauer-Ring. Built in 1938 as a Wehrmacht hospital, it had not yet been completed by 1944. It was taken over in June 1945 by the 317th Station Hospital of the U.S. Army, which ran the hospital as an inpatient center, while outpatient care was offered at dispensaries around the city. In 1947, the hospital, then known as the Wiesbaden Military Post Medical Service, provided "first and second echelon medical service to the entire Wiesbaden Military Post (…) [and] third echelon medical service to patients referred to this hospital from the entire European Command for the treatment of neuropsychiatric patients".[48] In the late 1940s the Wiesbaden hospital became known as a major psychiatric hospital and training center, but with the expansion of the U.S. defense commitment in the early 1950s, it took on an even larger role. In October 1953 the resident unit at the center – the 495th Medical Group – was redesignated as Headquarters, 7100th USAF Hospital.[49]

Together, yet separate: „This playground of the American school in Wiesbaden may be used by all children except Monday through Friday from 8.30–15.00, when it is reserved for American schoolchildren."

Continued Housing Shortages

Although the American community took steps to move out of German buildings and on to U.S. military installations, the availability of housing continued to deteriorate. Between 1949 and 1954, as the city began recovering from war and occupation, the housing situation reached crisis proportions. The number of Germans and other Europeans in the city had grown, partly because of the influx of expellees from Eastern Europe and partly because Wiesbaden was rapidly becoming a center for state and federal government, with several important administrative headquarters and offices located in the city.

The American community grew during this time as well, as the Wiesbaden Military Post became one of the most important U.S. military centers in Europe. The Air Force, by now a separate branch of the armed forces, was anxious to demonstrate its importance to the North Atlantic Treaty Organization (NATO) and the defense of the West, so it took every opportunity to expand its operations. USAFE in turn gained greater responsibility, which meant greater importance for Wiesbaden in the American constellation of bases, and larger numbers of personnel. For a time, the headquarters of the Twelfth Air Force was in Wiesbaden. Even the U.S. Navy arrived in February 1949, stationing around 150 personnel in Schierstein as a Rhine River Patrol to help control navigation of the river. The Army also had a number of units in Wiesbaden, totaling about 1,600 officers and enlisted personnel. Most notable was the headquarters of the 1st Constabulary Brigade, but other Army personnel were assigned to Air Defense Artillery (ADA) battalions and stationed at WAB. In 1953 they moved to Camp Pieri in Freudenberg and Rhine Kaserne in Biebrich, as the Constabulary and other Army personnel moved out and those installations became available.

Overall, in 1949 the number of Americans in Wiesbaden grew by one-third, from about 9,000 to over 12,000, and by 1951 to 16,000. The availability of housing, unfortunately, did not appreciably increase. Throughout 1949, the number of requisitioned buildings, mostly family homes, remained constant. By the middle of 1949 many units had moved from their locations in the center of the city to LAS or WAB, but while office buildings were returned to their owners, the moves did not open homes to Germans or Americans. Two new housing areas, built in Mainz-Kastel (seventy-eight apartments in 1949, and twenty-four in 1951), and Crestview (398 apartments in 1949) made no appreciable dent in the situation, and no properties were derequisitioned as a result.[50] Even the hotels had no space, and the housing office listed a backlog of hundreds of applications. In April of 1949, 619 families living in temporary quarters waited to receive news of permanent quarters. Fifty-five families of airmen stationed in Wiesbaden lived in the distant town of Bad

Mergentheim, and hundreds of others could only receive authorization to move to Europe if they agreed to live in Bad Mergentheim for an unspecified period of time. By May, USAFE was sending personnel and their families scheduled to return to the "ZI" (Zone of the Interior – the United States) home early in order to free up housing for waiting families. In early 1951 the situation was so grave that Wiesbaden was declared by EUCOM to be a "restricted city" – American personnel were required to make reservations to come to the city for temporary duty, and personal leaves to Wiesbaden, a popular destination for vacationers, were not allowed.[51]

While housing shortages caused frustration among the Americans, the situation for the German population became even more desperate. Housing was an almost daily topic in Wiesbaden's newspapers, and by

Neue Beschlagnahmen in Wiesbaden

Oberbürgermeister Krücke teilt mit:

„Vor wenigen Tagen sind neuerdings erhebliche Beschlagnahmungen ganzer Häuserblocks in der Gegend der Adolfshöhe erfolgt, die eine große Beunruhigung in der Bevölkerung hervorgerufen haben. Infolgedessen hat am 4. 6. 1946 eine eingehende Rücksprache von seiten des Oberbürgermeisters und Vertretern der politischen Parteien, der CDU sowohl als auch der SPD, mit dem Town-Major, der Militärregierung und einem Vertreter der Armee stattgefunden. Es wurde dabei erklärt, daß an der Beschlagnahme selbst nichts zu ändern sei, jedoch wurde eine faire Behandlung der Angelegenheit zugesichert. Über das Mobiliar soll in jedem Haus eine Bestandsaufnahme gemacht und den Bewohnern diejenigen Sachen überlassen werden, die sie dringend für sich benötigen und die die Armee nicht unbedingt braucht, wie z. B. Arbeitsgeräte, Fachliteratur, auch Bettzeug. Die Bewohner sollen entsprechende Anträge bei dem Besatzungsamt stellen, zwecks Weiterleitung an die Armee. Die Erträge der Gärten sollen zur Hälfte den Besitzern überlassen werden.

Durch die Beschlagnahme sind bis jetzt 120—130 Häuser betroffen. Die Häuser umfassen durchschnittlich drei Wohnungen, so daß etwa 300 Familien oder ungefähr 900 bis 1000 Personen, wenn auch nach und nach, anderweitig untergebracht werden müssen. Als Ersatz sollen zwar einige andere Häuser freigegeben werden, die jedoch nicht ausreichen. Die Gesamtzahl der Wohnungen in Wiesbaden betrug 1939 52 000, wovon aber 11 300 unbenutzbar sind, während die übrigen Wohnungen mehr oder weniger Schäden erlitten haben. Die Besatzung hat bisher 2600 Wohnungen beschlagnahmt, wozu jetzt die Wohnungen in den 120 Häusern hinzukommen. Die Einwohnerzahl betrug im April 1945 etwa 145 000, zur Zeit beträgt sie etwa 182 000 außer den etwa 12 000 Angehörigen der Besatzungstruppen und 7884 verschleppter Ausländern. Außerdem kommen in jeder Woche noch 400 bis 500 Personen hinzu, aus Kriegsgefangenschaft Zurückkehrende, Evakuierte und andere, ganz abgesehen von der erheblichen Zahl von Flüchtlingen.

Durch all dieses ist Wiesbaden in die geradezu katastrophale Lage auf dem Wohnungsmarkt geraten. Unter diesen Umständen hat der Oberbürgermeister mit Vertretern der Stadtverwaltung auch am 6. 6. 1946 mit dem Herrn Ministerpräsidenten, dem stellvertretenden Vorsitzenden des Landesausschusses und den politischen Parteien Rücksprache genommen und gebeten, auch bei den höheren militärischen Dienststellen Vorstellungen zu erheben, damit die Stadt von weiteren Beschlagnahmungen verschont bleibt und daß ein Abzug der verschleppten Ausländer erfolgt. Es ist zugesichert worden, daß die Angelegenheit Gegenstand einer Besprechung im beratenden Landesausschuß bilden soll."

„New Requisitioning in Wiesbaden" – during the Occupation, a headline seen all too often in Wiesbaden papers.

1950 complaints grew louder. Headlines in the local papers announced that around tens of thousands of Wiesbadeners needed apartments, while only a fraction of the needed space was available.[52] Moreover, the continued possession of hotels delayed ever further the revitalization of Wiesbaden's tourist economy. It seemed to be an insoluble problem.

In April 1951 a spate of articles in the *Wiesbadener Kurier* and the *Wiesbadener Tagblatt* accused the Americans, in harshly critical language, of not using requisitioned property fully. The Americans frowned on such criticism, but by 1951 they had no authority to censor the offending words. The Public Information Office (PIO) believed the articles to be distorted and arranged a meeting with representatives of the papers to explain the American view and correct misapprehensions. But in spite of efforts to blunt the bad publicity, the American position proved difficult to defend. Ever since the Berlin Airlift had forced the housing office to scramble for homes for the sudden crush of airlift personnel and their families assigned to Wiesbaden, the American policy was to retain some housing space for emergencies. As reasonable as this policy appeared to the Occupation authorities, the harm caused by civilian housing shortages seemed to outweigh any good it might achieve. At a conference between American authorities, the Wiesbaden mayor, the head of the hotel association, and other officials, Redlhammer seconded the German hotel association's suggestion that hotels be released back to their owners, who would then permanently set aside a number of rooms for the Americans. "Colonel Reed declared that this suggestion is incompatible with the military law, which prohibits a joint accommodation of Germans and Americans",[53] reported the USAFE historian; for security reasons, rules forbidding Germans and Americans from living in the same building remained in force in the early 1950s.

To make matters worse, the Germans and Americans calculated relevant figures, such as the hotel occupancy rate, in different ways. The hotel association estimated occupancy rates based on the number of beds in the hotels before they were requisitioned. Using this formula, American hotels were only fifty percent occupied. The Americans, on the other hand, used more space per person in the hotels, so according to their calculations, the hotels were full. Such semantic differences did not help negotiations on the issue.

In response to complaints from the mayor and individual property owners, General Fay R. Upthegrove, commander of the 7100 HQ Command Wing, announced in October 1949 that the housing office would have to justify keeping requisitioned property that was unused. In some cases this was difficult or impossible. If the property was needed again after it had been released, however, the procedure to recall it would be "almost prohibitively involved" – including a trail of approval from all the way from the Real Estate Officer of the Military Post, to the Twelfth Air Force, to EUCOM.[54] Rather than derequisitioning the buildings altogether, the housing office released some properties "under sufferance" – returned to the owner, but if an emergency required American use of the building, the owner was required to vacate it immediately.[55] While on paper this addressed the needs of the military and the German owners, it could hardly be considered a suitable solution in the longer term. Moreover, when housing was returned to its owners, complaints about the upkeep of the homes and furniture were not uncommon. The Civil Affairs office recognized that the poor condition of returned homes was yet another public relations problem that would affect German-American relations into the future, and by 1952 took steps to improve maintenance, or at least reimburse those whose property was damaged or destroyed.[56]

As the situation continued into the mid-1950s, occasional tragi-comic incidents arose. In the first part of 1955, one Herr Görgen, a city councilman, owner of Gotenweg 9, lost his patience with the Americans who had requisitioned his home. "He always maintained close vigil of his property and the morning the American occupant moved out, Herr Görgen and his family moved into the basement. He padlocked the garden gate and posted a large sign on the front door on which was written 'Off Limits to American personnel. I am the legal owner of this property and anyone who trespasses will be sued for house breaking.'" He eventually agreed to vacate the house so another American tenant family could move in. But as Herr Görgen and his family sat on the sidewalk with their belongings, "newspaper correspondents and relatives created a big scene".[57] Görgen's action was unusual, but his feelings on the matter were not.

Requisitioned homes engendered the biggest conflict between the Germans and Americans in the early 1950s, and it appeared to many

Germans that the Americans lacked the will to solve the problem in a timely fashion. But from the American point of view, continued requisitioning was an unfortunate result of the onset of the Cold War. The Office of the Land Commissioner for Hesse, which had replaced OMG-(G)H, discussed the issue:

> *It is readily understandable how the Germans feel. It's not pleasant to be removed from your home for 6 or 7 years, and to live in 2 or 3 rooms elsewhere. These people who have been dispossessed are beginning to complain, and we can sympathize with their situation, although to begin to understand it fully, we would have to imagine an army of occupation in – say – New York State.*
>
> *On the other hand, we are faced with certain responsibilities that make the release of further properties an extremely difficult matter. Were it not for the Berlin blockade and the Korean affair we would be out of Germany as an occupying power (…). Thus, instead of an anticipated lowering of our housing requirements, there has been to the contrary, an increase. To be sure, the old days of a VIP in a 17 room house are over (…).*[58]

In spite of efforts to ease the hardship, the problem threatened to harm the American reputation in Wiesbaden more permanently than any other issue.

American Housing Complexes

By 1951 it was clear that the Americans would not be leaving the city any time soon. The long-term solution to the housing crisis was to build additional housing for the Americans. In the 1950s, three large hotels were constructed for the use of American personnel – bachelor officers, families waiting for permanent housing, and military and civilians traveling to Wiesbaden on official business. These were paid for by the German government, but handed over to the Americans for their exclusive use. The first to open was the American Arms (Stern Hotel) on elegant Frankfurter Straße, built in 1950 on the grounds of the Hotel Kaiserhof, which had been destroyed in the bombing of Wiesbaden in February 1945. The Amelia Earhart went up in 1955, next to the USAF Medical Center, a convenient location for personnel stationed at the hospital or at nearby LAS, as well as for families of hospital inpatients. The General Von Steuben on Auguste-Viktoria-Straße, built in 1956, was the finest hotel of the three. Congressional representatives and VIPs from around the world stayed at the Von Steuben when they visited Wiesbaden; the hotel's most prestigious guest was President Kennedy, who visited Wiesbaden on his famous trip to Germany in 1963. All three hotels had been built for the Americans, but were paid for and owned by the West German government and had a total of 1,214 beds.[59]

An aerial view of the American Arms Hotel on Frankfurter Straße shows why Germans often called it the „Stern-Hotel" (Star Hotel).

In 1955, the Amelia Earhart Hotel was built next to the USAF Hospital.

The most comprehensive solution to the housing crisis, however, came in 1952, when plans for a large American housing complex were unveiled. The scheme was known initially as the Brewster Plan, named after Post Commander Colonel Brewster, who had designed it and introduced the idea to Air Force headquarters and Wiesbaden officials. It called for the construction of a virtually self-contained residential and shopping zone, including "a community center complete with offices, hotels and billets as well as apartment type billets (…)" according to the initial plans.[60] At first the mayor and other city leaders balked, asking that German housing be returned first. But Brewster pointed out that derequisitioning would follow the construction, as families moved into the new area. The federal government, realizing the worth of the idea, offered to build an additional 900 apartments if accelerated derequisitioning would take place.

The Brewster Plan went ahead, funded by the German government, and in 1954 the first families moved into what was by then known as Hainerberg Housing Area. When complete, Hainerberg included 200 buildings with a total of 1,146 apartments,[61] on 167 acres. In the early

The Hainerberg housing area includes an apartment complex, a large commissary, and a shopping center.

years, both communities were anxious to move Americans out of requisitioned housing and onto the new American complex, and families occupied buildings as soon as they were ready, well before the entire complex was complete. In 1955, German and American officials had a difficult time moving the last German farm families off land in the Hainerberg area, which had been requisitioned wholesale by the German government,[62] but in the end the project was completed, and the derequisitioning process took a leap forward.

Other housing facilities were built in the 1950s as well. Aukamm, a small area north of Hainerberg, near Crestview, was reserved for field-grade officers. It spread over ninety-three acres, had 188 apartment buildings with 581 quarters,[63] including single family homes and

Aukamm Housing Area was reserved for field-grade officers, of which Wiesbaden had an unusually large proportion.

duplexes. Other family apartments were built on Wiesbaden Air Base, as well as the small installations of Schierstein and Hindenburg. These were by no means large complexes like Hainerberg or even Crestview –

Schierstein housing, for example, had only one building with six apartments.[64] In addition to housing built specifically for the U.S. forces, German homes were leased for the use of American personnel; in Medenbach, seven miles outside the city, the Air Force rented twenty-six units of family housing.[65]

In spite of the extensive efforts to move as many Americans as possible into specially built housing, about half of the American families in Wiesbaden could not obtain apartments. Rather than live in requisitioned German homes, however, they lived "on the economy" – that is, they rented apartments just as any German resident might do. Of course, the American renters were very different from German families. For one thing, they usually only stayed for a few years, then moved on. For another, they received housing allowances and so could pay what was asked, within reason. And third, they generally did not understand German, nor were they familiar with German housing laws and conventions. These conditions created a somewhat dangerous situation, where Americans might be taken advantage of, and conversely, where the housing market might be distorted by an influx of American money. To avert these possibilities, authorities created the German-American Housing Committee, an organization which inspected housing that Americans proposed to rent, and controlled negotiations between landlord and tenant. In this manner, the Americans allayed "the fears that have been expressed by Wiesbaden citizens and the Oberbürgermeister that Americans are causing skyrocketing rent for mediocre apartments which place them out of reach of the average German family (…)".[66] The German-American Housing Committee later became the housing office, which accepted notices from landlords wishing to rent to Americans, and dealt with other housing issues.

Requisitioning in Wiesbaden ended officially on 5 May 1956. Not all homes were released on that day, however, because some new homes in Aukamm had not yet been completed. This did not please some homeowners, who wrote to the American occupants of their homes, saying that they expected to be able to move in on the official date. Hints of grumbling elicited a polite but firm response from the American and German leadership: "(…) relations between Germans and Americans in

Wiesbaden have reached the highest level of cooperation and friendship and it was not anticipated that the few remaining property owners would damage these excellent relations with the local government and population. The property owners were informed that strict measures would be taken to protect military personnel should violence erupt."[67] No violence was reported. In retrospect, it is clear that the construction of Hainerberg Housing Area and the return of property to its German owners was an important step in improving the shaky relations between the two communities.

Growing Resentment of the American Presence

After the currency reform in June 1948 and the formal creation of the Federal Republic of Germany (FRG) in 1949, the Occupation formally ended. With the attendant economic and political stability that came along with those two events, Germans began to hope that conditions would normalize and improve. The remaining signs of war and the subsequent German degradation would pass, and Germans could consider themselves, and expect others to consider them, as "normal" western Europeans.

As is clear, however, the Americans still occupied Wiesbaden, de facto if not de jure, and their presence constituted an increasingly resented burden. While Germans hoped to reach a greater state of equality with the Americans, some Americans continued to regard themselves as victors and occupiers. To be sure, much of this was simply careless acceptance of past social roles, and could be transformed through leadership. For example, the *Post* reported that Mrs. John McCloy, wife of the U.S. High Commissioner (successor to the Military Governor), encouraged wives of American Occupation personnel in Wiesbaden in 1950 to "remove from their doors 'Forbidden for Germans' signs and to take up closer relations with the German population".[68] Yet in June of 1951, a report on housing problems began: "With the Occupation well into its seventh year (...)",[69] a verbal slip that revealed the attitude of many Americans in Wiesbaden.

American personnel, too, displayed behavior which, while annoying and even dangerous to themselves and to German bystanders, could be put down, in part, at least, to a thoughtless assumption of occupation attitudes, or "Besatzungsrechtsdenken". This behavior included continued petty crime, and, more commonly, drinking and rowdiness. In 1950, EUCOM headquarters warned all commands that "instances of disgraceful, detestable and decidedly unmilitary conduct on the part of enlisted men while traveling on duty trains have been reported to this headquarters. Such conduct includes open drinking, drunkenness, molesting women, lewd profanity, slovenliness in the wearing of the uniform and other forms of disorderly conduct (…)."[70] Furthermore, as more Americans brought their autos to Germany from the United States, the traffic accident rate for Americans rose to absurd heights. Compared with Birmingham, Alabama, the U.S. city with the highest rate of accidents per 10,000 registered vehicles – 5.9 – Wiesbaden had a rate of 7.5. If only the Americans in Wiesbaden were counted, however, the rate rose to 18 accidents per 10,000 vehicles. The rates according to population were equally dismal: San Diego had the highest rate in the United States for its population, at 16.3, but the Americans in Wiesbaden registered a stratospheric 60. The problem, it appeared, stemmed from lax enforcement of traffic rules, which created a Wild West-like atmosphere of oversized American cars careening through the narrow streets of the city.[71]

This sort of thoughtless arrogance began to have its toll on German-American interaction. In February 1950, for example, the Provost Marshall described steps taken to prevent Americans and Germans from "clashing" during the late winter Fasching festivities. Americans were not welcome to take part: "many Germans felt it to be a celebration which they should be left free to enjoy without outside participation", said the Provost Marshall. Guards were posted at the bridge to Mainz, to make sure that personnel without proper authorization were unable to go to that city for the parade. In Wiesbaden, the Fasching parade was used as an opportunity to make digs at the Occupation forces. One report described a "particular float [that] showed a replica of the [requisitioned] Eagle Club with Uncle Sam standing over it. The caption read 'Uncle Sam in Wiesbaden', and on the Club replica was a sign reading 'Off Limits to Civilians'."[72] In another memo, the question of Americans using German buses instead of special American buses arose, but the commander of the Maintenance and Supply Group rejected the idea: "I don't think we should start riding the German buses to any great extent. People riding these buses run the risk of being insulted, and even spit on, particularly kids."[73] Clearly, German-American relations were not all they could be in the early 1950s. Although Civil Affairs and other organizations tried their best, the artificiality of Cold War-induced friendship was overwhelmed by real resentments stemming from tensions and frustrations at the local level. It would remain for the military community to take steps to reduce the amount of negative contact between the two populations, while increasing the number of positive interactions, both formal and informal.

---

1   "Nonfraternization, Occupied Germany, 1944–45", USAMHI RefBranch dv Aug 1989, 1.
2   Ibid, 2.
3   ETOUSA: VD Control; Letter from Brig. Gen. R.Q. Brown, Headquarters Commandant, Hq Comd, USFET, to Commanding Officers, 17 November 1945, 2.
4   "Nonfraternization, Occupied Germany, 1944–45", 2.
5   USAFE: "History of the HQ Command, USAFE and Assigned Units", January 1947, 22.
6   USAFE: "HQ Command Narrative", November 1946, 25; also, USAFE: "Venereal Disease Control Section Report", November 1946, 2.
7   PIR 1: Intelligence Report compiled by Investigator Otto Seeler, 6871st District Information Services Control Command (DISCC), September 1945, 2.
8   ETOUSA: Courts Martial and Discipline; Letter from Robert F. Bubier, Major, AG, Adjutant, Hq Comd USFET, to Unit Commanders and Section Chiefs, 26 February 1946.
9   *WP*, editorial, 7 November 1946.
10 USAFE: "HQ Command Narrative", November 1946, 16.
11 USAFE: "Proceedings of June Session, Wiesbaden Military Post Venereal Disease Control Board", June 1948, 2.
12 *WP*, 11 June 1948.
13 USAFE: "7122 AF Police Sq Report", November 1948, n.p.
14 USAFE: "History of the HQ Command, USAFE and Assigned Units", February 1949, 4.

15 Ibid., 5.
16 USAFE: "History of the HQ Command, USAFE and Assigned Units", April 1947, 9.
17 HESS4: "Relations of Tactical Troops to OMGH", 139.
18 The names of the family members of the first Wiesbaden contingent were: Ethel A. Beau, Martha Nunn, Jane Curtin and son Robert, Pauline R. Breedon, Kathleen J. Mann, Alva M. Prentice and son John, Dorothy Robbs, Kathryn N. Roberts and son John, Annah V. Estes and two sons Michael and Howell, Melba Goetcheus and daughter Gayle, Floy Hill, Peggy B. Keown, Norma B. Leisenring, Nelda A. Stipeck, Jane H. Sturdy, Ellna H. Weaver and daughter Killie Kae, G. Seywreata. From ETOUSA: Transportation of Dependents; Letter from Lt. Col. Peter Peters, Asst. Adj. Gen. Frankfurt, to Hq Comd USFET (Wiesbaden Det.), 25 April 1946.
19 USAFE: "History of the HQ Command, USAFE and Assigned Units", January–June 1953, 10.
20 USAFE: "Special Report on Dependents", January 1947, 12.
21 USAFE: "HQ Command Narrative", November 1946, 10.
22 USAFE: "Special Report on Dependents", January 1947, 12.
23 USAFE: "History of the HQ Command, USAFE and Assigned Units", January 1947, 7.
24 USAFE: "HQ Command Narrative", November 1946, 8.
25 Ibid., 9.
26 USAFE: "History of the HQ Command, USAFE and Assigned Units", March 1947, 15.
27 USAFE: "HQ Command Narrative", November 1946, n.p.
28 USAFE: "History of the Headquarters Command, USAFE and Assigned Units", February 1947, n.p.
29 USAFE: "History of the Headquarters Command, USAFE and Assigned Units", January 1947, 7.
30 USAFE: "History of the Headquarters Command, USAFE and Assigned Units", February 1947, 13.
31 OMG(G)H Information Control Division – Intelligence Branch, "Weekly Political Intelligence and German Opinion Review", no. 14, 14 September 1946, 9.
32 USAFE: "Dependent Report", April 1947, n.p.
33 USAFE: "History of the HQ Command, USAFE and Assigned Units", February 1947, 10–11.
34 USAFE: "HQ Command Narrative", December 1946, 10.
35 USAFE: "History of the HQ Command, USAFE and Assigned Units", May 1947, 15.
36 Ibid., 6.
37 USAFE: "History of the HQ Command, USAFE and Assigned Units", June 1947, 6.
38 Ibid., 5–6.
39 USAFE: "History of the HQ Command, USAFE and Assigned Units", July 1947, 5.
40 USAFE: "Air Installations Report", June 1947, 8.

41 USAFE: "History of the HQ Command, USAFE and Assigned Units", July 1947, 5.
42 USAFE: "History of the HQ Command, USAFE and Assigned Units", December 1947, n.p.
43 UNRRA 2: 24 September 1946, 4.
44 USAFE: "History of the HQ Command, USAFE and Assigned Units", February 1947, 8.
45 In 1954 Camp Lindsey was renamed Lindsey Air Base, and in 1958 Lindsey Air Station. Among the German population, however, it was always known as Camp Lindsey.
46 USAFE: "History of the HQ Command, USAFE and Assigned Units", February 1947, 10.
47 *WP*, 7 May 1948.
48 Jayne Traendly, "The History of the Wiesbaden Medical Center", DoD publication, 1993.
49 Ibid.
50 USAFE: "History of the HQ Command, USAFE and Assigned Units", May/June 1951, 33.
51 USAFE: "History of the HQ Command, USAFE and Assigned Units", January/February 1951, 2.
52 *WT*, "20 000 Wiesbadener suchen Wohnung", 18 April 1950.
53 USAFE: "History of the HQ Command, USAFE and Assigned Units", March/April 1951, 28–29.
54 USAFE: "History of the HQ Command, USAFE and Assigned Units", May/June 1951, 20.
55 USAFE: "History of the HQ Command, USAFE and Assigned Units", March/April, 1950, 10–11.
56 USAFE: "History of the HQ Command, USAFE and Assigned Units", November/December 1952, 9–10.
57 USAFE: "History of the HQ Command, USAFE and Assigned Units", January–June 1955, n.p.
58 USAFE: "History of the HQ Command, USAFE and Assigned Units", May/June 1951, 26–27.
59 7101st Air Base Wing, "Data Digest", 30 June 1966, 15.
60 USAFE: "History of the HQ Command, USAFE and Assigned Units", January–June 1953, 26.
61 "Data Digest", 10.
62 USAFE: "History of the HQ Command, USAFE and Assigned Units", July–December 1955, 71.
63 Erich Schmidt-Eenboom, *Wiesbaden – Eine Analyse der militärischen Strukturen in der hessischen Landeshauptstadt* (Starnberg: Forschungsinstitut für Friedenspolitik, E.V., Juni 1987), 60.

64 Ibid., 61.
65 United States Air Force, Office of Information, "Lindsey Air Station Fact Sheet" (n.d.), 2.
66 USAFE: "History of the HQ Command, USAFE and Assigned Units", January–December 1955, 61.
67 USAFE: "History of the HQ Command, USAFE and Assigned Units", January–June 1956, 82.
68 quoted in *WP*, 12 May 1950, n.p.
69 USAFE: "History of the HQ Command, USAFE and Assigned Units", May/June 1951, 18.
70 USAFE: "History of the HQ Command, USAFE and Assigned Units", July/August 1950, 21.
71 USAFE: "History of the HQ Command, USAFE and Assigned Units", July/August 1951, 35.
72 USAFE: "History of the HQ Command, USAFE and Assigned Units", January/February 1950, 46.
73 Ibid., 36.

German - American Friendship

At no time until the 1990s did U.S. geopolitical perspectives change more quickly than in the ten years after World War II, and these changing views deeply affected German-American relations. Initially, U.S. policy focused on punishment, but as relations with the USSR cooled, American attitudes toward the Germans became less rigid. In September 1946 Secretary of State James F. Byrnes gave his famous speech in Stuttgart, in which he promised that the United States would remain involved in Europe and work toward European recovery, even if that meant moving away from close cooperation with the Soviet Union. In July 1947, revised directives spelled out a new policy of aid and protection, and a year later the Berlin Airlift indicated that the U.S. was willing to act to defend a democratic Germany. By 1949, the Federal Republic of Germany had come into existence, and OMGUS became the much smaller and less intrusive U.S. High Commissioner of Germany (HICOG). In spite of an evolving policy of support, however, the number of U.S. troops stationed in Germany decreased annually, as military units deactivated and bases closed. Many policymakers believed that the United States would not keep large numbers of troops in Europe for any length of time. Only when North Korea invaded South Korea in 1950 did American leaders come to a strong consensus that West Germany and the United States must form a defensive partnership against the Soviet Union.

The new position signaled a decisive shift in relations between American military communities and their host towns. Rather than punishing the Germans, or trying to reeducate them, or even protecting them paternalistically, Germans were now to be treated as important friends and allies against the communist threat. West Germany was to be viewed, by and large, as a democratic ally of the United States, albeit one which was expected to be rather more obedient than true equality would imply. Suddenly, German-American friendship was a fact of life to be celebrated and emphasized – even called into existence, if necessary.

German-American Marriages and Families

In Wiesbaden, signs of close German-American contact on the most personal level could be seen well before the change in policy driven by

Cold War hostility. In the late 1940s, many American GIs had formed at least temporary attachments with German women – in 1949 the Oberbürgermeister reported that 800 airmen were living with German women in Wiesbaden.[1] German-American marriages were not illegal, but under MG regulations, German-American couples were required to transfer to the United States within ninety days of the marriage. The Alien Spouse Act, commonly known as the GI Bride Law, passed in 1946, enabled foreign wives and stepchildren of American military personnel and civilians serving in postwar Europe to enter the United States with their spouses without having to go through regular immigration channels. This rule was set to expire at the end of December 1948, after which non-American spouses would have to apply for a non-quota visa, including a background check which would take up to six months. Stepchildren would be considered normal immigrants and approval for them might take as long as ten years. As a result of this change, a rush of weddings occurred in the summer and fall of 1948. In Wiesbaden, 262 marriages were approved

German-American marriages were very common in the 1950s. The bride in this photo was originally from East Prussia and fled with her family at the end of World War II.

between January and November, the peak coming in August when 85 "alien" marriages took place. Most of the marriages were between Germans and Americans, but 64 out of the 262 were between Americans and other Europeans, sometimes of more complicated background[2] – DPs and ethnic German expellees whose original homeland had changed hands several times. Different marriage rules applied depending on the bride's original nationality, and a detailed form was used to determine what that nationality was.

In the rush to complete paperwork before the December deadline, many children were adopted in 1948. Colonel Franklin J. Potter, OMGH legal division chief, reported a five hundred percent increase during July, because GIs were adopting their stepchildren in order to receive permission to bring them into the United States. Under the Displaced Persons Act of 1948, which superseded the Alien Spouse Act, adopted children of American personnel could enter the United States like children born to American parents overseas. The act expired in 1952, and after that adopted children had to wait along with other nonrelatives wishing to enter the country.[3]

Even after 1952, adoptions continued to be, according to a USAFE report, "an important development in German-American relations during the postwar years".[4] Under Occupation law, German courts had no jurisdiction over American personnel and could not investigate prospective parents who were members of the Occupation; Colonel Potter was charged with approving American adoptions of German children. By 1952, however, EUCOM gave the German courts the authority to grant adoptions and investigate parents. There were fifty-two adoptions by Americans in Wiesbaden from October 1951 to August 1952, many of them not stepchildren, but orphans adopted by childless American couples. The report noted that "military personnel in Germany are particularly interested in adopting children in Germany because of difficulties encountered in America. [American] adoption and welfare agencies or organizations are prone to feel that military families cannot provide a normal home due to their nomadic life".[5] This trend continued into the 1960s – the *Tagblatt* noted as late as 1966 that Americans constituted a large proportion of adoptive parents in Wiesbaden.

As the rules and regulations governing family law became less Byzantine at the end of the Occupation, German-American marriages in Wiesbaden became very common. In 1955, for example, fifteen percent of the marriages announced in the *Tagblatt* and *Kurier* took place between German women and American soldiers. While consistent records are impossible to obtain, a conservative estimate based on newspaper announcements and occasional USAFE reports suggests that seven to ten percent of the marriages in Wiesbaden during the years 1955–1964 involved German-American couples.

Efforts to Improve German-American Relations

As noted in the previous chapter, numerous irritants hindered the development of a truly close relationship between the armed forces and the city. With the outbreak of the Korean War, however, USAFE made a systematic attempt to cultivate good German-American relations not only on the individual level (which in many instances had already occurred), but also between the two communities. In the fall of 1950, the Air Force Information and Education Program (I&E), a moribund source of make-work and kindly described by a USAFE historian as "relatively ineffective",[6] gained a new lease on life. The original mission of I&E had been to provide troops with information such as VD prevention techniques, but its new aim was to help Americans become familiar with German culture and to present the German point of view on issues from the very local to the international. The focus on interpreting the German perspective would, it was hoped, cement the newly formed NATO alliance and bring Americans to a recognition of the closer relationship between the two nations.

In the revamped program, personnel were required to attend lectures on matters ranging from geopolitical alliance systems, to the dangers of world communism, to how to behave as guests while in Germany.[7] The I&E Program was just one component of the Public Information Office or PIO, the organization responsible for all information and education efforts in the American community. The information efforts of the PIO targeted American personnel and family members stationed in Wiesbaden, and most of the information provided by the PIO was relevant only to the military community – pay raises, announcements of deadlines for filing paperwork of one sort or another, shopping hours of the PX, and so forth. The Civil Affairs office, also reinvigorated by the Korean War, addressed the German community directly and worked with German organizations to present an improved picture of the Americans. In time, these two offices were combined into the Public Affairs Office (PAO), an umbrella organization for disseminating information to both the German and American communities.

With the help of Civil Affairs and the PIO, American military commanders and the civilian officials of HICOG became more assertive in their attempts to curb disruptive behavior of Americans, one path toward improved relations. In February 1952, U.S. officials met with 100 tavern and hotel owners in Wiesbaden to discuss problems with American clientele. Colonel Laurence B. Kelley, the commander of the Wiesbaden Military Post, asked bar owners to refuse to serve drunk servicemen and to "call the Air Police if you have any difficulty whatever along this line". Taverns were given signs to hang in their establishments saying "Attention, U.S. military personnel: The owner of this establishment is in cooperation with the provost marshal and has been requested to call the air police in all instances of misconduct. Cooperate in maintaining good order and enjoy your stay."[8] The Wiesbaden chief of police, Herbert Becker, said it more bluntly to his countrymen: "Use your heads like good Germans (...). The troops are our guests, and our defenders."[9] According to Kelley, Americans spent close to 500,000 marks a month in Wiesbaden, and much of this was spent in bars and restaurants, a fact of which the owners were well aware.

American delinquency continued in spite of efforts to address the problem. Finally, in October 1952, a curfew was put in place for off-duty American military personnel. Between the hours of one and six o'clock in the morning they were not to be on the streets or in public places. Strictly speaking, this applied only to junior enlisted personnel, but officers and higher ranking enlisted men were advised to be off the streets if possible as well. According to a subsequent report, the curfew was "well received in all German official circles as it became a major factor in helping them solve many of the chronic public security and safety problems (...) [and] improved the behavior of troops on Wiesbaden streets and in public places".[10] Bar owners, however, suffered a sharp decrease in American customers, which affected their businesses adversely.

The curfew, and other measures through which Americans acknowledged their culpability in causing citywide problems and resolved to fix them, were important moves toward the strengthening of German-American friendship. But until the requisitioning situation was solved entirely (see previous chapter), the housing issue generated a great deal of resentment toward the American presence. Daily reports on new construction, the large numbers of homeless Germans, and the slow return of requisitioned buildings drew constant attention to the fact that Americans were a significant part of the problem. The end of requisitioning in Wiesbaden enabled the Civil Affairs office to work more smoothly toward its goal of enhancing German-American relations.

German-American Clubs

As the Americans moved into the housing areas built in the 1950s, their presence in Wiesbaden changed rather dramatically. On the one hand, they no longer courted resentment by living in requisitioned housing areas, and tensions reduced accordingly. On the other hand, Americans now could spend their entire tours in Germany without ever venturing off the American bases, and a certain intimacy and familiarity between Germans and Americans slowly began to disappear. In time, many members of both communities knew each other only through newspaper articles or through carefully orchestrated public relations events. The new model of German-American interaction could be described as "voluntary" – Americans and Germans were not forced to have dealings with each other if they chose not to.

It does appear, however, that this voluntary interaction became more common among those Germans and Americans who were interested in getting to know each other better. Servicemen formed the first German-American friendship organization in Wiesbaden, the "Wiesbaden Union", as early as 1947.[11] The German American Women's Club, founded in

1948 by ten American and ten German women, was one of the first of its type in the U.S. Zone. From its inception, the group served an important social function as well as raising money for charities. In its early years it was an important source of revenue for organizations providing food and clothing to local children. It continued to sponsor a number of charities even as the reconstruction of the postwar economy made emergency relief needs less dire, and it also formed a scholarship fund, which sponsored several German and American exchange students each year. While dozens of similar clubs were formed in other cities and towns, the Wiesbaden women's organization remained one of the mainstays of the Federation of German-American Clubs, a nationwide umbrella group.

In 1952, German civilians and American military officers formed a German-American men's group, known as the Good Neighbors, along the same charitable-social lines as the women's club. Both clubs organized frequent events throughout the year, both for their members and for the general public. Club leadership alternated between German and American members, and many members of the clubs were involved in German-American activities in other spheres. The beginnings of a longstanding German-American social circle were formed through these clubs.

The USAFE policy of nurturing good German-American relations showed signs of success as early as the end of 1951, when the PIO reported that "no derogatory material concerning the Air Force" was to be found in local newspapers, contrary to the previous year when negative comments concerning requisitioning outnumbered positive reports. In February 1954, the Office of Information Services (OIS, later Office of Information, or OI) replaced the earlier organization, but continued and expanded its mission – divided into the Historical Program, Public Information, Internal Information, and the publication of the *Wiesbaden Post* newspaper. The unit worked closely with Civil Affairs to disseminate information about German-American relations. Civil Affairs continued to act as the liaison between the American installation and the German community, dealing with issues ranging from hunting and fishing permits for Americans to German complaints about American-generated pollution. This office initiated regular "German-American Council" meetings with the commander of the American community, the Oberbürgermeister, and other officials to discuss issues of significance to the German and American communities. In the first half of 1954, for example, the major topics included "derequisitioning of buildings, apartment housing projects, construction of recreation facilities and discussions on controversial articles in the local press pertaining to official releases of information".[12] In these meetings, the Germans met the Americans more or less as equals, unlike the earlier years when the Americans held "oberste Gewalt", or supreme authority. Both sides began to perceive their relationship as an alliance, an impression fostered and encouraged by the federal governments of both nations.

German-American Friendship Week

In 1954, Americans and Germans worked together to celebrate this new phase of the relationship, in the first annual German-American Friendship Week, running from 10 to 16 May. The Federation of German-American Clubs sponsored the week Zone-wide, and Civil Affairs cooperated with the German-American Women's Club to organize activities in Wiesbaden. The OIS and German officials were also involved in planning and carrying out the Friendship Week.

The events of the first German-American Friendship week illustrate the types of officially sanctioned German-American interaction common from the mid-1950s until the early 1970s. Preliminary activities included an Air Force Band concert in the Kurpark, followed the next day by another Kurpark concert, this time classical music performed by German and American groups. Music performances remained an important element in German-American activities, as a form of entertainment that could be enjoyed by both communities in spite of language barriers. The 686th Air Force Band was stationed in Wiesbaden, and for over twenty years, until its reassignment elsewhere, performed frequently in the city. The band was a much-loved asset for both Americans and Germans.

The highlight of the official opening ceremony of the first Friendship Week was a lecture on Nazism by Dr. Max Horkheimer, a prominent scholar at Frankfurt University. The event proved to be one of the few of its kind. In later years, the Nazi era was rarely mentioned in the course of

German-American activities, and never by Americans. German dignitaries occasionally alluded to the progress made by Germany in the years since 1945, but open discussion of Germany's National Socialist past seemed to be generally taboo. Silence on this topic, it must be noted,

The German-American Friendship Week always included many musical performances by German and American groups.

reigned not only in German-American friendship circles; in the 1950s it became normal throughout West Germany and the United States. Other Friendship Week events included more music, a GYA handicraft exhibit, dancing, films, and sports. The celebration ended with church services at St. Bonifatius and the Marktkirche. "On the whole", reported Civil Affairs, "the programs during this week were a great success which is a proof that constructive work with gratifying results can be achieved through German-American cooperation".[13]

German-American Friendship Week became a tradition in Wiesbaden, with increasingly elaborate schedules of events. In 1956, a German-American military band concert excited a great deal of attention – the first time a German military band had played in Wiesbaden since the war. That same year, the annual convention of German-American clubs took place in Wiesbaden, with eighty delegates from twenty-four clubs. Another event, connected with the Friendship Week, began in 1956 when WAB held a daylong open house. The "Tag der Streitkräfte" usually coincided with Armed Forces Day, which came at the end of the Friendship Week, and offered Germans a chance to examine stationary displays of U.S. and Allied aircraft, observe demonstrations of military procedures such as first aid or air assault maneuvers, and sample American-style refreshments. Hot dogs, soda, and especially American ice cream from the PX became a major draw for the Armed Forces Day open house. The first event attracted 10,000 people, but attendance increased each year. Part of this increase was due to the inclusion of precision-flying demonstrations. In 1957 the "Sky-Blazers", a USAFE acrobatic aircraft team stationed at Bitburg Air Base, put on a show at the open house, helping to bring the number in attendance to 50,000, even though, according to Civil Affairs, the weather was cloudy and rainy. Throughout the 1950s and 1960s, the German-American Friendship Week was a popular event, garnering a great deal of publicity and attention throughout the city.

Other German-American Interaction

Americans also began to participate in German festivities. While in 1950, Americans were prevented from attending Fasching celebrations, by 1956 the Wiesbaden Fasching committee chose an American girl to be a carnival princess, and the USAFE and Army bands marched in the parade.[14] In fact, outside of German-American Friendship Week, most public German-American festivities occurred at traditional holidays, such as Fasching, Easter, and Christmas. In 1956, the Good Neighbors began their long tradition of sponsoring a Fasching Ball held at the Kurhaus, which raised money for German and American charitable causes. The Fasching Ball became, according the newspapers, one of the highlights of the Fasching season. This may have been an exaggeration, but in any case the Fasching Ball was usually attended by German and American dignitaries, including

In the 1950s and early 1960s, American personnel in Wiesbaden participated in holiday celebrations of all kinds, including the „storming" of the Rathaus, a Fasching tradition.

the USAFE commander, the Hessian Minister-President, the Oberbürgermeister, and others. In addition, beginning in the early 1950s, the city and the military community sponsored an annual German-American Christmas sing-along at the Rathaus courtyard. Each year the

Americans also invited the German public to a Christmas concert held in the theater at Hainerberg. The Chaplain's office held numerous Christmas parties for German and American children and other Christmas activities. At Easter, German-American religious services were held in German churches, especially the English language Anglican Church St. Augustine of Canterbury, which had served for several years as a U.S. military chapel.

African-Americans in Wiesbaden

Since 1945, African-Americans had been a presence in Wiesbaden as Occupation personnel. At first they served in segregated units – the Transportation and Construction units were "colored" –, but in 1948 President Truman desegregated the U.S. armed forces and African-American personnel were no longer limited to lower-status support units. African-Americans were more heavily represented in the Army than in the Air Force, and more often in the enlisted ranks than officers, but many were stationed in Wiesbaden nonetheless. In the early years, "colored" troops were said to be kind, friendly, and generous. Germans attributed this to the shared experience of being the underdog; whether this interpretation was accurate or not, it remained a widespread perception. On the other hand, African-Americans found themselves implicated, often unfairly, in crime and indiscipline. Venereal disease statistics, for example, generally indicated a higher rate for black units than for white units. Racist white officers used such information as evidence of black soldiers' inherently uncontrollable nature, but some analysts took a more insightful approach. In one report, for example, a venereal disease officer speculated that higher rates were attributable to the fact that German women fraternizing with black soldiers suffered such a drastic decline in social status among whites that they continued to associate only with the African-American subculture, so one carrier of the disease might have a disproportionate impact. Furthermore, both black soldiers and their German partners were less likely to use prophylactics or request appropriate treatment, fearing stigmatization. Higher rates, the officer concluded, were due to racism, not greater frequency of promiscuous sex, as whites often claimed.

The presence of African-Americans in Wiesbaden evoked curiosity in many Germans, but not as much as was the case in more isolated towns and villages. Wiesbaden maintained a long cosmopolitan tradition of international tourism, and after World War I the city had been occupied by French troops, some of whom came from French colonies in Africa. Many younger Wiesbadeners, however, had never seen Africans or black Americans until the Occupation years.

Was prejudice against African-Americans common in Wiesbaden? Many Germans and Americans, both white and black, have asserted that bigotry was a serious problem. Certainly children of German mothers and African-American fathers had no easy time of it. But black soldiers had different perceptions. Many enjoyed life in Germany enough to extend their tours as much as possible, and even married German women and remained in Europe after retirement. They preferred German curiosity and the relatively mild mistrust of a few to the harsh, bleak life of the segregated South, where black soldiers serving in the U.S. armed forces could not find habitable off-base housing because of racist Jim Crow laws, and where they would find themselves in physical danger if they associated with their white colleagues.

German-American Activities in the 1960s

Throughout the 1960s, clubs, groups and public affairs bureaus on both sides pursued German-American activities enthusiastically. The year 1966 opened with an official expression of interest in German-American friendship, as commander Colonel Gail L. Stubbs and the Office of Information sponsored a new German-American youth group. The goal of the group was to "promote and increase German-American friendship, to further cultural understanding and to overcome the language barrier". At its inception, the club had sixty members,[15] with German and American co-presidents.[16] However, it appeared that at least some of the American teenagers were encouraged to join with incentives such as school credit and time off from classes; many of the members did not stay in the club once the school year was over.[17]

German-American activities directed at adults were well attended through the mid-1960s. Officials from the Wiesbaden Carnival Association developed a custom of presenting American personnel with Fasching medals of honor in appreciation for their participation in the German holiday.[18] In February 1966 the Fasching ball was held with special fanfare at the Kurhaus, in honor of the tenth anniversary of the tradition.

Colonel Harold P. Sparks receives his 1965 Fasching medal of honor from Oberbürgermeister Georg Buch.

A noteworthy development in German-American friendship circles was the choice of Wiesbaden as the city where national German-American Friendship Week 1966 officially began, with a ceremony in the Kurhaus honoring astronaut John Glenn. Prominent Germans and Americans attended the opening ceremonies, including U.S. Ambassador George McGhee; Hessian Minister-President Georg-August Zinn; Oberbürgermeister Georg Buch; Gertrud von Berg, national president of the Federa-

John Glenn in conversation with Minister-President Georg-August Zinn.

tion of German-American Clubs; and General Andrew O'Meara, the commander of USAREUR. Remarks at the opening ceremony recalled the path of German-American friendship since the end of the war: "Aus dem Befehl 'Keine Verbrüderung' von vor zwanzig Jahren sei eine echte Freundschaft geworden" (From the non-fraternization order twenty years ago, a true friendship has grown), said one speaker.[19] After the reception in the Kurhaus, the traditional music festival took place at the Berliner Straße stadium, and the *Tagblatt* reported that "thousands saw the 'show of the year'" at which John Glenn spoke.[20] Many of the spectators apparently were motivated by the desire to see the famous American in person. Glenn received a great deal of attention in the newspapers; fully half the twelve newspaper articles during Friendship Week concerned Glenn's visit, which lasted just two days. "Wahrscheinlich ist der Höhepunkt der diesjährigen deutsch-amerikanischen Freundschaftswoche schon vorüber (...). Weltraumfahrer John H. Glenn ist dann nicht mehr dabei!" (Perhaps the high point of this year's German-American Friendship Week is already over (...). Astronaut John H. Glenn is here no longer) lamented the *Kurier*.[21] Other events during Friendship Week included the charity ball sponsored by the Women's Club and a musical performance in which several choral groups participated. Church groups got involved in the celebration: the Hainerberg Chapel Protestant group offered an "Evening of Sacred Music", in which Germans and Americans performed,[22] and the Catholic St. Anne's Society sponsored a party for forty orphan children of the St. Michael's Kinderheim in Wiesbaden.[23] The Friendship Week concluded with the traditional Armed Forces Day open house at WAB, where between

70,000 and 75,000 visitors arrived, far more than the 60,000 expected.[24] The day was counted as a success, but perhaps the theme of German-American friendship was beginning to wear thin; "Böse Zungen behaupteten nachher, der Flugtag sei für die meisten Besucher gar nicht das Wichtigste – vielmehr (...) die Aussicht auf eine Portion amerikanischer Eiscreme" (evil tongues claimed afterwards that Armed Forces Day isn't the most important thing for most people – their aim is to eat some American ice cream), reported the *Kurier*.[25]

Moreover, although John Glenn's visit added a great deal of excitement to the week, many of the smaller events held in previous years were not held in 1966. Lectures and museum exhibits went unannounced in both American and German papers. The 1967 Friendship Week offered even fewer activities. The *Tagblatt* mentioned only a choral concert at Hainerberg, a German-American concert at the American Community Center (ACC), a show of English and German books at the city library entitled "So sehen andere Völker unser Land" (How other people see our country), and the Women's Club charity ball.[26] The Armed Forces Day open house was as popular as ever, featuring a show by the Thunderbirds precision flying team; the Wiesbaden police estimated a crowd of 110,000.[27] However, while the *Tagblatt* covered the show with five articles, the *Kurier* devoted only one story, accompanied by a small photo, to the event.[28]

Overall, media coverage of German-American Friendship Week 1967 was much less than in the early 1960s, and this trend continued in subsequent years. It was due in part to personnel difficulties in the 7101st Office of Information. According to the OI records of 1966, "there is no manning problem (…) but there is an experience problem". With the exception of longtime community affairs chief Klaus Müller, airmen with "negligible training and experience" staffed the OI.[29] Airmen new at the job did not have the personal connections with staff of the *Tagblatt* and *Kurier*, and were perhaps not aware of the importance of alerting the media to newsworthy events.

In spite of decreasing media attention to Friendship Week, German-American activities in general did not subside significantly, because they relied on a core of dedicated members rather than on the interest of the broader public. The clubs, in particular, continued to sponsor charity events and social activities for their members. The highlight of the year for the German-American Women's Club was the charity ball, which the club scheduled during the Friendship Week. The event raised money for a scholarship fund to send German and American students to college, and enabled the women's club to donate items and money to the Nassau Home for the Blind and a school for special needs students.[30] The Good Neighbors also continued to sponsor their Fasching ball, donating proceeds to three local orphanages.[31] In December 1966 the newly formed German-American youth group took a trip to West Berlin, flying in an Air Force C-118 because German-American groups were not allowed to travel on the autobahn to Berlin. The trip gave the thirty-nine students an opportunity "zu erfahren, was die Berliner bewegt" (to find out what interests the Berliners).[32]

A well-publicized German-American event in 1966 was the "große Zapfenstreich" (Grand Tattoo), a farewell ceremony sponsored by the city of Wiesbaden for departing USAFE commander General Bruce Holloway. The Grand Tattoo, featuring an after-dark torchlight parade, was a Prussian tradition dating to the eighteenth century. It received extensive coverage in both the German papers and the *Post*. The public was invited to the Grand Tattoos, and many Germans and Americans attended. The ceremony was intended as an unusual honor, but in fact after General Holloway's departure it came to be held for every USAFE commander who served a full tour.

Other German-American events continued throughout 1966 and 1967. Two sources of small-scale but frequent German-American activities were the chapels and the American schools. The chapel communities of WAB and Hainerberg sponsored numerous activities directed toward the civilian community. At WAB, for example, the St. Anne's Society conducted clothing drives for the Spanish and Italian missions in Wiesbaden, while Protestant teachers from the German Bible Institute taught classes for the American congregation, and the Protestant Junior Choir sang Christmas carols at a retirement home in Biebrich and at an orphanage in Wiesbaden. At Hainerberg, the Protestant Women of the Chapel (PWOC) donated money to the German Baptist Church for a summer camp, the Protestant youth group hosted German members of a Biebrich church for socials, and American choirs sang at German churches. In December 1967 the combined Catholic and Protestant choirs performed a selection of Handel's *Messiah*: "Received many fine comments from German nationals", a report from the chaplain's office noted. During the same time period, a Protestant youth group collected food for "needy German families". Although this type of charitable activity was perhaps an anachronism by 1967, the youth group also organized programs entitled "Aspects of Sex" and "The Hippies and Drug Addiction"; these activities, more than the food drive, suggested the direction future social outreach would take.[33]

The DoDDS system also tried to foster German-American contact between students, but exchange programs and instruction in German language and culture were inconsistent because they were organized by individual schools, rather than as an element of central policy. Most notable in this regard were the Aukamm and Vandenberg elementary schools, at Aukamm Housing Area and Mainz-Kastel, respectively. These schools sponsored intercultural programs which included visits to German schools, cultural activities in Wiesbaden, and German language classes.[34] Aukamm arranged an exchange program with a German elementary school: German children celebrated Valentine's Day, Halloween and Thanksgiving at the Aukamm school with American children, while American children visited their German peers for other holidays.[35] It is perhaps significant that only children of higher-ranking officers were enrolled at Aukamm elementary school. Their parents, better educated and more influential than enlisted personnel, may have insisted that their children's educational experience include exposure to German language and culture.[36]

At the beginning of 1968, a USAFE management team inspecting the 7101st noted that "community relations within the area are very good; the support the commander and key staff officers render various community relations endeavors enhance the value of the program". Throughout 1968 and 1969, German-American activities continued to be popular among large numbers of Americans and Germans, but in spite of the efforts of the Information Office, promotion of German-American events in Wiesbaden's daily papers decreased dramatically. The decline was most evident in coverage of German-American Friendship Week festivities. In 1968, the two events publicized in the *Tagblatt* and *Kurier* were the women's club charity ball and the Armed Forces Day open house at WAB. The ball, according to the *Tagblatt*, was well attended and brought in 4,000 marks for the club's student exchange program.[37] In 1969, the charity ball was also "well attended", but aside from the open house, no other Friendship Week events were announced in the *Kurier*. The *Tagblatt* did not report on the 1969 ball at all, but a short article on the opening of the week reported that two concerts at the Kurpark would be held, one featuring the Frankfurt American High School band.[38] The lack of publicity for the week was particularly noteworthy because the national German-American Friendship Week held its opening ceremonies in Wiesbaden in 1969, as it had with much greater fanfare in 1966.[39]

The Armed Forces Day open house, in contrast, was very popular in 1968 and 1969; a big draw was the "Red Arrows" precision-flying team from the British Royal Air Force, which performed both years. In 1968, the *Tagblatt* noted that WAB was the only air base in Germany to offer an aircraft performance during the national Friendship Week.[40] This suggests that the level of German-American Friendship Week activities had been diminishing not just in Wiesbaden but on other U.S. military installations as well. It also helps to explain the large crowds from all over Germany that flocked to the Wiesbaden open house. Colonel Norbert Treacy invited guests to come and see "was wir tun. Und auch, dass wir eine Streitkraft des Friedens sind" (what we do. And also, that we are a force for

Colonel Norbert C. Treacy, commander of the 7100 ABW during the turbulent year 1968.

peace).⁴¹ The *Post* and the German papers produced conflicting estimates of the number of visitors, the *Post* estimating a crowd of 100,000 in 1968,⁴² while the *Tagblatt* reported that 80,000 people came, in spite of rain and wind, partly to purchase one or more of the 60,000 containers of ice cream sold. "Doch was wäre der 'Tag der Streitkräfte' ohne Eiscream!" (What would the open house be like without ice cream) the *Tagblatt* wondered. In 1969 the day was also plagued with bad weather, but in spite of thunder, lightning and hailstorms, "viele kamen, sahen, staunten und schleckten" (many came, saw, gaped, and ate). An estimated 65,000 visitors ate 52,000 cartons of ice cream and watched the Red Arrows.⁴³ The *Post* predicted a "Record Armed Forces Day Crowd",⁴⁴ but did not report any numbers after the event.

The year 1969 was the twentieth anniversary of the founding of NATO, and the Friendship Week was a logical time to celebrate such a milestone. The lack of publicity for the Week was especially surprising, therefore, and in part indicated financial pressure, political ambivalence, and public disinterest. However, German-American Friendship Week was not the only German-American event to suffer from a lack of attention. Other traditional activities like the participation of the 7101ˢᵗ ABW in the annual Fasching parade, and the German-American Fasching ball sponsored by the Good Neighbors, received no publicity in either daily paper. That the events were not promoted did not signal their actual demise – in contrast to the German papers, the *Post* reported heavily and enthusiastically on German-American activities. For example, according to the *Post*, twelve bands provided music for the 1968 Fasching ball, and "the crowd (…) is expected to break all attendance records". That year, the *Post* reported, the USAFE band marched in the Wiesbaden parade and a "Dixieland" float was entered by the 7101ˢᵗ, upon which Miss Wiesbaden Air Base rode. Americans also lent their convertibles for use in numerous parade floats, as they had in past years.⁴⁵

Throughout the 1960s, German-American friendship continued to be celebrated by those dedicated to fostering it. As has been noted, however, media coverage of activities decreased noticeably in the course of the decade. Military commitments in Southeast Asia pulled experienced personnel from the public affairs offices, and pressure from the German economic boom began to eat away at the ability of the Wiesbaden military community to pay for expensive public relations events. Decreasing interest in the German community was a factor as well. Events during the 1960s in West Germany and West Berlin, such as the growing student movement and the shooting death of protester Benno Ohnesorg, drew attention away from what to some looked like Cold War propaganda. Furthermore, over the years the Germans had grown accustomed the American presence. "It wasn't so new anymore, and it was clear that the Americans were here to stay. So people weren't as interested", observed one eyewitness.[46] German-American friendship activities had served their purpose – to accustom the two communities to each other's presence, and help them learn to live together harmoniously.

---

1 USAFE: "History of the HQ Command, USAFE and Assigned Units", November–December 1952, 24.
2 WP, "Alien Marriages Peak", 25 November 1948.
3 WP, [no title], 6 August 1948.
4 USAFE: "History of the HQ Command, USAFE and Assigned Units", July–August 1952, 16.
5 Ibid.
6 USAFE: "History of the HQ Command, USAFE and Assigned Units", July–August 1951, 25–34.
7 Ibid.
8 USAFE: "History of the HQ Command, USAFE and Assigned Units", January–February 1952, 43–44.
9 Ibid.
10 USAFE: "History of the HQ Command, USAFE and Assigned Units", November–December 1952, 15.
11 WK, „Die ‚Wiesbaden Union'", 25 July 1947.
12 USAFE: "History of the HQ Command, USAFE and Assigned Units", January–June 1954, 59.
13 USAFE: "History of the HQ Command, USAFE and Assigned Units", January–June 1954, 60.
14 USAFE: "History of the HQ Command, USAFE and Assigned Units", January–June 1956, 55.
15 7101 Air Base Wing History, "Historical Data Record: Office of Information", 1 January 1966–30 June 1966, 3.

16 *WP*, "Remy, Kelley Elected G-A Youth Club Heads", 14 January 1966.
17 Klaus Müller, former chief of community relations for the 7101st Air Base Wing, interview by author, tape recording, Wiesbaden, Germany, 2 March 1994.
18 *WP*, "Grand Fasching Medal", 28 January 1966.
19 *WT*, „Amerikas erster Astronaut wurde mit Jubel und Beifall begrüßt", 9 May 1966.
20 *WT*, „Tausende sahen die ‚Show des Jahres'", 9 May 1966.
21 *WK*, „Freundschaftswoche beginnt mit Paukenschlag", 9 May 1966.
22 7101 Air Base Wing History, "Historical Data Record: Hainerberg Chapel", 1 January 1966–30 June 1966, 2.
23 Ibid.
24 *WT*, „75 000 beim Tag der Streitkräfte'", 23 May 1966.
25 *WK*, „Die Air Force rief – und 70 000 kamen", 23 May 1966.
26 *WT*, „Freundschaften auffrischen", 6/7 May 1967.
27 *WT*, „110 000 Besucher auf dem Flugplatz", 22 May 1967.
28 *WK*, „Amerikaner gehen für Deutsche in die Luft", 20 May 1967.
29 7101 Air Base Wing History, "Historical Data Record: Office of Information", 1 July 1966–31 December 1966, 3.
30 *WT*, „Licht in das Dunkel", 28 July 1966, 4; *WT*, „Hilfe für Behinderte", 9 November 1966.
31 *WP*, "Tenth Annual G-A Benefit Fasching Ball Set February 12", 28 January 1966.
32 *WT*, „Flug in die geteilte Stadt", 3/4 December 1966.
33 7101 Air Base Wing History, "Historical Data Record: CHN", 1 July 1967–31 December 1967, 2.
34 7101 Air Base Wing History, "Historical Data Record: DoDDS", 1 July 1966–31 December 1966, 5.
35 *WK*, „In der Schule spukten Gespenster", 2 November 1996; *WK*, „Deutsche Kinder feiern mit Amerikanern", 22 November 1966; *WT*, „Deutsche Kinder erleben Valentinstag", 17 February 1967.
36 In 1967 the Wiesbaden schools were transferred from the jurisdiction of USAFE to USAREUR and their records have not been made available for this study.
37 *WK*, „Tanz in die Freundschaft", 11 May 1968.
38 *WT*, „Freundschaft enger knüpfen", 2 May 1969.
39 *WK*, „Könige der Lüfte kommen", 10 May 1969.
40 *WT*, „Fäuste und Pfeile als Attraktion. Am Sonntag: Tag der Streitkräfte", 16 May 1968.
41 *WK*, „Der Blick über den amerikanischen Zaun", 16 May 1968.
42 *WP*, "Armed Forces Day Show Draws 100,000 Spectators", 24 May 1968.
43 *WT*, „Icecream war beim Flugtag wieder die große Attraktion", 19 May 1969.
44 *WP*, "Record Armed Forces Day Crowd Expected", 16 May 1968.
45 *WP*, "More Autos Needed", 2 February 1968.
46 Rudi Schmitt, former Oberbürgermeister of Wiesbaden, interview by author, tape recording, Wiesbaden, Germany, 26 May 1994.

Economic Relations

The history of economic relations between the American armed forces and their German neighbors is one of the more interesting chapters of this story. During the early Occupation, the economic imbalance between Germans and Americans was at its most extreme – many Germans were reduced to begging, blackmarketing, and prostitution in their struggle for existence, while Americans could commandeer whatever goods and services they desired. In the early years, a job with the Americans, no matter how menial, was valued above all things, because with it came at least one hot meal daily and the opportunity to cadge cigarettes, PX rations, and other goods for trade on the black market.

While this peculiar situation had largely remedied itself in the 1950s, the economic disparity between Germans and Americans continued. Germans sometimes resented the PXs and commissaries that made American goods available to members of the armed forces, viewing the special shops as evidence of American disdain for German products. As the "economic miracle" gathered steam in West Germany, Germans became increasingly sensitive to suggestions that German standards stood below American ones.

Then, in the 1960s, the economic revival of West Germany brought a severe labor shortage, which hit American bases especially hard. Personnel offices struggled, usually without success, to retain "local national" workers who could earn more in a German firm, with better conditions and more job security. In addition to this burden, the expansion of the Vietnam War drained financial resources from the budgets of American bases in Europe, and funding for "extras" dried up. As West German standards of living rose, the quality of life on American bases in Germany declined, and the economic balance between the two cultures began to reverse. When, in the early 1970s, the Nixon administration took the dollar off the gold standard and allowed a floating exchange rate, the purchasing power of the American dollar plummeted, leaving many servicemembers in poverty. The redevelopment of West Germany, coupled with American monetary policy and international commitments, transformed the economic relationship between Germans and American

GIs; by 1973, the Germans were affluent and comfortable, while many American personnel were poor and demoralized.

The Americans as Employers

The U.S. forces in Wiesbaden depended on German help from the very first days of the occupation. Few Americans spoke the German language with any fluency, and those who did were often assigned to important tasks in intelligence gathering or positions with OMGUS in Berlin. In Wiesbaden, the MG was dependent on Europeans to act as intermediaries, and sometimes barriers, between the local population and the various units assigned to the city. The American sections of Wiesbaden, including housing areas, were guarded by units of Polish former DPs, many of whom remained in American employ well into the 1980s. On occasion, non-Americans were even employed to maintain barriers between different segments of the American population – for example, in 1945 and 1946, the MG hired German teenagers to guard the women's barracks from marauding male GIs.[1]

Germans, both male and female, worked for the Americans as domestic servants, office personnel, guards and laborers. Official policy was to hire DPs over Germans – UNRRA complained loudly when it found Germans doing work that DPs could have performed, and some Germans lost their American jobs as a result.[2] But many positions, such as translation, typing and other office work, or skilled craftsmanship, required special skills. In spite of DP preference policy, most of the employees of OMG-(G)H in Wiesbaden were German – in May 1947, for example, 264 U.S. military, 207 U.S. civilian, and 2,572 "Indigenous" or (mostly) German employees performed a variety of tasks for the military government.[3] Through the months and years of occupation, the numbers varied widely, but thousands of Germans were employed in some capacity by the American forces in Wiesbaden.

Many Germans viewed employment with the Americans as an excellent opportunity, primarily because the job came with daily hot meals. Another positive aspect of the employment was that Americans tended not to be overly concerned with evidence of training or

Economic Relations 107

Although the U.S. forces could not promise long-term job security, some workers stayed with the Americans for decades; this photo was taken in 1982.

qualifications, but rather demanded only that an employee perform the job adequately. This allowed workers who possessed skill and drive but no formally established credentials to advance fairly rapidly in American employment, an important advantage when formal education had been disrupted so severely by the war.

In many ways the history of the Occupation of Germany is a story of women. So many German men had been killed, imprisoned, or demoralized by suffering that for a few years they were all but invisible. The history of the Occupation as seen through the story of institutions – the rebuilding of the civil service, the courts, state and federal government, etc. – conforms to traditional gender roles and divisions. However, it can be said with great accuracy that women played many of the most important roles in the reconstruction of Germany.

Women struggled to find food and fuel for their families, trading, begging and scavenging. Young women who found a steady GI boyfriend enjoyed an enviable level of protection. Others provided for their families through work in amateur or, less frequently, professional prostitution. While it is most certainly unfair to contend that all women who consorted with American men were by definition engaging in prostitution, the immense power and status that American soldiers possessed, compared with the poverty and vulnerability of German women, made any alliance a somewhat unequal one. As noted in the previous chapter, however, thousands of these alliances ended in marriage and new opportunities in the United States.

Alternatives to prostitution existed, of course. Some of them were rather grim. "[There continues to be a] line of patiently waiting women outside the various enlisted men's billets, hoping to exchange laundry services for a few cigarettes, chocolate bars and soap",[4] remarked a USAFE report in 1947. German women were also an important part of the city workforce, clearing rubble from the badly damaged center city. Known as "Trümmerfrauen", the women cleared away bricks by hand, cleaning them for reuse.[5] The cleanup of the city is owed in no small part to the efforts of thousands of women, young and old, who made the best of their difficult situation, and worked hard to make a better future.

The Black Market

The black market – informal trading of goods and services for necessary items – flourished during the early Occupation years. The Reichsmark rapidly lost all value as the Allies adopted a "rigid monetarist policy"[6] in a misguided attempt to prevent a repeat of the hyperinflation of 1923. In-kind barter replaced buying and selling, often at what would have been considered outrageous exploitation in "normal" years: "Für ein viertel Pfund Butter verlangten sie von mir eine goldene Kette mit einem Anhänger, die ich von meiner Mutter geerbt hatte" (for a quarter of a pound of butter, [traders] demanded a gold chain with a pendant, which I had inherited from my mother), recalled one woman.[7] But in a short time, the standard unit of currency became the American cigarette, used by Americans, Germans, and DPs for all types of trade. One cigarette could buy food for an entire family, and cigarettes were so valuable that an entire industry grew up around their collection and reuse. Children would collect discarded cigarette butts from the ground where GIs had thrown them, and carefully shake out the last few shreds of tobacco. When enough had been gathered, the young entrepreneur could roll new cigarettes, to be traded or smoked to stave off hunger pangs.

The importance of the black market grew as the threat of hunger and even starvation dragged on in 1947 and 1948. German civilians simply could not survive on the rations allotted to them by the Allied authorities – at their lowest level, about 800 calories a day. American food items such as canned meat, milk, coffee, and sugar found their way into the black market trading system through the activities of enterprising GIs or local employees of the Americans. MG authorities in Wiesbaden considered creating a semi-official market, like ones in Berlin and Frankfurt, but rejected the idea as unlikely to do away with the abusive nature of black market trading.[8]

Although work with the U.S. forces was a valuable source of

Military Government - Germany
UNITED STATES ZONE

Notice

POSSESSION, SALE, AND BARTER OF ARTICLES OF UNITED STATES ORIGIN.

1. The existence of a black market in articles brought into Germany for the use of U.S. Forces constitutes a menace to law and order, to the security of the U.S. Forces, to the value of German money and to price control and rationing measures. The Military Government is resolved to take severe measures to repress illegal traffic in these goods.

2. Notice is hereby given that it is unlawful for any person to sell, barter or exchange articles supplied for the use of the U.S. Forces to a civilian or for a civilian to acquire such articles by sale, barter or exchange.

3. The possession by a civilian of food, cigarettes, clothing, gasoline, or other articles, issued or sold by the U.S. Forces will be held prima facie to be a violation of Ordnance No. 1, Section 31 and will be punished by Military Government courts unless possessor affirmatively proves the article was lawfully acquired. Any other act by any civilian contrary to the terms of paragraph 2 of this Notice will be punished by Military Government Courts.

4. The term "civilian" as used herein does not include nationals of the United Nations who are formally accorded the privileges of members of the U.S. Forces.

5. This Notice is effective 7 September 1945.

BY ORDER OF MILITARY GOVERNMENT.

The Military Government tried to suppress the black market, without success.

food, connections and scavenged cigarettes (the pay was not important, because shops offered few items for sale), as the economic situation grew increasingly dire, the attraction of a steady paycheck waned all the more. By early 1948 the American forces reported difficulty in recruitment of workers, as potential employees gave up working for worthless money and spent their days bartering on the black market. Air Installations, which needed large numbers of construction workers for its renovation projects, found that it was becoming "most difficult to retain laborers on the payroll, and it is felt that indigenous personnel feel that they can resort to other means of livelihood with greater earnings that wages offered by occupation forces".[9] The black market, while a logical method of obtaining scarce goods for the individual during such chaotic times, hindered the growth of a normal economy, and endangered Germany's reconstruction. A primary goal of the German and Occupation authorities, therefore, would be to set the German economy back on a legitimate footing.

Militärregierung - Deutschland
AMERIKANISCHE ZONE

Bekanntmachung

Besitz, Verkauf und Tausch von Gegenständen Amerikanischen Ursprungs.

1. Der Schleichhandel mit Gegenständen, die für den Gebrauch der Amerikanischen Streitkräfte nach Deutschland gebracht worden sind, bedeutet eine Gefährdung der öffentlichen Ordnung, der Sicherheit der Amerikanischen Streitkräfte, der deutschen Währung, der Preisüberwachung und der Maßnahmen zur Warenbewirtschaftung. Die Militärregierung ist fest entschlossen, energische Maßnahmen zur Unterdrückung des ungesetzlichen Handels in diesen Waren zu treffen.

2. Es wird hiermit bekanntgemacht, daß es allgemein verboten ist, Gegenstände, die für den Gebrauch der Amerikanischen Streitkräfte bestimmt sind, zu verkaufen oder zu tauschen. Zivilpersonen dürfen derartige Gegenstände weder durch Kauf noch durch Tausch erwerben.

3. Befinden sich Nahrungsmittel, Zigaretten, Kleidungsstücke, Betriebsstoff und andere Gegenstände, die von den Amerikanischen Streitkräften verausgabt oder verkauft worden sind, im Besitze einer Zivilperson, so gilt die Vermutung, daß ein Verstoß gegen die Bestimmungen des Paragraph 31 der Verordnung No. 1 vorliegt, der durch die Gerichte der Militärregierung bestraft wird, es sei denn, daß der Besitzer den rechtmäßigen Erwerb des Gegenstandes einwandfrei nachweist. Jede andere Handlung einer Zivilperson, die gegen die Bestimmungen des Paragraph 2 dieser Bekanntmachung verstößt, wird durch die Gerichte der Militärregierung bestraft.

4. Als „Zivilpersonen" im Sinne dieser Bekanntmachung gelten nicht Angehörige Vereinigter Nationen, denen die Rechte als Angehörige der Amerikanischen Streitkräfte eingeräumt worden sind.

5. Diese Bekanntmachung tritt am 7. September 1945 in Kraft.

IM AUFTRAGE DER MILITÄRREGIERUNG.

Currency Reform and its Effects

In June of 1948, the German government announced the creation of a new currency, the Deutsche Mark (DM), for the western zones, replacing the worthless Reichsmark. The almost legendary effects of the currency reform on the national economic situation are well known – overnight, it seemed, goods appeared in stores, the economy revived and Germany rejoined the family of modern industrial nations.

In Wiesbaden, as elsewhere, the currency change was a big surprise, but it did not provide for everyone the immediate benefits later ascribed to it. "Sources indicate that the German population is somewhat critical of the new mark, thinking that the lack of impressive and illegible signatures lessens its value", reported the *Post* sardonically.[10] However, the reform dramatically increased the number of applicants for jobs in the military community, as well as in German firms, a sign that the population did indeed have faith in the value of the new currency. Goods of all sorts appeared in stores for the first time in years. In July, the *Post* advised Americans in Wiesbaden, who had purchased a total of about 200,000 DM, not to spend them all at once, to prevent temporary inflation. Besides, the *Post* reasoned, "it seems only right that the German populace should get first crack at their own goods. Americans still have a fairly well stocked Post Exchange, Commissary, Swap Shop and Package Store. Why unnecessarily deprive someone of a chance to obtain something he has been 'sweating out' for years?"[11] In September, four months after the currency reform, the *Post* reported that the black market had not yet disappeared, but even on the black market, DM prices for scarce items had stabilized. Coffee and cigarettes were the most common products, selling for eleven to fourteen DM per pound of coffee, and forty to fifty DM per carton of cigarettes. Butter and chocolate were also traded illegally. Continuing shortages and high taxes on legally purchased goods kept the black market in business.[12] However, over the next six months, the black market in Wiesbaden gradually withered away for most products, a most beneficial effect of the currency change.

On the other hand, the reform had an ominous and unintended effect on international politics, hastening the advent of the Cold War. The Soviet

Union viewed the conversion to DM as a deliberate threat to its zone, and in retaliation announced a blockade of the divided city of Berlin. In response, General Clay organized a plan to supply the millions of people in Berlin's western zones with food, fuel and medication – all by air. Wiesbaden played a pivotal role in the Berlin Airlift for several reasons. First, Wiesbaden Air Base and Rhine Main Air Base near Frankfurt were the two American airfields involved in the project, although a much greater number of planes flew from Rhine Main's larger airstrip. Second, Wiesbaden was the location of Airlift headquarters, which took over the Taunusstraße buildings occupied earlier by UNRRA and ARC, then by the ATC, and finally by EATS. Much has been written about the effects of the Airlift on the international situation, and on the city of Berlin itself – without doubt the population most directly affected by the crisis. The Airlift, however, had a significant impact on Wiesbaden as well. Every few minutes, twenty-four hours a day, seven days a week, a plane would take off from WAB. Some residents, traumatized by air attacks during the war, found the incessant noise almost unbearable, though they recognized the importance of the cause. In addition, the airlift meant a large number of jobs for civilians, loading and unloading the planes.

The Airlift also led to a new influx of Americans, just when it appeared that the American presence would shrink sufficiently that most buildings could be returned to their German owners. The arrival of Airlift personnel and their families in Wiesbaden exacerbated the housing shortage and slowed the derequisition process. And, as noted earlier, concern that Soviet retaliation might bring new hostilities in Central Europe made the Americans somewhat loathe to return buildings, in case another airlift or similar emergency arose.

The Economic Miracle and German Employees

While the currency reform brought new applicants to the American employment offices, it also spurred job growth in the civilian sector. Most Germans preferred work among their own fellow citizens, so the Civilian Personnel Office (CPO) continued to have difficulty hiring "local nationals". Moreover, like employers everywhere, the Americans sometimes complained about the quality of workers. In a 1947 report, the Air Installations section noted that enlisted personnel supervising German workers had no management experience, and as a result the German workers were not as productive as they might have been. The report also mentioned a fair amount of stealing.[13] In 1950, General Upthegrove, commander of USAFE, ordered units in Wiesbaden to try to streamline work because of shortages of qualified labor. He noted that other American bases reported a higher productivity level for Germans than for Americans, but, he added, "if that is correct, they have better Germans than we have. Also, the majority of the stations stated that the Germans would rather work for the Americans than the Germans. That is not true here, particularly with the higher-class Germans whom we want for supervisory work. They not only would rather not work for us but will not because we can't pay them enough money."

A lot of this was probably the usual griping of any powerful group employing workers from another culture, similar to complaints from Europeans living in colonial lands in the nineteenth century and other such situations. Some German workers did probably steal, but pilfering and looting were endemic to postwar Germany, "symptomatic of a degree of lawlessness in thought and behavior on the part of both the German and American population (...)", as one report suggested.[14] As the German economy regained its stability and black marketeering disappeared, these problems faded away.

The Labor Shortage

U.S. policy on the employment of German workers fluctuated with changing circumstances. Budgetary cutbacks often shaped employment policy, dictating that new hiring be kept to a minimum or even frozen. Conversely, during times when active-duty personnel were needed elsewhere, the employment of Germans was expanded. In 1953, for example, USAFE implemented Project Native Son, which replaced American military and civilian workers with Germans or other Europeans in non-sensitive jobs as a result of personnel pressures of the Korean War and the resulting troop buildup in Europe. Four years later, however, in

German was spoken on the bases, not only by German family members, like the woman and child in this photo, but also by the many German employees of the Americans.

1957, the German personnel program in Wiesbaden was reduced substantially. Five hundred employees were laid off by the first reduction in Wiesbaden. In short, the American employment policy was not consistent, and German employees of the American forces could not assume long-term employment, although the Americans usually managed to shift laid-off workers into other positions.

Moreover, military communities were burdened with the instability of the U.S. mission in general. Before 1950, the U.S. created plans to decrease the number of troops in Europe, but the Korean War changed defense policy and signaled that the Americans would remain in Europe in large numbers. In spite of the apparent intractability of the Cold War, however, periodic rumors claimed that the Americans were planning to leave Germany, or reduce the numbers of forces stationed in Europe, or that units would be transferred to other installations. The city was not economically dependent on the bases, and local businesses or the city government could have used the space. Yet, as early as 1958, the city was rocked by unconfirmed tales that the Air Force was planning to leave Wiesbaden for a location west of the Rhine River. Civil Affairs reported that "the Wiesbaden community, including business men, hotel operators and others were gravely concerned about the news as were the many German civilian employees of the U.S. Air Force. Repercussions of this news resounded in many leading German newspapers."[15]

In retrospect it appears fairly clear that Wiesbaden was one of the last places that the Americans would have released to the German government, due to its advantageous location and excellent network of housing and installations. Unfortunately, however, the early uncertainty affected the ability of the military community to lure workers as the German economy began to hum in the mid 1950s.[16] In Wiesbaden, the labor shortage began in earnest in the late 1950s, and by the early to mid-1960s had reached crisis proportions. A lack of real job security was the first strike against the American employers. Second was pay rates. German firms competed for employees by raising pay, but the Wiesbaden CPO required authorization from the Department of Defense (DoD), a cumbersome process at best, usually made more difficult by competition from other areas of the defense budget. In addition, the DoD was unwilling to allocate funds for German workers in the early 1960s because of the growing offset-payments issue, discussed below.

American family members were a potential source of employees for the American community, but in reality this source was limited by several factors. First were complex rules set out in the NATO troop statute, which dictated that certain jobs must be reserved for local nationals. Second, American family members usually stayed only a short time in Germany before moving back to the United States. Third, American family members, who often had small children to care for, did not always need or want work outside the home. Finally, the notion that spouses, usually wives, of American personnel could or would take jobs as truck drivers, carpenters, electricians and maintenance personnel on military bases was simply implausible. In the 1950s and 60s, American family members were not a potential solution to the labor problem on U.S. installations.

Instead, the American community in Wiesbaden attempted to fill vacancies with non-German workers – "guest workers" – much like many German firms did. In 1966, the CPO had on its payroll approximately 200 non-Germans, mostly from Spain or Italy.[17] The employment of non-German workers, however, was not a simple solution to the problem. Of the total of 11,450 non-German workers in Wiesbaden in 1966, almost all had been sponsored by German firms, and were already employed.[18] Non-German employees, in other words, could not be found simply by advertising in local papers.

All units were affected by the labor shortage. To cite just one example, throughout the 1960s, the Motor Vehicle Operations Branch

(MVOB), which relied extensively on non-U.S. drivers, had a persistent deficit of about ten percent, resulting in almost 20,000 hours of more expensive overtime for the existing employees.[19] In 1967, the situation worsened. The CPO hoped that the short recession in the West German economy would alleviate the squeeze, but a USAFE report noted that "contrary to all expectations [the recession] had no major impact on the labor force in the Wiesbaden area, where the unemployment rate is less than half of the average unemployment rate of the Federal Republic; 1 per cent vs. 2.3 per cent".[20] In the second half of 1967, advertisements were placed in seventeen different German newspapers announcing positions available for non-U.S. personnel. However, because of low wages, a lack of skilled applicants, and adverse publicity surrounding job security, "the response to the massive advertising campaign fell far below expectations",[21] as the CPO noted. The problem would continue to bedevil the U.S. forces in Wiesbaden for years to come.

The Gold Flow

By the mid-1960s, another economic development began to worry accounting departments in Congress and the Department of Defense: the "gold flow", or the problem of too many American dollars being spent in Europe, and not enough money flowing the other way. The American forces in Germany alone did not cause the gold flow, but military communities and personnel contributed to the problem. The U.S. armed forces spent money in Germany in hundreds of ways, from constructing base facilities and paying monthly rent to thousands of landlords, to purchasing German automobiles and eating in restaurants. Much of this was an unavoidable part of the U.S. commitment to defend Europe, and periodically the U.S. and West German governments negotiated "offset payments" agreements to rebalance the deficit shouldered by the Americans.

Some of the gold flow, however, could be controlled by the individual decisions of Americans stationed in Germany, and as the problem grew in the early to mid-1960s, American officials attacked the problem at the local level. In 1966 the commander of the 7101st, Colonel Kendall S. Young, initiated a gold flow public awareness campaign, reminding personnel and family members that shopping at on-base facilities kept dollars in the American economy. The same year, the 7101st sponsored a contest in which personnel and family members could offer suggestions to reduce the gold flow. "The purpose of the Gold Flow contest is to get practical and workable ideas from the people who daily spend dollars on European goods and services that might otherwise be channeled into the purchase of American products and services", the *Post* explained. Creative suggestions were needed; "We don't want obvious suggestions that will deprive our military community of morale and welfare benefits", cautioned Colonel F. E. Fleming, the contest originator. First prize in the contest was a five day trip for two to Garmisch Recreation Area, a military vacation spot in Bavaria.[22]

In addition to encouraging creative ways to keep money from being spent on the German economy, the Wiesbaden command recommended conservation of utility services. In November, Colonel Young explained in an article in the *Post* that the annual consumption of utilities on the American installations in Wiesbaden had risen to over $ 4 million, including $ 480,000 for water, $ 1.33 million for electricity, and $ 2 million for heating. Coal for heating was purchased in the United States, but local firms sold electricity and water to the base. "The money [spent on utility services] flows directly from the U.S. taxpayer into the German economy. We get nothing back", he wrote.[23] Of course, the Americans received goods and services for their money – but except for their role as defenders, they had no goods or services to offer the Germans in trade.

In another attempt to decrease expenditures, the 7101st initiated a Cost Reduction Program (CRP).[24] The program was created to eliminate fraud, waste and abuse, inviting personnel to suggest ways to operate the base more efficiently. Suggestions leading to significant savings won cash prizes. Unlike the gold flow contest, which aimed to change the personal behavior of personnel and family members, the CRP was directed at the organizational structure of the 7101st. The program was based on the assumption that personnel knew their jobs intimately and could often devise more efficient procedures than those in place. The CRP also served as a morale-boosting program, emphasizing that the Air Force depended on skilled, experienced personnel, and that innovation could pay off. Approximately $ 1,000,000 was saved through the CRP in 1966, as the program met one hundred percent of its goals.²⁵

In spite of these efforts, labor shortages and the gold flow continued, and the costs of the Vietnam War began to affect the financial condition of the Wiesbaden community. "With the cost of supporting combat forces skyrocketing (...) many items taken for granted in past years, were suddenly labeled as luxuries and were either completely eliminated or drastically reduced", a 7101ˢᵗ report noted. In response, the CRP was expanded, and the savings goal for the first six months of the year was set at $ 685,000, which the Wing surpassed, saving a total of $ 745,000. The CRP made many operations more efficient, but the program also cut funding for many non-mission related budgets, such as the base libraries, which scrambled for scarce funding in 1967. The LAS library reported that "funds have been extremely scarce, if not completely unavailable. After considerable expenditure of effort, $ 5,425 were allocated for the purchase of periodicals for the library (...) $ 3,700 were approved for purchase of books", and at the WAB library, one employee lost her job while others were converted to part-time employees.²⁷

Base Support Services

Labor shortages and financial problems did not suffice to dim an extremely positive overall atmosphere in Wiesbaden during the first half of the 1960s. Air Force personnel and civilians generally viewed Wiesbaden as an ideal assignment. A former USAFE commander, General Maurice A. Preston, described his experience in the city:

> *Morale problems are just foreign to [Wiesbaden]. You don't really have morale problems (...). We never did certainly. Everybody is so delighted to be assigned there and they feel they are living so high on the hog that there is very little discontent (...). I never was in a more satisfied, happier, and better motivated command in my life (...).*²⁸

Many Americans enjoyed sightseeing, traveling, and getting to know the city, and in spite of the gold flow problem, commanders encouraged personnel to "Learn German Ways", in the words of one Public Affairs campaign. For the less adventurous, the installations offered numerous recreation and entertainment activities. The Air Force clubs on LAS and WAB remained extremely popular, averaging monthly sales of $ 217,630; the revenue available for club maintenance and improvement was bolstered by profits from slot machines, ubiquitous on military bases overseas, which in Wiesbaden totaled approximately $ 72,443 per month.[29]

Personnel Services, a morale and welfare unit which provided a variety of services from educational opportunities to burial, was also very busy in the early 1960s. The unit historian reported that Personnel Services organized such events as "pool, darts, pinochle, table tennis, badminton as well as Crazy Bingo, birthday parties, drawing contests, quizzes and Record Hops"[30] at the Skyhook recreation center on WAB, and "Spoken German, French, Volkswagen Maintenance, Typewriting, Shorthand, Goren Bridge (…) Drawing and Painting" and ballet at the Community Center near Hainerberg.[31] Personnel enjoyed athletic activities of all kinds, as inter-base leagues competed in football, basketball, baseball, soccer, track, and many other individual and team sports. The chapel system also held a number of events every year, including concerts, religious plays, lectures and family social evenings. Women's groups organized charity drives and social events centered on religious holidays.[32] In the first half of the decade, military life in Wiesbaden seemed to resemble that on a cruise ship, with numerous recreational opportunities for family members and personnel, both officer and enlisted.

The Air Force provided another familiar signpost for homesick Americans when it built a large commissary, or supermarket, at Hainerberg in 1962. The commissary, designed by a German architect, was the largest of the one hundred U.S. food stores in Europe[33] and it drew patrons from Army and Air Force installations throughout central Germany, as well as Wiesbaden. It impressed Germans and Americans alike, although only Americans with military IDs were allowed to shop in the store. By U.S. standards the commissary was not huge – American supermarkets of the time usually sold around 6,500 different products, while the commissary offered only 1,600 items. Compared with the smaller German shops, however, it was, according to the *Tagblatt*, "unheimlich großräumig" (tremendously large). The paper added that "überall davor

Parkplätze für die Autos [sind]" (parking spots are everywhere).[34] About 60,000 Americans shopped there each month, and the commissary conducted an average business of $ 25,000 each day, or over $ 9 million per year,[35] although on the twice-monthly paydays business could reach $ 46,000 per day.[36] By contrast, a more typical American commissary in Oslo, Norway, sold approximately $ 25,000 of goods per month.[37] The commissary did not operate as a for-profit business; the ideal was to break even and .5 percent was the maximum discrepancy allowed; if profits rose above that percentage, prices would be lowered. All items were tax-free, but a five percent surcharge was leveled on purchases, which helped to pay the salaries of civilian staff.

Increasing Economic Challenges

In 1968 and 1969 the Wiesbaden Military Post, like other U.S. installations, continued to suffer from an unfortunate combination of reduced budgetary allocations, logistical pressures of the Vietnam War, and increasing challenges from the strong German economy. In addition, economic tensions frayed German-American relations, as the offset-payments negotiation system collapsed, lack of job security alarmed the installation's non-U.S. employees, and some members of the U.S. Senate, led by Mike Mansfield of Montana, called for troop cutbacks in Europe.

Funding and staff shortages, seen in earlier years, grew worse in 1968–1969. Summaries contained in the official unit histories insisted that in spite of "austere budgeting and shortages of personnel", the 7101st operated at a high level of effectiveness. The 1968 report of the 7101st claimed that "the transition from ordering whatever one wanted to only what was considered to be mission essential" was achieved relatively easily. But even if the military community had indeed managed to balance needs and resources in 1968, a year later almost every unit described pervasive deficits and delays. Necessary maintenance projects in the housing areas, hotels and food service facilities, for example, could not be completed because of budget constraints or shortages in the workforce.[38] Though personnel officers in the CPO made extensive efforts to attract employees, both military manning and civilian recruitment lagged far behind optimum levels. Job security continued to be the biggest drawback for potential civilian employees, as even the CPO admitted that "no guarantee could be given as to the number of years the American forces would be guests of the Federal Republic".[39] The 7101st found it very difficult to attract many types of help: "cleaners; chambermaids; transportation laborers; garbage collectors; warehousemen; laundry workers; electricians; highly specialized mechanics and metal workers" were in especially high demand and short supply.[40] Newspaper and television campaigns enjoyed little success because the CPO could afford only monthly recruiting ads, rather than the weekly ads placed by German firms. This, of course, put the CPO at a disadvantage in the fierce competition for employees.[41] By 1968, the 7101st was actively searching for workers from other European nations. A number of Spanish workers were recruited for the Americans by the German labor exchange authority in Spain and sent to

In the late 1960s and 1970s, the Civilian Personnel Office advertised for employees. One of the benefits offered: „You can acquire or improve your English skills through daily use."

labor exchange authority in Spain and sent to Germany, where they lived in government quarters at Camp Pieri. Clerical personnel, who needed to have a good command of English, arrived from Britain, where the Air Force had several installations and could pursue recruiting efforts from those bases.[42] Eighteen English and Australian women began work in the first six months of 1968.[43] Nevertheless, the lack of workers "delayed work accomplishments, caused customer dissatisfaction and management frustration".[44]

On the other hand, some base operations improved in 1969. Due in part to success of the gold flow campaign, commissary sales increased in 1968, from $ 460,000 in May 1967 to $ 536,000 one year later, and the EES expanded its range of shops in response to booming business. Unfortunately, some of the EES outlets continued to offer a substandard range of goods unappealing to the evolving tastes of young military consumers. A USAFE management team inspecting the base in 1968 found, for example, that the LAS store sold "old, less popular phonograph records (1965, 1966 and 1967 selections)" and too few small ticket electronic items.[45] Because of the rapidly changing cultural climate in the United States and Europe, this lag was particularly distressing.

Another positive development of 1969 was a decrease in the waiting list for government housing. At the end of 1968, 819 enlisted personnel and 451 officers waited for quarters, but six months later, the list was down to 578 enlisted and 149 officers.[46] No new housing had been built, but personnel authorizations of the 7101st had been adjusted downward, so that fewer Americans were moving to Wiesbaden. German housing continued to be necessary for many families, however, which drained a great deal of money into the local economy; in the first six months of 1969, the average rent was DM 491, and the total amount paid by Americans was DM 408,248. "The Wiesbaden area definitely remained a high rental area", concluded a 1969 unit report.[47]

Financial Difficulties for American Personnel

The floating exchange rate instituted in 1971, while reflecting the relative value of the dollar and the DM more accurately, created a significant hardship for American personnel, especially lower enlisted personnel and those with families living in German quarters. Each month, rent and utilities costs rose as the dollar dropped in value, and cost of living adjustments did not cover added expenses. In late 1971 the Wing Command recommended that personnel below the grade of E-8 with four or more family members should not be assigned to the Wiesbaden area because of the considerable economic hardship involved.[48] Base services were affected by the revaluation of the mark as well. The billeting fund, which paid for temporary housing for personnel waiting for government quarters, reported deficits in 1970 and 1971.[49] The commissary noted a substantial increase in business due to the cost of food purchased in German stores.[50] In 1973 the situation became more severe, even coming to the attention of the German population. In February, the *Kurier* reported that bars and prostitutes who accepted dollars had raised their prices because of the exchange rate,[51] and in July the *Tagblatt* reported that family members of lower enlisted personnel were being sent home because of the rising costs, although "for obvious reasons it weakens troop morale", Public Affairs Officer Klaus Müller told the paper.[52]

In the span of approximately twenty-five years, the economic status of the U.S. forces in Wiesbaden underwent a complete transformation. While in the late 1940s, GIs were the most wealthy and generously supplied group in the city, by the early 1970s American personnel of all ranks scrimped and saved, and lower enlisted families were even impoverished. This was due partly to the remarkable redevelopment of the West German economy, of which Wiesbaden was a primary beneficiary, and partly to the Vietnam War, which drained resources from the American military communities in Germany. As military personnel led ever more constrained and impecunious lives, the deleterious effects of poverty on morale and on German-American relations would become increasingly apparent.

---

1   Erich Diefenbacher, former employee of OMG-(G)H, interview by author, tape recording, Wiesbaden, Germany, July 1998.

2 UNRRA 2: Monthly Report, 30 November 1946.
3 HESS4: "Administrative Organization and Development", 3.
4 USAFE: April 1947, 9.
5 In Wiesbaden rubble was also cleared away through the use of narrow-gauge trains, which, by the spring of 1948, had cleared about seventy-eight percent of the rubble – about 380,000 cubic meters. *WP*, "City Dinkies Girdle Globe In Job of Rubble Removal", April 1948, n.p.
6 Douglas Botting, *From the Ruins of the Reich: Germany, 1945–1949* (New York: Meridian, 1985), 235.
7 "Chewing-gum, Cigarettes and no fraternisation", Wiesbadener über den Nachkriegsalltag, oral history project produced by Elly-Heuss-Schule, 1987.
8 USAFE: "History of the Headquarters Command, USAFE and Assigned Units", February 1947, 15.
9 USAFE: "Air Installations Report", April 1947, 22.
10 *WP*, "Military on 30¢ March: Boost Hits US Prices; Finance Purchase Set", 18 June 1948.
11 *WP*, "To Buy or Not to Buy: Smart Money Says No!", 16 July 1948.
12 *WP*, "Black Market Stays Steady Since Reform", 17 September 1948.
13 USAFE: "Air Installations Report", April 1947, 5–7.
14 USAFE: "History of the Headquarters Command, USAFE and Assigned Units", April 1947, 7.
15 USAFE: "Civil Affairs Report", January–June 1958, 9.
16 The beginnings of a labor shortage are discussed in Henry Christopher Wallich, *Mainsprings of the German Revival* (New Haven: Yale University Press, 1955).
17 Ibid., 2.
18 Niederschrift über die 5. Sitzung der Stadtverordnetenversammlung am 7. April 1966, Anfrage Nr. 52.
19 7101 Air Base Wing History, "Historical Data Record: Motor Vehicle Operations Branch", 1 January 1966–30 June 1966, 3.
20 7101 Air Base Wing History, "Historical Data Report: USAFE Base Command", 1 January 1967–30 June 1967, 7.
21 Ibid., 4.
22 *WP*, "Gold Flow Ideas Wanted", 28 September 1966.
23 *WP*, "Commander's Comments", 4 November 1966.
24 7101 Air Base Wing History, "Historical Data Record: USAFE Base Command", 1 July 1966–31 December 1966, 2.
25 7101 Air Base Wing History, "Historical Data Record: DMAT", 1 January 1966–30 June 1966, 2.
26 7101 Air Base Wing History, "Historical Data Report: USAFE Base Command", 1 January 1967–30 June 1967, 2–3.

27 7101 Air Base Wing History, "Historical Data Record: Personnel Services Branch", 1 January 1967–30 June 1967, 2.
28 General Maurice A. Preston, USAFE Commander in Chief 1 August 1966–1 August 1968, interview by Mr. Hugh N. Ahmann, transcript of tape recording, 13–15 September 1973, USAF Oral History Project, Center for Air Force History, Bolling AFB, Washington DC.
29 7101 Air Base Wing History, "Data Digest", 1 July 1966–31 December 1966, 17.
30 7101 Air Base Wing History, "Historical Data Record, Personnel Services", 1 January 1966–30 June 1966, 3.
31 Ibid., 3.
32 7101 Air Base Wing History, "Historical Data Record: Hainerberg Chapel" and "Historical Data Record: Wiesbaden Air Base Chapel", 1 January 1966–30 June 1966, n.p.
33 *WT*, „Der größte Supermarkt Europas", 27 April 1966.
34 Ibid.
35 7101 Air Base Wing History, "Data Digest", 1 July 1966–31 December 1966, 12.
36 *WT*, „Der größte Supermarkt Europas", 27 April 1966.
37 7101 Air Base Wing History, "Historical Data Record, 7240th Support Squadron (USAFE), Oslo, Norway", 1 January 1966–30 June 1966, 10.
38 The historical records themselves changed. From the mid-1950s through most of the 1960s, the semi-annual unit histories of the 7101st were made up of lengthy reports written by each agency, such as Maintenance, Personnel Services, or Transportation. A complete history could cover hundreds of pages, with information about personnel, mission statements, and activity summaries for dozens of different offices. In July 1969, however, the format of the unit history changed; it was issued quarterly, and rather than including separate reports for the various agencies, it was written as a narrative summarizing the problems and achievements of the Wing, similar to the unit histories created in the immediate postwar years. The report was still lengthy, between eighty and ninety pages, and contained a great deal of information, but it was significantly reduced compared to the older reports. No reason was given for the change, but the lack of sufficient manpower and funding, as reported in the documents themselves, likely accounted for the shift. 7101 Air Base Wing History, "Historical Data Record: Special Activities", 1 October 1969–31 December 1969, 38–39.
39 7101 Air Base Wing History, "Historical Data Record: Foreword", 1 January 1968–30 June 1968, 9.
40 7101 Air Base Wing History, "Historical Data Record: Foreword", 1 January 1969–30 June 1969, 11.
41 Ibid.
42 7101 Air Base Wing History, "Historical Data Record: Foreword", 1 January 1968–30 June 1968, 9.
43 7101 Air Base Wing History, "Historical Data Record: CCPO", 1 January 1968–30 June 1968, 3.

44 7101 Air Base Wing History, "Historical Data Record: Special Activities", 1 July 1969–30 September 1969, 37.
45 7101 Air Base Wing History, "USAFE Management Inspection Report", 1 January 1969–30 June 1969, J2, J4.
46 7101 Air Base Wing History, "Historical Data Record: USAFE Base Command", 1 January 1969–30 June 1969, 8.
47 Ibid., 9.
48 7101 Air Base Wing History, "Historical Data Record: USAFE Base Command", 1 October 1971–31 December 1971, 1947.
49 7101 Air Base Wing History, "Billeting Office Report", 1 January 1972–31 March 1972, 1948.
50 7101 Air Base Wing History, "Historical Data Record: USAFE Base Command", 1 July 1971–30 September 1971, 23.
51 *WK*, (n.t.), 8 February 1973.
52 *WT*, „Dollar-Schwund wirkt sich aus auf die Truppe", 26 July 1973.

Vietnam and the 1960s

The years from 1968 to about 1975 encompass an era, inaccurately dubbed "the Sixties", during which the U.S. military suffered perhaps the most severe shock and dislocation in its history. The major cause of this shock, the Vietnam War, took its toll on the armed forces – physically, in lives lost and ruined; economically, through its absorption of available funds which otherwise might have been spent on defense missions around the world; and emotionally, and in terms of readiness, morale, and sense of mission.

Related to the Vietnam crisis but distinct from it were a number of pressures put on military communities in Germany. For one thing, personnel shortages, both military and civilian, reached crisis proportions. The shortage of civilian employees illustrated the continuing impact of the West German "economic miracle", as described in the previous chapter, and the Vietnam War drew away increasing numbers of qualified officers and experienced enlisted personnel for supervisory duties. Secondly, base construction and maintenance were virtually abandoned for lack of funding, at a time when many bases built in the 1930s were reaching obsolescence. During these years it was common for personnel to endure flooded lavatories, defunct heating systems, and rodent infestations in offices and barracks. Finally, a number of cultural changes transformed life in the armed forces, including a widespread mistrust of authority, experimentation with drugs, and growing racial pride among African-Americans that inflamed racist attitudes among some whites, leading to frequent clashes.

In 1973 the U.S. Army moved to an all-volunteer force, eliminating the draft. The other branches of service had always been "all-volunteer", but during the expansion of the Vietnam War effort in the mid-1960s, increasing numbers of "volunteers" in the Navy and Air Force were considered to be "draft-motivated", that is, they enlisted to avoid being drafted and sent to Vietnam. While technically volunteers, these enlistees, who saw themselves as victims of coercion, posed special challenges to military authorities struggling to build a sense of esprit de corps.

Changes in Base Life

Wiesbaden was relatively fortunate during this troubled period. Morale and discipline never reached the nadir that they did in many other U.S. bases in Germany – soldiers and airmen always considered Wiesbaden a desirable assignment. The unusually high proportion of officers and career personnel assigned to USAFE headquarters made the problems associated with "draft-motivated" volunteers a much smaller concern than elsewhere. The most significant challenge in Wiesbaden during this time centered on funding problems, and the lack of finances. Base authorities struggled to make the most of the money they had, to improve life on and around the base.

Financial difficulties emerged especially clearly in the area of base recreation and entertainment offerings. Because these activities were not "mission-essential" in the traditional sense, they were especially vulnerable to budget cutting. On the other hand, the need to spend recreation dollars wisely meant that base recreation and entertainment offerings should correspond as closely as possible to what the majority wanted. There were limits to the rule of popular taste, however, as officials searched for "wholesome" activities that would conform to the ideals of the military – patriotism, traditional moral values and gender roles, and cultural conservatism. An examination of base recreation and entertainment and the changes that took place in this area illustrates the difficult navigation between changing youth culture and a more traditional culture popular among the career military.

A new "audio club" opened in August 1966, whose main focus was selling new stereo equipment and repairing older components. The club also provided a tape duplicating room, an electronic hobby shop, and a library of popular rock and roll recordings. By 1968 it was the most lucrative club in the system. The success of the audio club indicates the growing importance of rock music among Air Force personnel; the unit historian noted that the club "create[d] another wholesome past-time for many members who would otherwise be idle or astray".[1] In the first six months of 1969, the audio club reported a gross income of $ 1.8 million, almost all from equipment sales. The two other special interest clubs, the

Rheinblick Golf Club and the Rod and Gun Club, offering more traditional pursuits, were also well-supported throughout 1968 and 1969.

The enlisted clubs at LAS and WAB, however, showed a large decline in net profit, and the civilian club showed a series of net losses. In fact, by 1970 the Civilian Club had closed its doors permanently. Some of the decline in enlisted club net revenues was due to construction and improvement expenses, as well as increasing labor costs, but much of the decrease was caused by lower sales than in previous years,[2] as younger personnel sought off-base amusement more suited to their tastes. In order to boost revenue, slot machines became omnipresent in 1968 and 1969. Euphemistically referred to as "amusement machines", the slots added a total of almost two million dollars to the club revenues, approximately double the amount brought in 1967. The slot machines, found at all the clubs except the Audio Club, helped to make up the difference in revenue when sales dropped.[3]

The two recreation centers in Wiesbaden offered the customary wide range of activities, although many of the free classes and lessons of past years had been replaced by special events, such as performances and tours. In 1968, the ACC presented six plays performed by the base amateur theater group, as well as an arts and crafts contest and two piano recitals; the ACC building was used for an annual Girl Scout Fair, a Boy Scout "Scout-O-Rama", and Court of Honor ceremonies.[4] The Skyhook center, under the leadership of director Jacky Wolfgang, held numerous German-American events, with the intention of bringing together single airmen and German women. In the second half of 1968 the Skyhook sponsored a German-American dance, and held monthly dances to which Germans were invited.[5] During this period Wolfgang also attempted to organize events that appealed to younger, more disaffected members of the service. For example, in early 1968 the Skyhook hosted a musical performance by a member of the Air Force who sang protest music: "Kein Hinausschreien im Stile ungezügelter Weltverbesserer, sondern mehr musikalischer Ausdruck innerer Unruhe, aufgebaut auf einer Synthese von Folklore und manierlichem Rock and Roll" (not a cry in the style of unrestrained idealism, but more of a musical expression of inner unease, created from a synthesis of folk and moderate rock and roll), according to a review in the *Kurier*.⁶ The event was attended by both Germans and Americans, and was notable for its attempt to provide entertainment of a distinctly nonmilitary bent. The performance at the Skyhook was one of the increasing number of events deliberately designed to draw those who felt alienated by the standard offerings of military recreation centers. It was an event popular or unusual enough to warrant an article in the *Kurier*.

Although all Americans in the Wiesbaden military community were welcome to participate in events at the recreation centers, many of the newer activities appealed to single personnel and married couples without young children. The center offered fewer family events, and some activities targeted to female participants, such as bridge and cooking classes, were discontinued.

The labor shortages afflicting the Wiesbaden CPO did not ease in the early 1970s. Out of approximately 2,000 authorized civilian positions, about one hundred went unfilled. In December 1969 several dozen non-U.S. civilian jobs were terminated in a planned reduction in force (RIF), a money-saving measure. The employees were offered other positions with the Air Force in Wiesbaden, but not all were happy to be uprooted. The RIF made the labor shortage worse in 1970, as workers, fearing that they might be next, scrambled to find jobs with German firms. More importantly, non-U.S. workers were forced to confront the unpalatable fact that the American forces could leave at any time, if political and strategic circumstances dictated. In 1966 the U.S. forces had left France altogether, when French president Charles de Gaulle withdrew his nation from the NATO alliance and demanded that all NATO forces leave France. There was no threat of such measures in West Germany, but some in the United States called for drastic cuts in troop levels in Europe, for reasons of economy. "Continuing publicity concerning the possible reduction of U.S. military forces in Europe has increased the apprehension of the non-U.S. citizen employee towards U.S. employment", the January–March 1970 unit history reported.⁷ Uncertainty continued to beleaguer the CPO well into the 1970s.

The constant shortage of personnel negatively affected life on the installation: long lines, slow service, maintenance neglected. In the commissary, "the hiring of German personnel dwindled to the point of nonexistence";[8] and long lines "made weekly shopping a tiresome chore" throughout the early 1970s,[9] according to 7101st reports. On paydays, two hour waits in checkout lines were common. The main factor keeping personnel and family members shopping at the U.S. facilities was the weak dollar, which made shopping in German stores prohibitively expensive (see previous chapter).

Maintenance, conducted by Civil Engineering, became more of a challenge as civilian employees found other work. In the first nine months of 1970, 135 non-U.S. civilians resigned, most because they felt "a lack of confidence in the future of positions with the United States forces in the Wiesbaden area".[10] The upkeep of housing and office buildings was a vital service affecting morale and cohesiveness among the 20,000 personnel and family members in Wiesbaden. Americans living in military housing, whether single airmen or more established "career" Air Force families, moved from place to place, according to their orders, and generally became accustomed to having little control over their physical surroundings. However, when they lived and worked on an installation surrounded by peeling paint, broken windows, loose floor tiles, and vermin, their attitudes toward military life soured. In family housing, washers and dryers broke down and were not replaced.[11] In the single airmen's dormitories, "washrooms, showers, and toilets in these old buildings were continuously in need of repair and presented a run down appearance",[12] which encouraged a sense of anarchy and disrespect among those using them. The dilapidation of the physical surroundings added to the already pervasive sense of alienation felt among many airmen in Wiesbaden. The problem of dilapidated airmen's quarters became so serious that the West German government gave one million dollars to the military community to be used for improving dormitories in Wiesbaden. German contractors replaced plumbing, electrical wiring, doors, windows, and lavatory tiles, and plastered and painted walls.

Declining Morale

As an organ of the Public Affairs Office, the *Wiesbaden Post* weekly newspaper was carefully controlled by the 7101st ABW, and as such it could not reflect entirely accurately the thoughts and feelings of enlisted men and women. But in the 1970s, the *Post* took on a didactic tone remarkable even for the normally educational paper. While the paper never made explicitly clear at whom or what this material was aimed, the subject matter of inspirational articles hint at what military authorities viewed as the most serious problems: a decline in patriotism, pride in military service, and respect for authority and the law.

In 1970 and 1971, for example, Colonel R. G. McKittrick, the commander of the 7101st ABW, contributed weekly articles to the *Post*, the majority of which focussed on discussions of virtues and ethical behavior. "What are some of the qualities that earn our highest respect (…)?", he asked in one column. "Modesty (…) industry (…) initiative (…) integrity (…) these qualities must be self-developed (…)."[13] McKittrick often praised the pursuit of positive German-American relations in his essays, suggesting that American personnel serve as informal "ambassadors" to their hosts. On the eve of German-American Friendship Week 1970, he noted that "the personal contacts that each of us foster with our German friends are fundamental to our nation's 'people-to-people' program."[14] He addressed the question of German-American interaction on the occasion of "Law Day U.S.A.", again with a didactic purpose: "The people of Germany (…) expect us to obey their laws as they do. By showing respect for their laws we in turn gain their respect."[15] He also discussed German-American council meetings[16] and other German-American events.

Many articles openly criticized the main contours of contemporary youth culture and the anti-authoritarian movement, as it was called in West Germany. Authors exhorted young soldiers and airmen to reject what they saw as the self-indulgence of youth culture and the antiwar movement. A piece entitled "Take the 'Pro' Test", attempted to use reverse psychology to encourage military personnel to see themselves as rebelling against a repressive and conformist "counterculture":

> *(…) the distinction between individualism and protest becomes distorted. Protest for its own sake becomes the fashion and individualism becomes more regimented and*

uniformed than the 'establishment' itself. The dissenters fail to recognize this and continue to see the man who shines his shoes and salutes as conforming to the 'establishment' (...). But is he? (...) Who is this man and what are his goals? He is an American and part of the mightiest machine the world has ever seen. When his flag goes by, he gets a lump in his throat and he thrills at the power of his service and his country.[17]

"*Take the 'Pro' Test*": through media such as the Wiesbaden Post, *the military command tried to oppose the anti-military, countercultural messages in the wider youth culture.*

In addition to the editorial campaign in the *Post*, McKittrick also took concrete steps to improve morale. For example, in April 1971, he gave permission for women to be allowed to visit the enlisted men's dormitories. Although this was a "radical departure from military tradition", after one month airmen and officers agreed it was "a smashing success".[18] More importantly, in 1971, the Wing established a program to improve airmen's facilities on base, known as "Better Living". Under the Better Living program employees renovated bathroom facilities, installed new washers and dryers, and allowed airmen to choose a variety of "rugs, bed headboard and footboard covers, room dividers, bookcases, wall lockers, drapes, bedspreads, light fixtures, and paints" for their rooms.[19] However, the Department of Defense did not provide extra funding for the Better Living program; "a critical Congress will be looking to trim dollar requirements", reported the *Post*. Decision makers in Washington, D.C., did not consider living programs to be mission essential.[20]

Drug Use

For many airmen, declining morale merely meant feelings of boredom, dissatisfaction, and a desire to go home. Some, however, turned to drugs. By 1969, many military personnel throughout the world, including Air Force members, used marijuana or hashish. The impression of universal drug use sometimes recalled by participants and observers was an exaggerated one, but drug use was indeed very common among lower ranking enlisted personnel. Career NCOs and officers were more likely to abuse alcohol than use illegal drugs, and military authorities pointed to a qualitative difference between recreational use of alcohol and use of drugs, a distinction seen as artificial and self-serving by younger enlisted men, fed a huge "culture gap" between airmen and their more traditional superiors, and increased perceptions of alienation on the part of younger personnel.[21]

In Wiesbaden, however, whatever the actual rate of drug use, few arrests of Americans for drugs were noted in the German papers until mid-1971. The relatively late onset of negative publicity in Wiesbaden contrasted with the experience of many other garrison towns, which struggled with flourishing American drug cultures, including drug dealing by American soldiers, from the late 1960s until the early 1980s.

In 1970, newspapers reported only two drug arrests in Wiesbaden involving Americans, and both were treated as sensational anomalies. In the first case, police arrested a group of Americans and runaway German youths living in a deserted building, and in the second, an "international drug ring" including American deserters, was arrested with large quantities of hash and LSD.[22] Both of these cases, in other words, involved "dropouts" who had been marginalized from the mainstream military and German communities, and had already committed a number of offenses, such as going AWOL and desertion. The next year, however, the number of American drug arrests reported in the *Kurier* rose to nine, while the *Tagblatt* reported a total of twelve. These arrests involved active-duty American personnel who were apparently otherwise law-abiding, but who used drugs in their free time. Many Germans used drugs as well; according to the Wiesbaden police, the number of drug arrests in Hesse increased more than one thousand percent between 1960 and 1970.

Wiesbaden found itself in an unfortunate location, a police spokesperson explained in the *Kurier*: "Die Landeshauptstadt gehört durch [ihre] Nähe zu Frankfurt mit zum deutschen Rauschgiftzentrum" (as a result of its proximity to Frankfurt, [Wiesbaden] is a part of the drug center of Germany). The police blamed much of the drug trade on Americans: "Außerdem gibt es viele amerikanische Schüler als Käufer und US-Soldaten als Verkäufer" (moreover, there are many American high school students purchasing drugs, and U.S. soldiers as sellers).[23]

The attention given to drug crimes in the two daily papers does not reveal the actual numbers of Germans or Americans using drugs, nor did news reports accurately reflect the numbers of users arrested by the police. The papers reported only the most sensational and newsworthy events, and in any case they did not report arrests by the Air Police within the American installations. However, the publicity of American drug arrests increased the increasingly common image of the American armed forces as a scourge and a danger to German communities. Interestingly, Germans and Americans both claimed that Wiesbaden's American population was not responsible for drug commerce; rather, they attributed the problem to less-elite U.S. Army troops from Mainz and Frankfurt, who enjoyed visiting Wiesbaden on weekends. Whether this was accurate or simply a function of civic pride is not entirely clear, but rates of drug use were indeed higher in the Army than in the Air Force, according to Department of Defense studies, so the explanation is plausible.

Strangely, there were no drug arrests of Americans reported in the newspapers in 1972, a precipitous drop-off that did not reflect a similar steep decrease in use. Anecdotal evidence suggests that the police stopped arresting people they found using drugs, and it is likely that arrests of this type ceased to be newsworthy. Drug use remained endemic among German and American young people in Wiesbaden until at least the mid-1970s, but as early as 1970 the 7101st began a wide-ranging anti-drug program. With assistance from the Department of Defense, the Bureau of Narcotics and Dangerous Drugs, and other federal agencies, school officials and the 7101st Command sponsored informational seminars for students, parents and active duty personnel on the dangers of drug abuse. In September 1971, USAFE instituted urinalysis for all personnel with the help of an expanded testing laboratory at the USAF Medical Center.[24] In 1971 General David C. Jones arrived in Wiesbaden to take command of USAFE, and he hired a colorful and dynamic drug abuse counselor named Cal Espinoza, with whom Jones had worked in California, to combat drug abuse in Wiesbaden and throughout USAFE.[25] The *Post* also published frequent warnings against the abuse of drugs, including testimonial-style tales and poems allegedly from former drug addicts themselves. "So now Little Man you've grown tired of grass, L.S.D., acid, cocaine, and hash. And someone pretending to be a true friend said, 'I'll introduce you to Miss Heroin'"[26] began one anti-drug poem, reprinted several times. Drug use may not have been the plague for the Air Force in Wiesbaden that it was in other areas, but the 7101st took the problem of drug abuse by American servicemembers in Wiesbaden very seriously.

Crime

Along with drug abuse came an increase in crime and disorderly conduct among Americans in the city. The Wiesbaden police noted that "mit dem Steigen der Rauschgiftfälle schnellte auch die Anzahl der Straftaten empor, die im Rauschzustand stattfanden oder bei denen sich Süchtige Geld für Drogen beschaffen wollten" (with the rising number of drug cases comes an increase in crime, which is done under the influence of drugs or because addicts want money for drugs).[27] Some of the crime committed by Americans was doubtless for these reasons, but other reasons for the increase of crime were less clear. A certain amount of criminal behavior came from the Army soldiers at Camp Pieri and the Army personnel at Rhine and Hindenburg Kasernes. The paratroopers at Rhine Kaserne, in particular, had a reputation for being very tough and causing trouble, and on 31 December 1973, they were moved to Vicenza, Italy,[28] to the great relief of many citizens. In 1971, Army troops at Camp Pieri refused orders to begin a three-day exercise, and began rioting. One account, from the socialist newspaper *Vorwärts*, described Camp Pieri in ominous terms:

> *Refusal to obey orders, overstepping of boundaries, and above all offensive rallies in reference to American policy in Vietnam have long been the order of the day at Camp*

Pieri (...). Drill and drugs preoccupy the thinking of the U.S. boys and produce all those aggressive impulses which they also occasionally display in public as unsoldierly behavior (...). The fact cannot be denied: harmony between Germans and Americans is not the best in Wiesbaden.[29]

While this was in part an distortion by the anti-military left-wing press, the Army troops stationed in Wiesbaden and those who visited the city from Mainz did earn an increasingly bad reputation. However, Air Force personnel, too, instigated a growing number of violent incidents. Beatings, fights involving large numbers of people, stabbings, and muggings became distressingly commonplace. In November 1970, the *Tagblatt* announced, "Gewaltdelikte nehmen wieder zu" (rape crimes increase again) in an article about three crimes committed by "farbige Amerikaner" (colored Americans).[30] Random violent attacks were more frequently reported in the papers, especially in 1971 and 1972.

An especially disturbing incident occurred in the vicinity of Hainerberg Housing Area in late May 1972, when a gang of teenagers – American high school students and one high school dropout, all under the influence of alcohol – attacked several elderly pensioners, delivering life-threatening wounds to one man. The German police spotted the gang near the high school, where they were involved in another fight, this time with Americans.[31] When the police attempted to arrest those identified as assaulting the elderly Germans, the mob, which had grown to about 200 people, rioted and prevented the arrest of the youths. Several officers suffered fairly serious injuries such as broken bones, and finally they were forced to draw their weapons, an unusual event for the Wiesbaden police at the time.[32] Oberbürgermeister Schmitt contacted base commander Colonel Warren T. Whitmire by letter, asking American personnel and family members to help end the violence; "einige von ihnen [verhalten sich] in höchstem Maße kriminell in einem Land (...), in dem sie zeitweise zu Gast sind" (some of [the youths] behave to the largest extent as criminals in a country where they are temporary guests), Schmitt noted. The mayor also expressed the fear that such episodes would erode the good German-American relations that the city had enjoyed for years.[33]

Whitmire replied that he was also working to prevent further episodes, and that the youths involved, "dependents of members of the U.S. Army in Mainz", had been expelled from the country. He described measures taken to improve security, and concluded: "Lassen Sie mich Ihnen gegenüber noch einmal meine von Herzen kommende Entschuldigung dafür zum Ausdruck bringen, daß Amerikaner für solch ein Benehmen in dem Lande, in dem wir zu Gast sind, verantwortlich gewesen sind" (let me again extend my most heartfelt apologies that Americans have been responsible for such conduct in a land where we are guests).[34] Later in June, the *Post* reminded its readers that parents of children who caused damages to persons or property were liable for the costs of damage, and under German law, children between the ages of seven and eighteen were personally liable in most cases.[35]

In spite of measures taken by the command, the upward spiral of crime did not abate. In July 1972 the *Kurier* reported that a twenty-one-year-old German woman was kidnapped and raped by three Americans, a sixteen-year-old American girl was attacked and

In the early 1970s newspaper articles decried the „Wild West" atmosphere brought about by American Criminality.

Wildwest in Landeshauptstadt
Soldaten überfallen Mädchen

Von US-Soldaten überfallen, entführt und vergewaltigt wurde eine 21jährige Schwesternschülerin aus Wiesbaden. Das Mädchen befand sich auf dem Heimweg in der Lessingstraße. Plötzlich hielt neben ihr ein amerikanischer Straßenkreuzer. Die drei Insassen zerrten sie in das Auto und fuhren mit ihr in einen verwilderten Garten am Hainerberg. Dort wurde sie von den Amerikanern vergewaltigt.

Die Tat fand bereits am Dienstag gegen 21 Uhr statt. Da die Überfallene unter Schock stand, konnte sie bis gestern keinen Bericht über ihr Erlebnis geben.

Die Polizei sucht nun Zeugen für diesen Vorfall. Die Täter werden wie folgt beschrieben: Der Fahrer, ein Weißer, war etwa 30 Jahre alt, 170 Zentimeter groß und schwarzhaarig. Er trug blaue Jeans und ein kariertes Hemd mit kurzen Ärmeln. Der Beifahrer war ein Farbiger, schlank und 180 Zentimeter groß. Er trug ein kurzärmeliges weißes Hemd. Im Fond saß ebenfalls ein Weißer, der etwa 26—28 Jahre alt, 170 Zentimeter groß und von kräftiger Gestalt war. Er trug eine gelbe Windbluse und blaue Jeans. Bei dem Wagen handelte es sich um ein viertüriges weißes Fahrzeug amerikanischer Marke.

Seltsam ist, daß der Entführten in der Lessingstraße niemand zu Hilfe kam. Trotz der Hilferufe hatte auch niemand die Polizei alarmiert.

Zwei Stunden nach dieser brutalen Tat kam es erneut zu einem Überfall. Diesmal mitten in der Wilhelmstraße am Theater. Das Opfer war eine 16jährige Amerikanerin, die Täter wiederum US-Soldaten. Die beiden Männer versuchten, dem Mädchen die Kleider vom Leib zu reißen und sie zu vergewaltigen. Sie wurden jedoch gestört und flohen. Möglicherweise handelt es sich um dieselben Täter.

Wird Wiesbaden zum heißen Pflaster für US-Soldaten? In der Landeshauptstadt häuft sich die Zahl der Vorfälle, in die Amerikaner verwickelt sind. So wurde ein Taxifahrer vor dem Camp Lindsey von einem US-Soldaten um das Fahrgeld betrogen und anschließend von rund 20 Soldaten bedroht. Er konnte nur noch mit gezückter Gaspistole seinen Rückzug sichern. In der Goldgasse trat ein US-Soldat Beulen in die Karosserie eines Taxis und wurde anschließend gegen den Fahrer handgreiflich. Derselbe Täter hatte bereits in der Webergasse ein Taxi beschädigt. Der letzte spektakuläre Vorfall fand am Sonntag statt. Wie bereits berichtet, wurde ein Deutscher von einer größeren Gruppe Amerikaner überfallen, mit einem Messer verletzt und beraubt. ca her American attackers attempted rape, and two taxi drivers were mugged by Americans – all on the same evening. "Wird Wiesbaden zum heißen Pflaster für US-Soldaten?" (Is Wiesbaden endangered by U.S. Soldiers?) asked the *Kurier*. "In der Landeshauptstadt häuft sich die Zahl der Vorfälle, in die Amerikaner verwickelt sind" (In Wiesbaden the number of incidents that Americans are involved in continues to rise).[36] Four days later, on 11 July, a band of Americans attacked a group of young men, and the same evening another group of Americans attacked and robbed a thirty-five-year-old. This time, the criminals were not soldiers, but teenagers between the ages of fourteen and sixteen.[37] One week after these crimes, a seventeen-year-old girl was attacked by a soldier, and a group of Americans mugged a Yugoslavian guest worker.[38]

On 21 July, a German-American council meeting was held to discuss the wave of crime. "In Wiesbaden lebende Amerikaner haben in den letzten Wochen von sich reden gemacht" (In the past few weeks Americans living in Wiesbaden have been the topic of many conversations), the *Kurier* reported, "allerdings nicht im positiven Sinne" (but not in a good sense). At the council meeting, German and American leaders agreed that American crime was a serious threat to good German-American relations, and needed to be addressed. The council agreed to beef up German and American police patrols, and to institute a program where German and American police patrolled high-crime areas together.[39] These patrols proved very successful, and the frequent reports of random, violent crime committed by Americans decreased somewhat in 1973. However, many of the crimes which were most damaging to German-American relations, such as the mob attacks of May 1972, were committed by family members, thus were more difficult to control. In November of that year, the *Post* reported that teenagers repeatedly pelted German homes with eggs and stones, and soaped the windows of German autos. "What have we done to anger these neighborhood children?" asked one resident.[40]

Racial Tension

The problem of racial tension was a third factor in the strained atmosphere in Wiesbaden, although like drug abuse and crime it was not as severe a problem as on many other American military bases in

Germany. The Air Force counted lower percentages of African-Americans than the other services, and especially low percentages of African-American officers. This meant, on one hand, that the race-related mass unrest seen on some Army installations was unlikely to occur in Wiesbaden, but on the other hand, African-American personnel may have felt much more isolated and discriminated against in Wiesbaden than on installations with more diverse populations. In any case, the 7101st experienced no serious outbreaks of racial unrest, but articles in the *Post* reflected growing racial awareness. In the early 1970s the paper published explanations of the "Dap" handshake and other cultural expressions, special reports on black history, and discussions of the way African-American personnel suffered racism in daily life. Many of these articles were distributed throughout USAFE by the Public Affairs division in the United States, and were dismissed with scorn by prejudiced whites. When USAFE instituted mandatory race-relations seminars in 1972, expressions of resentment could be heard among white personnel: "I am more prejudiced now then [sic] before I went into this seminar", complained one white airman.[41]

The Student Movement, Protest, and the GIs

Among Germans, on the other hand, the plight of African-Americans aroused sympathy and support. This was especially true among younger Germans who were active in or sympathetic to the student protest movements of the 1960s. In 1970 a group of university students founded the New Left Federation (Föderation Neue Linke, or FNL) which professed support for movements such as the North Vietnamese and the Black Panthers. The FNL wrote and distributed a newsletter in January 1970 describing the persecution of the Black Panthers by the American government, and proclaimed a "Solidaritätskampagne" with the Panthers. Around the same time another leftist newsletter appeared, entitled "Guerilla: Agitprogramm für Arbeiter, Schüler, Studenten". On the cover page was the Black Panther motto, in English: "We want an end to the robbery by the capitalists of our black community." It, too, explained the history of the Black Panthers and called for support from high school students.

Many young Germans sympathized with the plight of African-Americans, and voiced support for groups like the Black Panthers.

This feeling of sympathy for African-Americans proved complex and frustrating for young Germans, and led to some difficult and tragic incidents. In first week in May 1973, for example, the traditional time of the German-American Friendship Week, the *Kurier* reported that a black civilian American was sentenced to two years in prison for kidnapping and raping a Mainz college student. The student, it was reported, had studied in the United States, and "[sich] vor allem für die Rassenfrage interessiert" (was above all interested in the race question), and did not want to offend the American.[42] Newspaper reports of violence involving African-Americans were likely to arouse a complex mix of anger and sympathy when the race of the suspect was prominent in the story, as it often was. In 1972 the Federation of German-American Clubs asked the German Press Council to advise German newspapers and magazines to stop mentioning the race of the subjects of articles, "except in cases where it is of overriding relevance".[43] Apparently the request was honored, because the practice of reporting race, especially among crime suspects, disappeared in the 1970s.

Interviews with former members of local protest groups suggest that in the 1970s, agitation in support of the Black Panthers and against the Vietnam war and U.S. government repression did not merge into protest activity against the American armed forces in Wiesbaden, nor did it translate to anti-American sentiment against individual Americans. One participant explained: "We were never against the American forces. The Soviet invasion of Czechoslovakia showed us how bad the Communists were. We all supported the Czech freedom movement. When I heard the news of the invasion in 1968, I walked down through downtown Wiesbaden with tears running down my face."[44] Another member recalled that, although the groups protested against U.S. government policy, they had an "ambivalent relationship" with America, because "at the same time, so many cultural things came here from America (...) clothing, the peace movement was from there and television and above all, music. Back then, you protested against the Vietnam War, that is, against the USA, and also listened to AFN."[45] The ambivalence of most protesters extended to the U.S. forces in Wiesbaden, who were not targets of protest against the Vietnam War, perhaps because there were a significant number of soldiers and airmen who were against the war as well, and against the "military industrial complex". In Wiesbaden, about eight issues of the underground GI newspaper FTA (Fuck the Army) were printed between 1971 and 1972. The crudely printed sheets contained articles detailing problems with base housing, overbearing officers and military life in general, and many cartoon depictions of soldiers being harassed by career NCOs and officers. For its part, the command dealt with leaders of GI resistance simply by reassigning them to other regions of the world, effectively breaking up active groups.

German-American Activities

American culture continued to influence the culture of West Germany as well as other European nations in many diverse and complicated ways. In Wiesbaden, however, the outward signs of German-American friendship that had been so prevalent from the mid-1950s had diminished by the 1970s. One sign of the relative dormancy of German-American relations was the lessening importance of German-American Friendship Week. While a core of prominent Germans and Americans continued to attend the Week's events and emphasize the importance of maintaining German-American friendship – former Oberbürgermeister Georg Buch, widely known as an energetic socializer, was a prestigious guest at many events

– the actual number of events during the week continued to decline and the publicity surrounding them diminished, particularly in the German press. In 1970, for example, the week opened with the traditional ceremony at the Kurhaus, but in contrast to past years, neither the Oberbürgermeister nor the USAFE commander attended the ceremony. Albert Osswald, Minister President of the state of Hesse, spoke at the ceremony however, suggesting a continued level of support on many levels. The ceremony ended with a performance by the USAFE band, the Wiesbaden string quartet, and an American vocal group called the "Revelation Generation", which sang "religiöse, patriotische und volkstümliche Lieder" (religious, patriotic, and traditional songs) according to the *Kurier*.[46] The *Tagblatt* did not mention the ceremony at all, but the *Post* reported that "Gala Concerts and Shows Highlight German-American Friendship Week".[47] In contrast to previous years, just one additional concert was scheduled during the week. The only other events held during the week were a meeting of German-American Boy Scouts, a German-American coin show, and the charity ball sponsored by the German-American Women's Club.

The WAB open house ended the week; it was as popular as ever, with an estimated 150,000 visitors.[48] The event had become a regional draw by 1970; not only did visitors come from all over, but NATO forces from many nations contributed their performing talents to the day. The West German Army provided band music; precision air shows came from the Burda flight team and the Falcons, Blades and Lightnings of the Royal Air Force, as well as the Red Devils from the Belgian Air Force; and West German, Canadian, Danish and U.S. Army units organized aircraft and weapons displays. USAFE bases from around the area contributed personnel and equipment.[49] The event seemed to be celebrating NATO and European military strength, rather than simply the U.S Air Force, or Wiesbaden's German-American friendship, and was probably more popular for its broad appeal.

The following year, the only event announced during German-American Friendship Week was the women's club ball;[50] even the normally upbeat *Post* admitted it was "one of the few events taking place during German-American Friendship Week 1971".[51] The WAB open house was scheduled for the middle of June, rather than at the end of the Friendship Week. The 1971 festival was even larger than the previous year's, and included eleven international air exhibitions from Belgium, Italy, Great Britain, West Germany and the U.S. The *Post* claimed that

Open house at WAB, June 1971.

the event attracted 250,000 visitors. The *Kurier* estimated a more modest 150,000, but reported that "it was never so crowded", according to experts.[52] However, after 1971 the traditional WAB festival was not held for several years, because of budgetary problems. In 1972, instead of the open house, the 7101st planned a three-day "Expo" to be held at the ACC. Events included music, dancing exhibitions, and films, and the planners of the Expo took care to include multicultural events, such as "eine Afro-amerikanische Studentengruppe (…) ein Hawaii-Klub (…) eine jüdische Vereinigung" (an Afro-American student group (…) a Hawaiian Club (…) a Jewish Organization). The program acknowledged the difficult state of race relations in the United States with a lecture on

"Minoritäten in Amerika" and the film "Wenn es keine Schwarzen gäbe, müßten sie erfunden werden" (If there weren't any black people, they would have to be invented). The reason for canceling the WAB open house was money: "Der Flugtag war nicht billig, im vergangenen Jahr hat er uns 100,000 Dollar gekostet" (The open house wasn't cheap; in the past year it cost us $ 100,000), said Whitmire. The Expo was held at the beginning of the Week, which continued with a concert in the Kurpark, a flea market organized by the German-American Women's Club, and a rock concert. The *Tagblatt* hoped that "der akute Geldmangel, der alle US-Dienststellen, aber auch die einzelnen Soldaten und ihre Familien durch Dollar-Abwertung und Preissteigerungen auf dem bundesdeutschen Markt getroffen hat, zu einer neuen Ära verbesserter deutsch-amerikanischer Beziehungen führ[t]" (the acute money problems that all U.S. personnel, especially the soldiers and their families, suffer from because of the falling dollar and price increases in Germany, will lead to a better German-American relationship).[53] But after 1972, German-American Friendship Week ceased to be mentioned in the two Wiesbaden papers.

In addition to the Expo at the ACC, in 1972 Wiesbadeners were invited to a day-long festival at Camp Pieri. The army's open house was not as big an attraction as the Air Force day, with its exhibits of aircraft, parachute teams and precision flyers, but Camp Pieri offered the public a chance to view "schwere Waffen (...), Haubitzen auf Kettenfahrzeugen und Raketen" (heavy weapons ... howitzers on tracked vehicles and rockets), as well as electronic communications apparatus. Several musical performances were also offered. Camp Pieri's festival was intended to compensate for the cancellation of the Air Force open house, and to improve the damaged reputation of the Army in Wiesbaden, but the field artillery unit could not compete in glamour or popularity with the USAFE headquarters or the Air Force at WAB. The festival was held again in 1973, and Army spokespeople hoped that the event was "ähnlich erfolgreich (...) wie im letzten Jahr" (successful ... like it was the last year).[54] But no numbers of attendance were given, and the following year WAB held the open house once more. It was more popular than ever, suggesting that the tensions of the early 1970s were not enough to overcome widespread participation in what had become a Wiesbaden tradition.

In the early 1970s, elementary school teachers at the Aukamm and Hainerberg schools and at several German elementary schools continued to try to arrange exchange activities for their students. This, perhaps was one of the easiest and most successful paths toward German-American relations because the young children – kindergarteners through fifth graders – were not aware of tensions, prejudices or culture gaps between the two communities, and were not as encumbered by language problems. In 1971, thirty German and American eleven and twelve year olds spent a two-week spring vacation together at a hostel in Allgäu, along with several teachers. The Wiesbaden Jugendamt played a role in organizing the venture, whose purpose was "Kontakte mit jungen Amerikanern in unserer Stadt herzustellen" (to encourage contact with young Americans in our city).[55] The notion caught on in 1971, when the elementary school at WAB proposed a student exchange day with German students in the fifth grade. The Aukamm school held a Halloween party for German students, and Aukamm kindergarteners visited the German school for the traditional German St. Martin's day procession a week later. In 1972, the German-American school vacation was repeated, with forty-three students, ages thirteen and fourteen, involved.[56]

The city of Wiesbaden attempted to encourage contact between German and American children through the schools, setting aside funds for programs and activities, but there was declining interest in contact with Americans among some German schools. In spite of outreach attempts by the principal of Aukamm school, few German elementary schools were interested in forming a partnership, according to the *Kurier*. A 1972 report to the Magistrat noted that "Die Beziehungen zwischen deutschen und a-merikanischen Lehrern sind besser als dies vielfach angenommen wird. Sie sind aber auch nicht so gut, wie mancher es sich erhofft" (the relations between German and American teachers are better than is often supposed. They are, however, not as good as might be hoped).[57]

A new and popular activity that served as a German-American bridge for residents of all ages was the Volksmarch, a ten or twenty kilometer organized hike, with medals for those who completed the course, and food and beverages at the end of the route. Volksmarches became common in Germany in the early 1970s, and Americans became especially enthusiastic participants. In one German-sponsored march, the *Kurier* reported, "Erstaunlich war (...) die starke Beteiligung der Amerikaner, die etwa 40 Prozent der Teilnehmer ausmachten" (the number of Americans was amazing ... about 40 percent of the participants). The paper went on to report that the map and program of the Volksmarch were printed in English and German, and a three star general from Frankfurt was spotted in the crowd. Over four hundred American elementary school students attended.[58] Noticing the popularity of the events, American installations sponsored several Volksmarches of their own; in September 1972, WAB hosted a march, at which around 4,000 people showed up. The Good Neighbors club gave every 500th person who finished a transistor radio.[59] The following year's American-sponsored march was even more successful, and about half the participants were German.[60]

Other traditional German-American activities, such as summer concerts with the USAFE band at the Kurpark, and the Christmas sing-along, occurred regularly throughout the 1970s. The Christmas concert held at Hainerberg for several years, however, was not repeated after 1969.

Oberbürgermeister Georg Buch (on the left) was committed to good relations with the American military community and was always present at German-American friendship activities.

German-American clubs continued to foster contact between the two communities. The women's club sponsored their traditional charity ball during German-American Friendship Week. In 1970, the USAFE band performed at the event, and guests of honor included General Simmler, the vice-commander of USAFE, and Colonel McKittrick. The city was represented by Stadtkämmerer Dietrich Oedekoven and Oberbürgermeister Georg Buch.[61]

In 1971, the ball was billed as "semiformal", unlike past years when formal dress was required, another small sign of changing times.[62] Tickets cost two dollars, one dollar less than previous years, in an attempt to encourage interest, but 1971 was the last year the ball took place. "It did not make enough money for the effort we put into it", recalled one member. So the charity ball was discontinued, a victim of evolving tastes and customs. In 1972 the club held a flea market in downtown Wiesbaden instead. The flea market, scheduled during German-American Friendship Week, proved to be very popular, and was held in succeeding years, becoming a new tradition. The flea market, however, did not encourage Germans and Americans to become acquainted; rather, it was a bargain-hunter's opportunity to shop. The women's club also tried new methods of raising money for charity, such as organizing an Oktoberfest dance, sponsoring a fashion show, and participating in a Christmas bazaar with the German Red Cross. In 1971 the club held a "Roaring Twenties Show" at the ACC; although the show was apparently successful – "Hurra, wir sind ausverkauft!" (Hurrah, we're sold out!) proclaimed the club's president[63] – the effort was not repeated in succeeding years. Reorientation and reconsideration of the club's fundraising activities was necessary to ensure continued interest and support, but the club went through a period of disorganization as well. Club records, meticulous for the decades of the 1950s and early 1960s, as well as the 1980s, were virtually absent for the period 1970–1979.

The Good Neighbors men's club also held its traditional activities during this period. The club continued to sponsor the Fasching ball, although it attracted less attention in German papers than in years past. The club sponsored the event until 1988, but only until 1973 was the ball publicized in the *Tagblatt* or *Kurier*. On the other hand, the *Post* reported on the ball every year; Klaus Müller, who was an active member of the Good Neighbors club, also had a hand in publishing the *Post*, so this is perhaps not surprising. The *Tagblatt* reported in 1972 that the attendees of the ball were mostly Americans, which may have explained some of the lack of publicity.[64]

The club was involved in other programs: in August 1970, the Good Neighbors presented Schmitt with a check for 3,000 marks, to help Wiesbaden begin searching for a "sister city" in the United States. The forty-five members of the club also supported a scholarship program,[65] and in 1973, the club sponsored a German-American bowling tournament, which attracted around 150 people,[66] as well a German-American dance for teenagers. In December 1971, the club proudly celebrated its fifteenth anniversary.[67] Other clubs, such as the German-American coin collectors and the German-American stamp collectors clubs, continued to hold regular meetings, and organized shows several times a year throughout the early 1970s.

By 1970, the German-American youth club founded in 1966 had disappeared and a new club formed, this time by young people themselves rather than by the Office of Information. The *Tagblatt* reported that six Americans and three Germans founded the "Deutsch-Amerikanischer Beratungsausschuß" from the remains of the old club, which "sich im Sande verlaufen hatte" (had sunk into the sand). The club proposed to help publicize German-American relations and work to involve more people; "Wenn junge Deutsche Amerikanern den Eintritt in Jugendlokale verwehrten und amerikanische Highschüler offen erklärten, daß sie Deutsche nicht mögen, sei es höchste Zeit, daß etwas getan werde" (When young Germans don't allow Americans into meeting places for young people, and American high school students openly admit that they don't like Germans, then it is high time to do something), concluded the paper.[68]

German youths, too, continued to express complex attitudes toward the United States. On one hand, they rejected American policy in Vietnam and were very critical of other aspects of American society, including racism and the exploitative tendencies of free-market capitalism. On the other hand, however, they embraced many elements of American popular culture with increasing enthusiasm. A radical antiwar protester explained his complicated feelings about Americans:

> *On Friday nights there was live music [at the American Arms Hotel] and Germans couldn't go, but I knew one of the musicians, and he always let me in through the back door. It was great. So, I listened to the music with the GIs, and the next day I would be in Frankfurt burning American flags.*[69]

Ironically, some German young people attempted to participate in the culture of the installation when possible, unlike many American teenagers who sought to distance themselves from the GIs and the military bases.

By the 1970s much of the interest Germans and Americans had for each other diminished as German-American activities continued to fade away and serious social problems appeared among military personnel. Among German youths, America was still a cultural beacon, and interest in American music and style, including drug use, was still strong. Among other Germans and Americans, friendship clubs were maintained by a core of interested participants, many of whom had been members for many years. Some remembered the early 1970s as "the best time (...) for German-American relations (...) we did so very much together".[70] The *Post* continued to print a large number of articles on travel in Germany, and on German customs and laws, which indicates that the Office of Information and the 7101st command pursued a policy of encouraging Americans to interact more often with their German neighbors. The Wiesbaden Volkshochschule announced in September 1972 that it was offering a series of American-oriented classes: Introduction to Germany, Contact – German/American, Living in Wiesbaden, Conversational German I, and German Cooking were designed for Americans.[71] According to some witnesses, German-American friendship remained alive and well.

But other sources disagree. The pattern of crime in the Wiesbaden papers and the dwindling of German-American Friendship Week suggest that German-American relations grew more distant, or even became somewhat antagonistic during the early 1970s. Other clues can be found: for example, in a brief article about the Wiesbaden animal shelter in the *Post*, a German volunteer at the shelter "expressed concern about lack of contact with the American community. Until two or three years ago Americans would come to the Tierheim to pick up a house pet or dispose of one. In the past years this contact has discontinued (...)".[72] By the early 1970s, a combination of German opposition to the Vietnam War and to the military in general, installation problems with money, and personal problems with crime and drugs united to create alienation between Germans and Americans, even among those who were well-disposed toward American culture, such as young people. Although some Germans and Americans reached out to one another, most no longer made the attempt.

1   7101 Air Base Wing History, "Historical Data Record: Wiesbaden Audio Club", 1 July 1967–31 December 1967, 2.
2   7101 Air Base Wing History, "Management Looks at the Wing", 1 July 1969–30 September 1969.
3   7101 Air Base Wing History, "Historical Data Record: USAFE Base Command", 1 January 1969–30 June 1969, 10.
4   7101 Air Base Wing History, "Historical Data Record: Personnel Services Branch", 1 July 1968–31 December 1968, 3.
5   7101 Air Base Wing History, "Historical Data Record: Personnel Services Branch", 1 July 1968–31 December 1968, 3.
6   WK, „Musik wirbt um Verständnis", 29 February 1968.
7   7101 Air Base Wing History, "Narrative", 1 January 1970–31 March 1970, 5.
8   Ibid., 53.
9   7101 Air Base Wing History, "Narrative", 1 July 1971–30 September 1971, 23.
10   Ibid., 1.
11   7101 Air Base Wing History, "Narrative", 1 January 1970–31 March 1970, 51.
12   Ibid., 50.
13   WP, [no title], 22 January 1971.
14   WP, [no title], 24 April 1970.
15   WP, [no title], 1 May 1970.
16   WP, [no title], 16 October 1970.
17   WP, [no title], 16 January 1970.
18   WP, "Departing from Tradition Girls Visiting Dormitories", 21 May 1971, 1.
19   7101 Air Base Wing History, "Narrative", 1 July 1971–30 September 1971, 20–21.
20   WP, "Fiscal year fizzles – Prospects for dollars not improving in USAFE", 14 January 1972.
21   See Ingraham, *Boys in the Barracks*, for a detailed discussion of the cultural differences between lower enlisted and career personnel.
22   WK, „Blüten, Hasch und Deserteure", 14 July 1970.
23   WK, „Alarmierende Bilanz: immer mehr greifen zum Rauschgift", 2 October 1971.
24   WP, [no title], 3 September 1971.
25   WP, [no title], 26 November 1971.
26   WP, [no title], 13 October 1972.
27   WK, "Alarmierende Bilanz", 2 October 1971.
28   Klaus Müller, interview by author, tape recording, Wiesbaden, Germany, 2 March 1994.
29   *Vorwärts*, (Bonn), 26 August 1971, quoted in Daniel J. Nelson, *A History of U.S. Military Forces in Germany* (Boulder and London: Westview Press, 1987), 106.
30   WT, „Gewaltdelikte nehmen wieder zu", 3 November 1970.
31   WK, „Amerikaner schlagen Deutsche blutig", 31 May/1 June 1972.
32   WP, "Local Teenagers Arrested", 9 June 1972.
33   WK, „Die blutigen Zwischenfälle am Hainerberg dürfen sich bei uns nicht wiederholen", 2 June 1972.

34 *WK*, „US-Echo zum Hainerberg-Skandal", 3 June 1972.
35 *WP*, "Parents are Liable", 30 June 1972.
36 *WK*, „Wildwest in Landeshauptstadt: Soldaten überfallen Mädchen", 7 July 1972.
37 *WK*, „Bande überfällt Passanten", 11 July 1972.
38 *WK*, „Notzuchtversuch an 17-jähriger", 18 July 1972.
39 *WK*, [no title], 21 July 1972.
40 *WP*, "Vandals Destroy More than Windows", 10 November 1972.
41 *WP*, "Color Questions??", 6 October 1972.
42 *WK*, [no title], 10 May 1972.
43 *WP*, "Press Pressured by Writers", 24 March 1972.
44 Axel Ulrich, interview by author, tape recording, Biebrich, Germany, 15 March 1996.
45 Jürgen Zettlitz, interview by author, tape recording, Wiesbaden, Germany, 10 March 1996.
46 *WK*, „Freundschaft ist unerläßlich", 27 April 1970.
47 *WP*, "German-American Friendship Week", 24 April 1970.
48 *WK*, „Wolken-Stürmer und Himmels-Taucher", 11 May 1970.
49 *WP*, "Armed Forces Day", 15 May 1970.
50 *WT*, „Die Vorurteile sind beseitigt", 10 May 1971.
51 *WP*, "G-A Wives Slate Ball", 7 May 1971.
52 *WK*, „Luftakrobatik in Vollendung", 14 June 1971.
53 *WT*, [no title], 20 April 1972.
54 *WK*, „Zweiter Tag der Verständigung", 16 May 1973.
55 *WK*, „Jugendfreizeit für deutsche und amerikanische Schüler", 24 April 1971.
56 *WK*, „Deutsch-Amerikanische Jugendfreizeit beginnt", 27 April 1972.
57 *WK*, „Gute Beziehungen zu amerikanischen Schulen", 22 June 1972.
58 *WK*, „5000 Wanderer auf dem Weg ins Grüne", 23 May 1972.
59 *WK*, „Immer an der Rollbahn entlang", 18 September 1972.
60 *WK*, „Freundschaftliche Wanderung rund um den Flugplatz", 30 July 1973.
61 *WK*, „Freundschaft ergänzt die Politik", 9 May 1970.
62 *WP*, "Friendship Ball", 7 May 1971.
63 *WT*, „Kabarett der tollen Zwanziger", 22 March 1971.
64 *WT*, „'Gute Nachbarn' verzauberten das Kurhaus", 7 February 1972.
65 *WK*, „Gute Nachbarn gesucht: Deutsch-amerikanische Partnerschaft?", 26 August 1970.
66 *WK*, „Kugel rollen um die Freundschaft", 16 April 1973.
67 *WT*, „'Gute Nachbarn' seit 15 Jahren", 8 December 1971.
68 *WT*, „Junge Leute zweier Nationen am runden Tisch", 20 January 1970.
69 Interview with Jürgen Zettlitz.
70 Mr. and Mrs. R.M.A. Hirst, interview by author, tape recording, Wiesbaden, Germany, 18 March 1996.
71 *WP*, "Learn About Your Host Country", 8 September 1972.
72 *WP*, "Animals Find a Home in Tierheim", 30 June 1972.

USAFE LEAVES WIESBADEN

The decade of the 1970s saw major transformations in the visibility of American military communities in Germany, as the Americans withdrew behind their walls and receded from sight. One reason for this withdrawal was the economic difficulties caused by currency fluctuations – Americans were suddenly poorer than they had been. A second reason was the decline in confidence and morale caused by American involvement in Vietnam – Americans no longer had the optimistic self-assurance of earlier decades, and were less inclined to see themselves as "ambassadors" to the world. Thirdly, scarce resources increasingly went toward improving military readiness, combating drug use, and improving low education levels endemic in the lower enlisted ranks, rather than public relations outreach.

In Wiesbaden, the American military community changed drastically in 1973, when USAFE headquarters moved from LAS, where it had been since 1953, to Ramstein Air Base in the small Rhineland-Palatinate town of Ramstein, while the U.S. Army took over WAB. This reorganization had serious implications for German-American interaction in Wiesbaden, although WAB's first Army commander, Brigadier General Alfred J. Cade, did much to ease the strain. Cade was one of the American community's most popular and energetic leaders, and he successfully handled the difficult transition from Air Force to Army, cultivating excellent relations with Wiesbaden officials and dealing with potential problems before they grew out of control. But the Army personnel now stationed in Wiesbaden tended to be younger, less experienced, and of lower rank than the Air Force had been. As a result, they were less comfortable participating in social activities such as formal dances, banquets and the like, events typical of traditional German-American interaction.

The depressed decade of the 1970s came to an end in Wiesbaden when fifty-two American hostages, held by Iranian revolutionaries for 444 days, were released and brought to Wiesbaden Air Force Hospital for treatment. The hostage situation had symbolized American malaise, and its long-awaited conclusion signaled the beginning of a new era.

USAFE Moves from Wiesbaden

General David C. Jones was USAFE commander from 1971 to 1974 when the Secretary of Defense decided to transfer USAFE headquarters from its imposing building on LAS to Ramstein Air Base. In an interview a decade later, Jones reflected on the reasons for the move:

> *[USAFE needed] to get into a wartime posture and attitude that you couldn't do in the city. We would get people to come to Wiesbaden, members of Congress and the Defense Department. They would stay at the Von Steuben Hotel, and we had the beautiful music and the fine wine. We would take them down the Rhine River. They would visit the headquarters and be just as happy as could be. They would go back to Washington and talk about those fat cats living in the middle of Wiesbaden. You just couldn't get anyone – even my own people or the people who visited – feeling that we were really thinking about anything except to get the next glass of wine.*[1]

There were other reasons for the move, of course. Air Force policy in the late 1960s decreed that all major headquarters be located on active air bases, where aircraft could take off and land, and LAS was merely a small air station. Another policy goal involved moving major commands away from large urban centers.[2] A third aim was to reduce costs by relocating to less expensive areas. As early as 1968 Air Force planners considered moving USAFE to Ramstein as part of the Reduction of Cost and Forces in Europe (REDCOSTE) proposals. Ramstein Air Base was already a major NATO installation, the headquarters of the NATO 4th Allied Tactical Air Force (4ATAF). The commander of 4ATAF "wore two hats", in the favored American phrase – he also commanded USAFE. "Colocation", then, was an additional point recommending the move.

There were drawbacks to the idea as well. Demerits included increased overcrowding in an already cramped region, which would decrease morale as well as present security concerns. Secretary of the Air Force Harold Brown observed that the move "would result in a further concentration of an excessive number of key facilities in the Ramstein/

Kaiserslautern complex and make it a likely target for heavy attack".³ In 1968, nothing came of the idea.

Two years later, cost-cutters raised the question again, and USAFE commander General Joseph Holzapple agreed to move the USAFE staff from LAS, not to Ramstein, but to WAB. The Americans agreed to vacate LAS and return it to the German government; in return, the German government would pay for seventy-five percent of the cost of the move and would finance the construction of a new 127,500 square foot headquarters building. The German government also offered to provide $ 4,000,000 credits for housing and billet construction and other costs incurred by the move.

While a move from LAS to WAB would have kept USAFE headquarters in Wiesbaden, the plan was not favored by all, particularly neighbors of WAB. The Erbenheim town council (Ortsbeirat), for example, complained about possible increases in noise if an expansion of WAB took place. "Der Magistrat wird gebeten, sich dafür einzusetzen, daß der Militärflughafen Erbenheim nicht verstärkt angeflogen und benutzt wird" (The Magistrat is asked to assure us that WAB will neither have new units stationed there, nor be used more) resolved the Ortsbeirat in July 1970.⁴ The *Kurier* and *Tagblatt* both ran numerous stories emphasizing popular opposition to any expansion of WAB.

If USAFE headquarters moved to WAB, what would become of LAS, prime real estate close to the center of Wiesbaden? The Wiesbaden city government pressed for the installation's release back to its German owners. In March 1971, plans for vacating LAS were announced in the papers, and speculation over the fate of the former German base began. "Ein Freizeitpark, ein Büro- und Geschäftszentrum, der Fachhochschulbereich (…) [oder] Wohnungsbau" (a park, an office or business center, the technical college … [or] apartment complexes) were some of the options, according to Wolfgang Nierhaus, a Wiesbaden city council representative.⁵

When Jones assumed command of USAFE on 31 August 1971, however, the agreement fell apart. On 27 September, not a month after Jones had taken command, the papers announced that USAFE headquarters would move to Ramstein, not WAB. LAS, meanwhile, would remain under American control even after the headquarters was gone. The true reasons why Jones decided on this course are not entirely clear. The decision not to release LAS can be attributed to the unwillingness of the U.S. forces to relinquish any property that might have been needed in the future, and in fact other civilian and military units quickly filled up the space vacated by USAFE headquarters.

The choice of Ramstein over WAB was more complicated. USAFE histories suggest that Jones rejected the move to WAB because he had "grave reservations about sinking deep roots on one of the least desirable bases in Germany".[6] Furthermore, the sound strategic reasons for moving to Ramstein that had been evident in 1968 still existed. Jones claimed that the move would "enhance the USAFE wartime role and day-to-day operating environment".[7]

However, other, unofficial reasons for the move have been proposed. One source claimed that the real reason for the move was because General Jones and Oberbürgermeister Schmitt had a serious personality clash, and could not abide each other, which made negotiations over LAS impossible.[8] Schmitt, however, denied this, and remembered his relations with the Americans, including Jones, as very cordial.[9] Another reason given for the move was that the Americans demanded an unreasonable amount of money for the transfer of LAS, and would not compromise with German negotiators.[10]

Whether the rumors of dislike and disagreement had any basis in fact is unclear, but they were fairly widely known and believed, especially among individuals who were involved in German-American affairs. As a result, the circumstances surrounding the move, particularly the sudden disintegration of the negotiations over LAS, had a somewhat negative impact on German-American relations. While financial negotiations were still underway, the German papers reported that a plan for a technical college was widely favored; subsequent revelations that these plans would not bear fruit led to a sense of betrayal on the part of many Wiesbaden residents.

The news that USAFE headquarters was moving to Ramstein, thus leaving only about 15,000 out of 21,000 Americans in Wiesbaden, was likely not as upsetting to German residents as it might have been. The previous five years had seen a decrease in attention paid to German-American relations, as Vietnam and economic hardship took their toll. Crime, race tensions, and drug use connected with the U.S. forces, not only in Wiesbaden but also throughout West Germany, had chipped away at the positive reputation of the American forces. Thus, the announcement that U.S. forces were planning to leave Wiesbaden brought to many residents a sense of relief, rather than dismay.

In any event, the relocation, known as "Creek Action" for its move across the Rhine River, took place as scheduled, and on Tuesday, 13 March 1973, the USAFE headquarters held formal retreat ceremonies on the parade field at LAS. Creek Action was only one part of a larger reorganization among several bases in the states of Rhine-Palatinate and Hesse. While USAFE headquarters moved out of LAS, a number of other Air Force and civilian DoD units moved in to the installation on Schiersteiner Straße. The 2nd Mobile Communications Group and the 601st Tactical Control Wing moved from Sembach to LAS, for example. Other units traveled shorter distances to fill up the space vacated by the USAFE transfer. The 2nd Weather Wing and the CPO of the 7101st ABW moved from WAB, and some units already located on LAS took up quarters in other buildings.

Brigade 76

With the most important Air Force unit gone from Wiesbaden, WAB was no longer needed by the Air Force as it had been before 1973. In June 1975 the commander of USAREUR received authorization to assume control of the Wiesbaden military installation. With the exception of LAS, the USAF Medical Center, and the tiny intelligence base at Schierstein, all real estate parcels comprising the Wiesbaden military community were transferred from the Air Force to the Army. In exchange, USAFE received ten properties in the Kaiserslautern area. In addition, several small installations were returned to the German government. Polizei Kaserne in Biebrich, housing the 1361st Photo Squadron, the USAFE Library Service Center and the EES Dry Cleaning Plant were released in 1975. Hindenburg Kaserne, where a dog training unit had been located, was also returned. Finally, USAFE announced that the Von Steuben Hotel would no longer be used as officers' and VIP billeting, but would be turned over to the German government.

Wiesbadeners learned soon enough to what purpose the U.S. Army would put their new acquisition. In response to Warsaw Pact troop increases, NATO planned to beef up conventional weapons units in Europe, and WAB would be the new home of a tank brigade of the 4th Infantry Division. According to preliminary reports, the unit would include a total of about 3,800 men, fifty-four tanks, and 493 other heavy vehicles. The unit would transfer to Wiesbaden in several stages from its home in Fort Carson, near Colorado Springs, Colorado.[11]

Officials of the city government immediately registered opposition to the plan. They protested on the grounds of safety, that the presence of large numbers of Army soldiers would harm the character of the city, and that tanks would cause unacceptable damage and inconvenience in such a heavily populated area. As Oberbürgermeister Schmitt recalled, fears of the negative impact the army might have on the city were compounded in the minds of many with the loss of one of the most prestigious organizations in the entire NATO defense system.

Given the many difficulties Army command had experienced in the late 1960s and early 1970s, it was no easy feat to counter objections of residents who feared that the U.S. Army would bring destructive social problems in its wake. But General Cade, in a brilliant public relations move, invited city leaders and members of the press to visit Fort Carson and see for themselves what the unit was like, its state of discipline, and the quality of the officers commanding it.

The trip, which duly took place in the last week of January 1976, succeeded in assuaging the concerns of city leaders. Army officials and civilian leaders of Colorado Springs feted the German delegation, which included reporters from both local newspapers. The *Kurier* and *Tagblatt* ran a series of upbeat stories reported directly from the United States, impressing on readers the commitment to good relations that leaders of the brigade embraced. Further, many of the specific concerns that Wiesbaden officials had entertained – for example, that there might be

1,000 tanks in Wiesbaden, and maneuvers within city limits – turned out to be false or highly exaggerated. Upon their return, city leaders proclaimed their willingness to welcome Brigade 76 to Wiesbaden. As one of the most outspoken opponents of the brigade concluded, "es ist keine Schande, wenn man seine Meinung erheblich ändern muß" (it is no shame when one must change one's mind).

The vanguard of Brigade 76, arriving by C-141 from Fort Carson on 14 March, was welcomed with ceremonies and press attention.[13] It was noted that approximately three-quarters of the personnel had volunteered to come to Wiesbaden, and they were on average twenty-one years old – not quite the teenagers many had expected. The Wiesbaden military community had always included small numbers of Army personnel, ranging from 2,000 in 1957 to 400 in 1969. In the early 1970s the numbers remained steady at about 1,800. Single enlisted personnel were billeted at Camp Pieri (families lived in Hainerberg), and the army units

already in Wiesbaden included a Nike Hercules Air Defense Artillery (ADA) battalion and several Sergeant York ADA battalions, as well as maintenance and staff units. Beginning in 1976, however, the number of Army personnel stationed in Wiesbaden grew precipitously. Some of the older units were moved out, but the new units at WAB more than compensated for the loss. By March 1977 the city hosted a total of 4,649 Army personnel, including the tank personnel of Brigade 76, an infantry unit, as well as field artillery and armored cavalry units.[14]

General Cade, the commander of the Wiesbaden Military Post throughout the Brigade 76 controversy, became perhaps the best-loved American commander ever to be assigned to Wiesbaden. When he was

Brigadier General Alfred J. Cade receives a welcoming gift from the Hessian Minister of the Interior Hanns-Heinz Bielefeld. Cade proved to be one of the most popular and successful commanders of the American military community.

reassigned back to the United States in July 1976, there was a genuine and heartfelt wave of sadness at his departure. He had shepherded the German and American communities through a difficult time that could well have resulted in lasting bitterness on both sides – but as many city leaders noted in the days of festivities and ceremonies before his departure, General Cade did more for German-American relations than almost anyone else.[15]

American Ghettoization

In spite of General Cade's skill at fostering compromise and smoothing tensions, the late 1970s saw a general decline of a positive American presence from city life. Much of this was because of waning interest and knowledge on the part of American personnel. Studies of daily life among GIs in this period reveal widespread isolation and ignorance, exacerbated by casual drug and alcohol use in the barracks. For example, in *Die GIs*, a book by German journalist Signe Seiler detailing the daily existence of Army personnel in neighboring Mainz, apathy and boredom dominated the lives of lower enlisted personnel, and most had little or no contact with their civilian neighbors. Another study by Larry Ingraham reveals similar characteristics in the lives of enlisted personnel stationed on bases in the United States.[16]

In Wiesbaden, the causes and effects of low morale and discipline became a regular issue for those involved in German-American relations, especially when the problem spilled out into the German community. With the arrival of increasing numbers of army personnel in the mid-1970s, disruption in the vicinity of the Hauptbahnhof, particularly at the park across the street known as the Reisinger-Anlage, increased. On weekends, Wiesbaden officials alleged, GIs from Bad Kreuznach, Mainz and other army installations converged on the spot to drink, buy and use drugs, and other activities. Fights broke out frequently and German residents were afraid to walk through or near the park. Rowdies also threw trash, beer bottles and drug paraphernalia on the ground and in the water of the fountain and pool. In the first half of 1977, according to German police, there were almost two hundred arrests of American soldiers.

Dr. Ender, the chief of police, noted, "Ich mache mir große Sorgen über den Zuwachs der durch Amerikaner verübten Delikte (...)" (I am very concerned about the increase in crimes committed by Americans).[17]

Both sides tried to address the issue in periodic German-American council meetings. German representatives asked that American commanders take steps to control troop behavior and punish miscreants. This was certainly in the best interests of the American community as well. In 1977 commanders distributed a booklet to American personnel detailing exactly what behavior was tolerated in public places and what was not allowed – for example, playing radios at high volume, and playing football in crowded areas,[18] so that citizens would not be bothered by "lärmende Soldaten" (noisy soldiers). Steps taken to combat more dangerous activities included increased German-American police patrols of the area. And in August 1977, after several weeks of especially disruptive behavior on the part of Americans and well-publicized complaints in the papers, army commanders ordered a work detail of several hundred American soldiers to spend a day cleaning up the Reisinger-Anlage. The *Tagblatt* noted that although Americans received the lion's share of blame for filthy conditions at the park, Germans as well as Americans were responsible. The paper congratulated the Americans on attempting to rectify the issue. As one GI participant said, "Niemand kann sich vorstellen, wieviel Unrat im Wasser liegt, bis man es herausholt!" (You can't imagine how much garbage is in the water until you have to take it out!)[19]

But the Americans had complaints as well. A major issue on the American side was discrimination against GIs, particularly black soldiers. In several German-American council meetings, American officials raised the question of "off-limits" designations; in contrast to the occupation years when an "off-limits" designation from the U.S. command was a punishment, in the 1970s German bartenders placed their own "off-limits" signs on their bars, to indicate that Americans were not welcome.[20] The issue proved to be difficult. On one hand, if American soldiers were frequently disruptive or violent, then their exclusion was understandable and even necessary. On the other hand, discrimination and rejection of American GIs might be an important factor in creating the loneliness and alienation which led to thoughtless behavior, and in any case tarred all Americans with one brush.

An editorial in the *Tagblatt* suggested that the problem of "randalierende junge Amerikaner" (rowdy young Americans) should be solved by Germans: "Die jungen GIs bewegen sich ja nur in eigenen Gruppen, weil man ihnen, wenn sie Kontakt suchen, so wenig entgegenkommt." (Young GIs travel only in groups, because when they look for contact they get so little of it.) The paper challenged German youth organizations to pursue real and sustained contact with American soldiers, which, they argued, would prove more important than the holiday invitations and other superficial forms of interaction encouraged by the German-American council.[21] In late 1976, when Brigade 76 had been in Wiesbaden for almost six months, Stadtverordneter Armin Klein initiated a new friendship club known as "Aktion Partnerschaft".[22] This club was not intended to replace the older German-American clubs, but to promote contact between Germans and American GIs, the Army soldiers who had so recently arrived in the city. As Klein explained: "Unsere Initiative aber gilt partnerschaftlichen Beziehungen zwischen Wiesbadener Bürgern und den einzelnen, einfachen US-Soldaten." (Our initiative creates partnerships between the citizens of Wiesbaden and single common soldiers.)[23] Another program was the "Kontakt Club" a German-American club targeting single soldiers. It offered elementary German classes, get-togethers, and other guided German-American activities.

These efforts were fundamentally different from earlier German-American relations activities. In the past, clubs and special events brought together Germans and Americans of similar class and educational levels, who were genuinely interested in socializing with each other and fairly knowledgeable about each other's cultural and social expectations. Germans and Americans had viewed each other as social equals. Efforts in the 1970s to reach out to GIs, by contrast, had more of an educational and relief function. The GIs were assumed, correctly in most cases, to be largely ignorant of German customs, history and language, and German participants, whatever their initial expectations, were compelled to view their involvement as a charitable activity, rather than an opportunity to become acquainted with people like themselves. This transformation of German-American activities highlights the change in the social status of American personnel by the late 1970s.

One reason for this change in Wiesbaden was, of course, the switch from Air Force major headquarters, with its numerous field-grade officers and glamorous atmosphere, to an Army combat arms unit, comprised of larger numbers of low-ranking enlisted personnel. Another reason was the overall decline in quality, readiness, and morale of the post-Vietnam armed forces, whether Army or Air Force. The extremely divisive war had left scars on the personnel of all branches of service, and even before the Air Force had left Wiesbaden, the impact of Vietnam could be detected. A third, perhaps most important reason was that in 1973 the Army had switched to an all-volunteer force (AVF). While many military and political leaders argued that this change was necessary, it meant that when the status and attractiveness of military service among potential recruits was low, as it was in the 1970s, the quality of personnel would be lower as well, and the leveling factor of the draft did not pertain.

So, while the number of Americans in Wiesbaden did not substantially drop, and some traditional German-American activities continued to be held, the attention placed on those activities by both Germans and Americans declined. A few other activities grew in popularity, especially the LAS Volksfest, a German-style carnival, or Kerb, featuring rides, food booths and games. The air and equipment shows of past years were gone, and the fest was almost indistinguishable from innumerable carnivals held throughout the summer months in Germans towns. A few distinctly American aspects remained: "Gut gehen auch die Eiscreme-Pakete, fast schon Familienpackungen, die als Ein-Mann-Portionen gedacht sind." (The ice cream packets, which are almost family packs but are thought of as single portions, also go over well.)[24] Also, potential visitors were assured that the gates of LAS would be open and IDs would not be checked by guards during the festival.

Hostages Released and Taken to Wiesbaden

The decade of the 1980s, if measured by the election of Ronald Reagan as president of the United States, began in the American community in Wiesbaden in January 1981 with the release of fifty-two Americans held hostage for 444 days by Iranian extremists. This exciting and joyous event brought worldwide attention to the American military community and the city of Wiesbaden when the hostages were brought to the USAF Medical Center for medical treatment. Relatives of the hostages flew in from the United States and stayed with American families in the city or at the Amelia Earhart hotel. More than 1,100 journalists and news cameras descended, according to the *Tagblatt*.[25] The front page of the *Kurier* showed a photo of a banner saying "Free at Last!!! Iran is in the past! Welcome to Wiesbaden!"[26]

Arrival of the released Hostages in Wiesbaden.

The entire city was swept up in the excitement – individual German families offered their homes to the hostages and the Aukamm Thermalbad made itself available for them. "Der Jubel war unbeschreiblich, die allgemeine Stimmung ähnelte der eines Volksfestes", (The jubilation was indescribable, the general tone resembling that of a festival) observed the *Tagblatt*. "Die halbe amerikanische Wiesbadener Kolonie scheint vertreten zu sein." (Half the American colony seemed to be there.)[27] Ex-president Jimmy Carter, whose bid for re-election was crushed in part by the long hostage crisis, made a brief stop in Wiesbaden on January 21, a day after Ronald Reagan officially took office. Arriving in Frankfurt, he and former secretary of state Cyrus Vance went to the USAF Medical Center to visit with the hostages. The next day recently elected Oberbürgermeister Oschatz visited for about forty-five minutes. During the week they stayed in Wiesbaden, the former hostages shopped at Hainerberg for new clothes and personal items, and wandered around the center city of Wiesbaden. On Sunday morning, 25 January, at 9:30 a.m., the hostages left the city to go home. Their week-long stay in Wiesbaden had been an emotional experience for all.

1. General David C. Jones, USAFE Commander in Chief 1 September 1971 – 1 July 1974, interview by Lt. Col. Maurice Maryanow, with Dr. Richard H. Kohn, transcript of tape recording, 5 August and 15–17 October 1985, 20–21 January, and 13–14 March 1986, USAF Oral History Project, Center for Air Force History, Bolling AFB, Washington DC.
2. WP, "USAFE Hqs Will Transfer From Lindsey to Ramstein", 29 September 1972; WT, „Wiesbadener US-Hauptquartier wird verlegt: über 6000 Amerikaner verlassen die Stadt", 27 September 1972.
3. Internal memo from Secretary of the Air Force Harold Brown, 22 November 1968, quoted in R.M.A. Hirst, *Ninety Years at Lindsey or How to Goldplate an Antique* (unpublished manuscript, 1987), vol. 3.
4. Beschluss des Erbenheimer Ortsbeirats, 6 July 1970.
5. WT, „Für die Stadt ‚sehr interessantes' Gelände: Die Amerikaner wollen Camp Lindsey räumen", 20/21 March 1971.
6. Patricia Parrish, *Forty-five Years of Vigilance for Freedom: United States Air Forces in Europe, 1942–1987* (Ramstein Air Base, Germany: Office of History, Headquarters, United States Air Forces in Europe. 1987), 171.
7. HQ USAFE letter, Headquarters USAFE Relocation, 26 September 1972, from General Jones to all offices.
8. Former Stadtverordneter Horst Milch, interview by author, written notes, 9 March 1994, Wiesbaden, Germany.
9. Former Oberbürgermeister Rudi Schmitt, interview by author, tape recording, 10 April 1994, Wiesbaden, Germany.
10. Viktor Herrfurth, U.S. Forces Liaison Office, interview by author, written notes, 3 March 1994, Wiesbaden, Germany.
11. WK, „Wer kommt denn nun nach Erbenheim?", 27 January 1976.
12. WK, „'Es wird keine Panzerrollbahn Erbenheim geben!'", 27 January 1976.
13. WT, „'Starlifter' nonstop von USA nach Germany", „Militär-Zeremonie bei strahlender Sonne", 25 March 1976; WK, „US-Army im Rathaus", 31 March 1976.
14. Annual troop lists, DoD, Center for Military History, Washington, DC.
15. WK, „'Wie schade, dass der Cade jetzt geht …'", 18 June 1976; WT, „'Ausgezeichneter Repräsentant der USA'", 25 June 1976.
16. Signe Seiler, *Die GIs: amerikanische Soldaten in Deutschland* (Reinbek bei Hamburg: Rowohlt, 1985); Larry H. Ingraham, *The Boys in the Barracks: Observations on American Military Life* (Philadelphia : Institute for the Study of Human Issues, 1984).
17. WT, „Amerikaner wollen jetzt hart durchgreifen", 10 August 1977.
18. WT, „Kein Wirt darf Amerikaner einfach aussperren", 18 October 1977.
19. WT, „'Aktion Grünanlage': Amerikaner werden aktiv!", 16 August 1977.
20. WT, „Kein Wirt darf Amerikaner einfach aussperren", 18 October 1977; WT, „Wenn an der Lokaltür das 'off limits' hängt …", 29/30 July 1978.
21. WT, „WI in dieser Woche", 20 August 1977.
22. WK, „Neu: Aktion Partnerschaft", 4 November 1976.
23. WT, „US-Soldaten fanden Trainer", 17 March 1977.
24. WT, „Jahrmarkt auf amerikanisch", 16/17/18 June 1978.
25. WT, „Am Tag, als alle von Wiesbaden sprachen…", 22 January 1981.
26. WK, „Die 52 US-Geiseln sind frei – Heute in Wiesbaden", 21 January 1981.
27. Ibid.

MODERNIZATION AND OPPOSITION

The 1980s proved to be an interesting decade for the U.S. forces in Germany. German-American relations were at perhaps their most ambiguous since the early 1950s when the U.S. role in Germany had shifted from occupation of a defeated nation to protection of an ally. During the 1980s, the discerning observer might have noted a similar ambiguity surrounding the American presence. On the one hand, the readiness and discipline of U.S. troops dramatically improved in the early 1980s, decreasing the type and number of conflicts involving U.S. servicemembers and German civilians so frequent in the early 1970s. On the other hand, the modernization and expansion of U.S. installations drew opposition from German neighbors, who objected to the increased noise, traffic, danger, and environmental hazards of military activity. This opposition, combined with burgeoning peace and anti-missile movements, contributed to a sense of unease for many American personnel in West Germany. While most Germans continued to support the presence of NATO and the U.S. forces, many also began to question the true level of threat posed by the USSR, wondering if perhaps the western response to that threat went too far. Scholars and military experts have pointed out that this development was to be expected, as a wealthy and democratic West Germany emerged from under the shadow of the United States.[1] Moreover, younger Germans with little or no memory of war and occupation focused on such concerns as the environment, nuclear disarmament, and the freedom to determine quality of life on a local level.

Environmental Damage

Brigade 76's tenure in Wiesbaden was on balance a peaceful one, but several irritants kept the German-American council busy during the late 1970s. Above all were complaints of environmental blight of various types, which increased during the period. One form of destruction caused by the tank units was known as maneuver damage. The tank units held frequent exercises, both to improve skills and to keep the soldiers occupied, and these maneuvers, held in woods and fields, often left their mark on the countryside. Tank treads churned crops into mud, scraped off the bark of trees or knocked them over, and heavy vehicles even took their toll on stone sidewalks. Property owners who suffered maneuver damage were well compensated for their losses; from the American point of view maneuver damage was actually very lucrative for farmers and municipalities. Although genuine concerns – over the presence of tanks in Wiesbaden and the destruction of the environment – accounted for the new attention paid to the issue, some Americans resented what they perceived as selfish griping. U.S. officials, however, took great pains to prevent or minimize maneuver damage when they realized the level of public concern.

Another environmental problem arose from oil spills at WAB. It seemed that when soldiers changed the oil in the tanks at the former air base, much of it leaked into the nearby Käsbach Creek, causing bird and fish kills and other destruction. When the oil spills were first reported in January 1977, rumors pointed to the Americans as culprits. Then, on 26 August, a defective oil disposal apparatus on the American installation caused many liters of oil to flow into the creek, sufficiently dangerous that the police and fire departments were alerted.[2] In the German-American council meeting of late May 1978, environmental experts reported that the spill might cost ten million dollars to clean up. By that point, however, most of the cleanup had already occurred, and an environmental officer was appointed to oversee safe disposal of used oil and other hazardous wastes.[3]

As residents of Wiesbaden grew more aware of threats to the environment, they also became increasingly likely to blame the Americans for shoddy practices and less likely to believe American protestations of innocence. In January 1983, *Der Spiegel* ran a piece about the careless disposal of radioactive waste in a regular dumpster at Mainz-Kastel Storage Station. According to the article, a certain Sergeant Elijah Davis attempted to report the danger, but was ordered by his commander to say nothing. By the time the story broke, no one knew where the material had been taken. The event was just one more example, many Germans believed, of the careless arrogance of the Americans.[4]

Complaints about the damage and annoyance of maneuvers grew in the early 1980s, as the NATO modernization program got underway. This policy, initiated by West German Chancellor Helmut Schmidt and President Jimmy Carter and continued by President Ronald Reagan, provided funding for better equipment and training for U.S. forces. High on the list of training measures were the "Reforger" exercises, large-scale war games involving troops from the NATO nations as well as reservists and active duty personnel from units stationed in the United States. Reforger 81, held from 7 to 25 September 1981 in central Hesse, necessitated the use of the airfield at WAB for Air Force A-10 and C-130s flown from stateside bases. Wiesbaden itself was spared a great deal of irritation because most of the flying took place over the north Taunus Mountains, but residents of the Rhine-Main area generally eyed the endeavor with misgivings. During the exercise, the *Tagblatt* gleefully reported that in the confusion of the exercise the Americans accidentally arrested one of their own officers, and in a separate incident long-time Public Affairs Officer Klaus Müller suffered the same fate. Environmental umbrella groups such as the Bundesverband der Bürgerinitiativen Umweltschutz (BBU) criticized the huge exercise and vowed to disrupt the next maneuvers "durch gewaltfreie Aktionen" (through nonviolent actions).[5]

In January 1982 criticisms of U.S. maneuvers continued. Chair of the Wiesbaden Stadtparlament environmental council Wilfried Ries, joined by Klaus Bensberg, the sport and recreation spokesman of the liberal-left SPD party, charged that military exercises on the Platte, a scenic creek on the outskirts of Wiesbaden, were polluting the air, ruining footpaths and destroying wildlife feeding areas. The German armed forces could not hold exercises in this area so the Americans should not either, the two argued; "[es] drängt sich die Frage auf (...), wie weit wir eigentlich Herren unseres eigenen Landes sind" ([It] raises the question (...), how much are we really in control of our own land).[6] In February, when the Americans announced further training in the Platte, Stadtverordneter Ries brought the issue up in the Stadtparlament. He proposed an alternative site, but the Americans rejected it as not providing sufficient space and terrain.[7]

The maneuver controversy continued into the spring and summer of 1982, after a surprise exercise in the Taunus Mountains enraged citizens and led to many complaints. According to news reports, approximately fifty tanks chewed up streets in Igstadt, Auringen and Heßloch, and residents complained that "nachts in der Gegend herumgeballert wurde" (at night the area is shot up) as one Bierstadter put it.[8] The Americans contended that noise was kept to a bearable minimum, a claim disputed by the populace. Local town councils petitioned the Magistrat to prohibit tank exercises in villages and residential areas. When the papers announced further maneuvers to be held between July and September in the Rheingau-Taunus-Kreis, former Oberbürgermeister Rudi Schmitt, now SPD-Bundestagsabgeordneter, brought the matter to Staatssekretär Dr. Willfried Penner in the Bundeshaus. Unannounced maneuvers in residential areas, Schmitt warned, could harm cordial relations between the two communities.[9]

The maneuver damage issue was sufficiently serious that it crept into even the most formulaic expressions of German-American friendship. In early January 1983, for example, Brigadier General Glenn H. Watson, commander of WAB, left Wiesbaden to go back to the United States, and along with the usual expressions of "tiefe Verbundenheit und Freundschaft" (deep alliance and friendship), the general made a more potent reference to "mancherlei Kritik und Belastungen" (various criticism and aggravations). He added, however: "Diese Belastungen (…) haben allenfalls zu Irritationen, nicht aber zu Beschädigungen der Freundschaft geführt." (These aggravations have led to irritations but not to damage of the friendship.)[10] That the general would refer to German-American disagreements in a formal farewell speech suggested that they were too well known to ignore completely.

Stationing Aircraft at Wiesbaden Air Base

In the early 1980s, West Germany was rocked by huge protests against the deployment of Pershing II missiles, nuclear weapons targeted at the Soviet Union. The NATO plan was to negotiate disarmament with the Soviets while in the meantime continuing to deploy new nuclear weapons in Europe, known as the "two-track" policy.[11] Widespread outrage over the deployment of nuclear weapons in Germany culminated in the "Heißer Herbst" (hot autumn), the fall of 1983, when nationwide protests crescendoed in anticipation of the Bundestag vote on the matter. As it happened, the Pershing II missile system was endorsed by the German government, but the opposition struggle had not been fruitless. It had stimulated debate over the military presence in West Germany, and provided valuable organizational experience for anti-military activists, developments which would come into play in later years in Wiesbaden.

In addition to the deployment of nuclear weapons, a second component of the NATO modernization program was the stationing of conventional weapons in forward areas throughout West Germany. As part of this new policy, on 16 November 1979, the 12th Aviation Combat Group was deployed to LAS to "command and control" V Corps aviation units.[12] The announcement of this move merited only the briefest mention in one of Wiesbaden's local papers, and did not appear in the other. That the 12th Aviation Combat Group would include aircraft was evident, but officials cited no definite numbers.

It was the stationing of aircraft, not the arrival of personnel of the 12th Aviation Combat Group per se, that sparked a reaction in Wiesbaden. By January 1980, a little over a month after the announcement, the two major political parties had stated their positions on the move, the conservative CDU party cautiously accepting the plan and the SPD rejecting it outright. (At this point, the moderate FDP followed the lead of the Social Democrats, but in future debates they would side with the CDU, their coalition partners.) This basic disagreement would hold throughout the decade. For ten years, the SPD led opposition to the deployment of aircraft in Wiesbaden, on grass roots and municipal levels as well as in the state and federal governing bodies, while the CDU supported the federal government's policy of strengthening defense capability, including the deployment at WAB.

Little was known about the stationing plan for the first few years. Other pressing public debates, especially the controversial expansion of Frankfurt Airport and the deployment of Pershing II nuclear missiles in

West Germany, took attention away from the issue. By 1982, however, American and German officials were formulating more concrete plans for the aircraft. Unfortunately, the stationing issue was characterized throughout the decade by confusion, contradiction, and suggestions of dishonesty, which, though probably not intentional, fed opponents' suspicions of treachery on the part of the Americans and the federal government of West Germany.

In the summer of 1982, V Corps secretly informed the state government that by 1988, a total of 135 Apache attack helicopters and twenty-six Starfighters would be stationed at WAB. But in October, Watson assured Wiesbaden Oberbürgermeister Hans-Joachim Jentsch that no Apaches would be stationed in Wiesbaden. Watson reported that WAB would receive fifteen transport helicopters (Blackhawks, it was later reported) in early 1983, but that additional aircraft would strain the capacity of the airfield. In the future, he said, the only military aircraft in Wiesbaden would arrive for temporary maneuvers.[13] Watson, operating at the local level, may not have been privy to negotiations occurring among federal officials, because on 9 November, the Bundesverteidigungsministerium (BVM) confirmed the numbers of aircraft in the V Corps report. As late as 9 December 1982, however, 12th Aviation Combat Group commander Andrew J. Miller, and Allen Russo, commander of the aviation unit of the 8th ID in Mainz-Finthen – both local officials like Watson – assured the public at a press conference that there would be no attack helicopters at WAB.[14]

City and State Reaction

From the beginning, city officials discussed and debated the stationing plan. In June 1983 the SPD faction in the city council, led by Günter Retzlaff, proposed a motion that the Magistrat should, in the interests of the citizens of the area, oppose the helicopters with all possible means. Retzlaff's motion ignited a ferocious debate, which accentuated the deep divisions between the SPD and the CDU on the matter. While the SPD reiterated its unwavering opposition, CDU member Hildebrand Diehl forcefully stated the case for support of the stationing plan. "Erbenheim und die Soldaten dort sind Teil unseres Verteidigungskonzepts, ihnen verdanken wir, daß wenigstens ein Teil der deutschen Bevölkerung in Frieden und Freiheit leben kann." (Erbenheim and the soldiers there are part of our defense; we have them to thank for the fact that at least part of the German population can live in peace and freedom) he argued. The SPD motion was defeated with the votes of CDU and FDP opponents, and a more moderate resolution substituted urging the Magistrat to ensure that the Wiesbaden population would not be unduly burdened by any stationing that might take place at WAB.[15] Given the level of controversy, a V Corps announcement a week later that Brigade 76 would move to Fulda by April 1984 could hardly have come at a worse moment, raising suspicions that the tanks were being moved to make room for helicopters.[16]

At the same time, SPD Landtag representatives Frank Beucker and Herbert Schneider demanded information from the BVM about the possible reactivation of WAB. Like their party colleagues in the city government, they opposed the stationing, but even more stringently and for additional reasons. They cited the noise issue and charged that the Americans had no understanding for the geography of West Germany, especially the Rhine-Main region – "Erbenheim ist nicht Texas!" (Erbenheim is not Texas!)[17] they reminded planners. They also brought up the problem of congestion from Frankfurt airport, which would, they claimed, rise to dangerous levels if the proposed stationing took place. They cited a study by the Bundesanstalt für Flugsicherung on the carrying capacity of Frankfurt airport, which concluded that "Es sollte im Interesse der Flüssigkeit der Verkehrsabwicklung am Flughafen Frankfurt und damit der Erhaltung der Kapazität auf eine permanente Reaktivierung der Wiesbadener Air Base – insbesondere für langsam fliegende Luftfahrzeuge – verzichtet werden." (It is in the interests of the fluidity of traffic development in Frankfurt ... that a permanent reactivation of WAB – especially for slow flying aircraft – be renounced.)[18] A third objection addressed the military necessity of the aircraft at WAB; the two representatives asserted that the helicopters would not be for the defense of West Germany but would serve the military interests of the United States. Beucker and Schneider promised to raise the question of the stationing in the Landtag when it resumed its meetings in October.[19]

The SPD state government itself opposed the stationing. Minister President Holger Börner supported the efforts of citizens' groups (see below),[20] and in late 1983, when the Americans stationed a small contingent of Mohawk aircraft at WAB, he promised "Gift und Galle [zu] spucken" (to spit poison and bile) to prevent any further deployments. He strongly criticized the Kohl administration as well as the Americans for the underhanded dealings, and demanded to know exactly what the federal government knew about American activities at WAB.[21] In a letter to Defense Minister Manfred Wörner, the MP expressed his frustration about the deployment of the Mohawks: "Weder die Bundesregierung noch die US-Streitkräfte haben es für nötig befunden, die Hessische Landesregierung über diesen Schritt zu unterrichten." (Neither the federal government nor the U.S. forces have found it necessary to inform the Hessian state government about this step.)[22] Börner reminded the defense ministry of the study conducted by the Bundesanstalt für Flugsicherung, and accused the BVM of having decided to reactivate WAB in advance of the report's findings.[23]

BI „Keine Reaktivierung des Flugplatzes Erbenheim"

In the fall of 1982, residents of towns near the base formed a citizens' initiative (Bürgerinitiative – BI) known as "Keine Reaktivierung des Flugplatzes Erbenheim" (Against the Reactivation of WAB) to fight the stationing. Headed by Horst Domes, an active member of the SPD, member of the city council and veteran of anti-nuclear energy and anti-missile campaigns, the BI functioned as an umbrella organization of individual town groups. The BI attracted a great deal of support from those of all political persuasions who were alarmed at the prospect of more aircraft noise and threats to public safety. There were, of course, many in the BI who harbored more fundamental objections to NATO and to the western alliance in which the Kohl administration cemented itself. The 1980s was a decade when the defense consensus fell apart, and many, especially those affiliated with the Green Party, and to a somewhat lesser extent the SPD, disagreed with the general direction of the new Cold War.[24] In spite of these concerns, the BI avoided questions of larger policy or ideology, having learned from previous experience how divisive those issues could be. In an interview in 1997, Domes recalled that support for the grassroots movement was almost universal in the towns directly affected by the reactivation plans, as long as opposition was based on the concrete issues of aircraft noise and flight safety. He acknowledged his own long involvement in peace and anti-missile activism and his fundamental opposition to the Reagan Administration's military buildup, but pointed out that the BI deliberately avoided discussion of the larger issues of the NATO modernization, the U.S. forces in West Germany, and the arms race. He noted that a focus on the direction of defense policy would have probably hurt the BI, alienating those who fundamentally supported NATO but thought the WAB plan unacceptable.[25]

The BI, as a grass-roots organization, worked in tandem with local town councils of the villages most affected by the deployment, including Nordenstadt, Igstadt, Breckenheim, Auringen, Erbenheim, and Delkenheim. They debated the issue in their meetings in the fall and winter of 1983. The split between CDU and SPD could be seen in these deliberations as well, with SPD motions asking that the Wiesbaden Magistrat to try to prevent the stationing, while CDU leaders questioned specific aspects of the plan but refused to reject it outright.

The BI not only worked with local governments, but also made its voice heard at the federal level. In January 1984, representatives of the BI met with Wörner in a two-hour meeting in Bonn. Domes recounted the meeting in positive terms; the minister, he said, made it clear that he was against the stationing and was actively looking for an alternative to WAB.[26] Wörner agreed with Domes that the Americans were not dealing openly, but he said it was unlikely that any aircraft would suddenly appear at WAB without warning. The meeting, according to Domes, was an "offene und konstruktive Unterredung" (an open and constructive talk).[27] Unfortunately, his positive impressions of the meeting did not stand. Barely a week later the local papers reported that Wörner, when asked to confirm his opposition to WAB, denied that he had expressed clear opposition to the stationing. Rather, he said, he was aware of citizen concerns but the stationing was part of defense strategy and would have to be undertaken. The federal government would try to minimize the irritation of the stationing, but would not try to prevent the Americans from moving their aircraft to the airfield.[28] "Jetzt kommt es uns vor, als seien wir auf einer ganz anderen Veranstaltung gewesen" (it seems to us that we were at a totally different meeting), responded Domes.[29]

Concrete Plans Announced

At the end of 1983, Börner wrote to the BVM, requesting permission to conduct public hearings on the impact of the deployment, which were required under § 30 Abs. 3 Luftverkehrsgesetz when a significant change in the use of an airfield was contemplated. On 27 January 1984, Wörner denied the request, reasoning that the proposed deployment was not a "significant change".

A week later, Jentsch had the unpleasant duty of announcing an updated plan for the airbase, and it was even worse than expected: by 1990 there would be 156 Apache attack helicopters and twenty-five Starfighters stationed at WAB, a total of 181 aircraft. Jentsch emphasized that the city would do everything possible to prevent the full contingent of aircraft from coming to WAB. "Ich warne allerdings davor, in eine falsche Hektik zu verfallen" (I counsel against falling into a false frenzy about this), said Jentsch, who said that his information was unofficial and the sources wanted to remain anonymous.[30] The huge deployment planned for WAB galvanized opponents, who vowed to continue pressuring the BVM to allow hearings before new aircraft were stationed.

On 21 March, city leaders from the three major parties met to try to form a united position on the deployment, but they were unable to come to an agreement. The SPD wanted a statement of full opposition, while the CDU and FDP wished for a more moderate approach. In Mainz, meanwhile, representatives of the three parties met and agreed immediately to oppose the stationing at WAB, an unity of approach hailed by the Wiesbaden SPD and the BI.[31] Meetings and discussions continued throughout the spring, but little was accomplished aside from statements of concern and support. To make matters worse, at the end of the summer, it was rumored that WAB might receive 400 aircraft and become the largest U.S. military airfield in the world outside the United States. The Oberbürgermeister denied these rumors, calling them "ein weiterer Flop" (yet another Flop).[32]

In September when a Mohawk RV-1 D stationed at WAB crashed along the Bundesstraße 455 connecting Wiesbaden and Erbenheim, American public relations officials struggled with the bad publicity. Fortunately no one was killed – the pilot and co-pilot ejected safely, and the crash occurred early Saturday morning when few drivers were on the roads. The plane crashed because birds had gotten caught in the engines. Flocks of birds were attracted to the garbage dump near WAB at the Dyckerhoff Deponie, and they posed a serious hazard to aircraft. In the Stadtparlament the SPD attempted to show a film about damage caused by the birds, but was prevented from doing so by the CDU and FDP. Diehl charged that the SPD was trying to ignite a panic, and the Oberbürgermeister said that the population was more in danger from car traffic than airplane crashes. Another SPD motion to try to stop the stationing failed in a vote, but a motion to commission a risk analysis passed.[33]

In late summer 1984, the state government announced that it would bring charges against the Defense Ministry if its demand for hearings were not addressed by 31 October.[34] The challenge seemed to have no effect; on 21 September a spokesman for the defense ministry replied that the stationing at WAB was going to occur, and nothing would prevent it.[35] This was followed on 5 October by a unusually frank statement by General Robert L. Wetzel, commander of V Corps, who said that the 181 aircraft were coming to Wiesbaden as planned: "we've stationed aircraft all over, but nowhere has there been as much complaining as in Erbenheim", he maintained.[36] As Börner had promised, on 8 November the state government brought charges against the federal government in the Bundesverwaltungsgericht in Berlin, demanding that Hesse be permitted to hold hearings before any deployment took place.[37] The Bundesverwaltungsgericht met in a private session on 10 November to consider the case, and on 20 November, the court ruled for the state. The federal government immediately appealed the ruling.

Meanwhile, the city received some good news at the end of January 1985, when Jentsch announced that the German negotiating team had bargained the Americans down to one hundred helicopters, from 180. The Americans were looking for an alternative to WAB for the other aircraft. "In unseren Bemühungen (...) sind wir einen wesentlichen Schritt vorangekommen!" (We've taken a significant step forward in our efforts) the Oberbürgermeister said. The news was hailed by CDU and FDP members, who warned against a false choice of "all or nothing" as being unrealistic and bound to fail.[38] Diehl defended the compromise: "In einem so dicht besiedelten Gebiet wie der Bundesrepublik, das eine lange gemeinsame Grenze mit einem totalitären Gewaltsystem hat, werden notwendige Verteidigungsmaßnahmen immer zur Belastung der Zivilbevölkerung führen" (In a heavily populated nation such as the Bundesrepublik, which shares a long border with a totalitarian system, it will always be necessary to have defense measures which lead to inconvenience of the population), he noted, adding that it seemed as though the SPD were fighting with all its strength against any military installations, "insbesondere gegen amerikanische" (especially against American ones). The SPD rejected this criticism, and the debate in the Rathaus raged. The *Tagblatt* opined: "Und wären am Donnerstag Abend ganze Schwärme von Hubschraubern übers Wiesbadener Rathaus gedonnert, die Akteure im Stadtparlament hätten sie vermutlich nicht gehört." (If on Thursday evening a whole swarm of helicopters thundered over the Wiesbaden Rathaus, the participants probably wouldn't have heard them.)[39]

The BI Court Case

In 1985, attorney Michael Hofferbert advised the BI that there had never been a legal agreement with the Americans about conditions under which the airbase could be used, and particularly in what circumstances the airbase would be relinquished. So, according to the NATO Troop Statute (NTS), the American use of the airfield was illegal. Based on this interpretation, BI member Gabriele Thomas sued the federal government on behalf of the residents of the area.[40] The Thomas lawsuit demanded that the federal government conduct negotiations with U.S. officials to codify American use of the base – because, the BI asserted, the airbase had been deactivated in 1976, when it was converted for use as a parking lot for tanks. The Bonn government, on the other hand, claimed that land confiscated by the Americans in 1945 was, in effect, extraterritorial – the Americans could do what they wanted with those areas, and courts could not compel them to consider the interests of nearby communities or individual citizens. This was especially so, the Bonn lawyers argued, in the case of military land.[41]

On 6 August 1985 the court rejected the Thomas suit, ruling that a citizen could not sue the federal government to force it to take a certain position with a foreign country. The Occupation forces had confiscated the airbase in 1945, and, the court decided, it continued to be an airbase even if it had not been used since 1976. The Americans contended that the airbase had in fact been used throughout the 1970s even if no aviation units had been stationed at WAB. This ruling was a disappointment to opponents, as might be imagined. The BI, however, did not give up; it immediately brought the suit to a higher level court in Kassel.

American Life in Wiesbaden

How did American personnel and family members view this controversy? Evidence suggests that few Americans were aware of the variety of measures taken to prevent the stationing at WAB, but in general Americans perceived a less friendly atmosphere in Wiesbaden than in past decades. In December 1982, military officials decried the isolation and alienation of American soldiers stationed in West Germany. The peace movement made them feel unwelcome and unappreciated, reported the *Tagblatt*, and the fifty-three bomb attacks against U.S. installations in 1982 led to feelings of insecurity. Americans were often discriminated against in bars and restaurants, they had neither money nor command of the language, and attempts at welcoming them on the part of Germans were half-hearted and not successful. Small wonder, then, that "Den amerikanischen Soldaten wird die Wirklichkeit in der Bundesrepublik Deutschland immer unheimlicher." (Life in the Federal Republic is for the American soldiers ever more unfriendly.)[42]

The perception that U.S. soldiers were unwelcome, or even in some danger from opponents, was based on impressions coming not so much from Germany as from other parts of the world. Personnel stationed in Wiesbaden were reminded frequently of threats to Americans overseas. Beginning in 1980 with the fifty-two Americans held by Iranian radicals, the USAF Medical Center in Wiesbaden cared for a number of victims of hijackings, kidnappings and bomb attacks. These included: five victims of the fatal attack on Egyptian President Anwar Sadat, October 1981; several dozen Marines injured in the bomb attack in Beirut, October 1983; thirty-nine hostages from an aircraft hijacking in Athens, July 1985, and individual kidnapping victims from Lebanon.[43] The USAF hospital, officially redesignated as a Regional Medical Center in December 1982 to denote its size and importance, gained fame in the United States and throughout the world because of these events. The medical center also treated lesser-known but no less tragic cases, such as many victims of the war in Afghanistan.

In Wiesbaden, the most ominous sign of anti-American sentiment in the early 1980s was a rash of bomb threats targeting American properties. Some of these were hoaxes, some were real. While no bombs were actually detonated, the security situation was serious enough that in 1982, the Lindsey Air Station Volksfest, a relatively recent innovation, was cancelled.[44] In 1985, Wiesbaden was linked with one of the most stunning terrorist acts against Americans in West Germany, when, on 8 August, Red Army Faction terrorists detonated a car bomb on Rhine-Main Air Base. Two Americans were killed and eleven wounded. Investigators soon connected the case with the mysterious murder of Private Edward Pimental, a soldier stationed at Camp Pieri, whose body was found in the Taunus Mountains in the morning of 9 August. He was last seen with a woman he had met in the "Western Saloon", a bar that was frequented by Americans – a woman, who, it turned out, was a member of the RAF. The terrorists had lured Pimental to the isolated spot in the Taunus, killed him, and took his mili-

The popular LAS Friendship Fest was cancelled in 1982 because of concerns about terrorism, but was later resumed.

tary identification card and license plates. They used these to gain access to the heavily guarded Rhine-Main Air Base. In a later communique, the RAF explained the act as a strike against the American war machine, and dubbed it "Kommando George Jackson", after a member of the Black Panthers killed in a prison riot in 1971.[45]

News of "Kommando George Jackson" and other terrorist acts kept many civilian Americans home in the mid-1980s, depressing profits from tourism and travel. In spite of these frightening (but isolated) events, American military personnel and family members had good reason to rejoice in their assignments to Germany. The dollar gained strength for several years, reaching a peak exchange rate of about DM 3.40 to the dollar, which, on top of pay raises, meant that Americans could shop, travel, even buy BMW and Mercedes automobiles. The relative affluence of American personnel meant that they were not limited to base recreation and eating establishments, and many Americans in Wiesbaden enjoyed exploring the city and its environs.

Another development which increased the likelihood that Americans would learn more about their temporary home was the improved educational level of the armed forces. American military personnel were better educated than ever; all enlisted personnel entering the services were required to have a high school diploma or GED, and all officers were college graduates. The services could afford to be choosy, regularly turning away applicants with low test scores or records of disciplinary problems in favor of better qualified recruits. Moreover, opportunities for continuing education expanded with increased demand. American universities such as the University of Maryland, Troy State, Embry-Riddle, and Boston Universities, and City Colleges of Chicago offered undergraduate and graduate degrees to enlisted personnel, officers, family members, and civilian employees. For active duty personnel, most of the tuition costs were covered through military tuition remission programs or VA benefits. As a larger percentage of recruits joined the services for the chance to get an education, opportunities grew in variety and quality. These included courses on the German language, art, music, and history, which stimulated appreciation for the rich cultural heritage of Germany.

In many ways, life on the American bases in Wiesbaden improved drastically during the decade. In the late 1970s, base maintenance had been an intractable problem, in spite of increased funding for renovations. In a 1978 letter to Air Force personnel in Wiesbaden, then-commander Colonel George J. Vehrs described his first impression of LAS: "I was (...) appalled at the exterior appearance of the facilities (...) [and] the amount of trash I saw and the lack of a good lawn maintenance program." Vehrs acknowledged attempts to secure building and dormitory upgrade funds, but warned that poor appearances might lead inspectors to think, "Why spend money there? They don't even take care of what they have."[46] By the early 1980s these problems were on their way to being solved. In 1981 DoD allocated $ 14 million to improve Wiesbaden installations;[47] of that amount, $ 6 million was spent on renovating and expanding hotels and troop billets, enabling billeting officers to place no more than two enlisted personnel in each room – an improvement over earlier practice. In addition, buildings were painted, shrubs, lawns and flowerbeds spruced up, playgrounds and public spaces made useable. Recreation and entertainment options were upgraded – movie theaters at Hainerberg, WAB and LAS renovated, gymnasiums expanded, and recreation centers improved. A new bowling alley was built on LAS, at a cost

During the 1980s the American military community enjoyed many morale and recreation activities on base, such as this football game.

of $ 1.75 million, and the Rocker Club (LAS Consolidated Mess) received a $ 1 million facelift.[48]

By the mid-1980s, then, life in the American military community in Wiesbaden was markedly better than a decade earlier, even as the stationing controversy dragged on. In 1987, Colonel Ralph S. Rothstein, commander of the 7100st Command Support Wing (CSW), successor to the 7101st ABW, told the Wiesbaden Post: "I think our families are happy. We live in a great city. There's a wide range of things to do to enjoy ourselves and enrich our lives and we're doing that. As for political issues, like the stationing of aircraft, they should be handled at the political level (...). That shouldn't have anything to do with relations between the citizens of Wiesbaden and the people of the military community (...). We must remember we are the guests in this country."[49] Although Rothstein was speaking to a semi-official arm of the military community, his optimistic portrayal of American life in Wiesbaden reflected reality for many soldiers and airmen and their families.

Oberbürgermeister Achim Exner

In July of 1985, Achim Exner (SPD) was elected Oberbürgermeister of Wiesbaden, and almost immediately activists demanded that he take a firm stand against the reactivation. He had his chance soon enough. Over the summer, the Hessian Landesanstalt für Umwelt had conducted a series of tests of aircraft noise. The results were released in November, and they indicated that citizens in the Rhine-Main area were indeed plagued with aircraft noise.[50] The measuring station at Fort Biehler, adjacent to WAB, showed that noise from the airbase measured at the same level as the noise reaching Fort Biehler from Frankfurt airport – the residents of Erbenheim and nearby towns, in other words, suffered from two equivalent sources of noise. In his first step taken on the issue, Exner sent the results of the test to the BVM with the hope that they would strengthen the state government's bid for impact hearings.

At the end of November, Exner received General McGrath, commander of the Wiesbaden community, and General Ayers, the USAREUR second in command, at the Rathaus for a courtesy visit. Ayers

Oberbürgermeister Achim Exner was a persistent opponent of the reactivation of Wiesbaden Air Base, but he remained friendly with U.S. officials in spite of the controversy.

told Exner that USAREUR was willing to find an alternative location for the aircraft, but the problem was financing. The U.S. Congress would not finance a new site when WAB was available, so the Germans would have to pay for it – and this they would not do.[51] Later, Exner gave the *Tagblatt* his opinion of the issue – "Für unseren Widerspruch ist das Bundesverteidigungsministerium zuständig, nicht die Amerikaner." (The Defense Ministry is responsible for our opposition, not the Americans.)[52] The BI blamed the BVM as well – Domes and attorney Michael Hofferbert pointed out that there was no known case where the Americans had stationed aircraft against the will of the West Germans, so the federal government could easily stop the stationing by refusing to agree to it. They urged Exner to consider pressing charges to halt the reactivation, and vowed to continue their fight in court.[53]

The year 1986 saw a new determination in governmental opposition to the reactivation. On 14 March 1986, Exner founded an Arbeitsgemeinschaft (AG) "Flugplatz Erbenheim" to coordinate local efforts against the stationing. Initially, the AG membership included the mayors of Mainz, Hofheim, Hochheim, Niedernhausen, and of Landkreis Main-Taunus and Landkreis Rheingau-Taunus; in later years other towns joined the group. The primary goal of the AG was to prevent the stationing of military aircraft at WAB. A second, broader goal was to decrease aircraft noise in the area from all sources – Frankfurt airport, Finthen Army Airfield, and other NATO installations.[54] The AG announced a "Null-Lösung" as their goal – that is, they demanded that no aircraft be deployed at the airbase, in contrast to the CDU position that a compromise could be found.

Dr. Bernard Löwenberg, Landrat from Main-Taunus-Kreis, was careful to note that "Die amerikanischen Freunde sollten dies nicht als Abkehr von Amerika verstehen" (the American friends shouldn't understand this as a move away from America), and Mainz' Oberbürgermeister Herman-Hartmut Weyel pointed to the good relations between the Americans and Mainz city government as evidence countering suggestions of anti-Americanism.[55] The AG would meet every few months for the next seven years, and it became a major part of the opposition to WAB. In May, for example, the AG brought the federal government to court to stop the construction of a flight simulator at WAB. If completed, the flight simulator would initially decrease air traffic by replacing some real flights, but city officials feared that it would only make WAB a more central location for U.S. Army aircraft, and thus would have a negative impact in the long run.[56] Throughout the summer, moreover, the AG pushed the BVM to consider its Null-Lösung plan, garnering much attention in the papers,[57] and raising the awareness of citizens who were not directly plagued by the noise.

The AG had some initial successes: at the end of the year, the BVM announced

ARBEITSGEMEINSCHAFT
FLUGPLATZ WIESBADEN-ERBENHEIM

Informationsveranstaltung

Was wird aus dem Flugplatz Wiesbaden-Erbenheim?

Dienstag, 19. 8. 1986, 19 Uhr
Bürgerhaus Wiesbaden-Erbenheim

Teilnehmer:
für die Arbeitsgemeinschaft: Oberbürgermeister **A. Exner**, Wiesbaden
Landrat **Dr. B. Löwenberg**, Main-Taunus-Kreis
sowie Vertreter der übrigen Mitglieder
Vertreter der Bundesregierung, der Hessischen Landesregierung und der US-Streitkräfte

Arbeitsgemeinschaft Flugplatz Wiesbaden-Erbenheim:
Landeshauptstadt Wiesbaden   Main-Taunus-Kreis   Kreisstadt Hofheim am Taunus   Gemeinde Niedernhausen
Landeshauptstadt Mainz   Rheingau-Taunus-Kreis   Stadt Hochheim am Main   Stadt Eppstein

The Arbeitsgemeinschaft or working group, opposing the stationing of aircraft at Wiesbaden Air Base, held frequent meetings to muster support for the issue.

that construction of the flight simulator would be postponed until the court ruled on the state request for impact hearings. Moreover, in December, Exner announced that the Americans would delay the deployment of thirty-four helicopters and twenty-three Starfighters, which were due to arrive in 1987. Although Exner, the AG, and the others in the opposition movement were justly proud of their victories, Exner vowed to continue the struggle, to prevent plans from changing in the future.[58]

In December 1986, a "Risk Analysis" commissioned a year earlier by the Magistrat finally was completed. The BVM and the American forces had been slow to cooperate with the privately owned Air Traffic Services Consulting (ATSC), and the study's author, Wolfgang Kassebohm, which delayed the publication of the report.[59] Earlier, Bundestag representative Hannelore Rönsch (CDU) criticized the commissioning of the project, saying that publication of military information was a security breach.[60] The BVM concurred, alleging that the study went "far over the boundaries" of acceptable opposition to the stationing. Nevertheless, the study was available at the end of January 1987, and its conclusions were not encouraging. It predicted more flight hours per year, and said that the simulator would not decrease flight hours as much as the BVM had claimed. Kassebohm wrote that if the plans went through, the Wiesbaden area would have the heaviest air traffic of all V Corps airfields.[61]

One of the concerns of the Risk Analysis was that aircraft accidents would rise because birds would get caught in aircraft engines or rotors as they had in the 1984 Mohawk crash. According to a detailed report by the Deutscher Ausschuß zur Verhütung von Vogelschlägen, between 1968 and 1983 birds were the cause of twenty-four helicopter crashes.[62] The group asserted that the stationing would cause this number to rise, "eine weitere Grundlage bei unseren Bemühungen gegen eine Reaktivierung" (another reason for our efforts against a reactivation), said Exner.[63] Yet another argument for the opposition appeared at the end of March, when researchers from the Forschungsinstitut für Friedenspolitik in Starnberg submitted an analysis of Wiesbaden area military forces, German and American, to the city government. Information in the report had been gathered from public sources such as newspapers and unclassified USAREUR archives, and detailed the remarkably heavy concentration of military forces in the area. The analysis had a slightly different purpose than the air traffic report, as it showed that Wiesbaden was indeed bearing its share of the defense burden. "Wenn die Amerikaner trainieren und fliegen wollen", said Exner, "dann haben sie in Amerika viel bessere Möglichkeiten!" (If the Americans want to train and fly, they have a better opportunity in America). The report suggested that, due to its military presence, Wiesbaden would be among the main targets in a war. 2.7 percent of the land in Wiesbaden was given over to military purposes, compared with the national average of 2.3 percent.[64] Exner acknowledged that changing the deployment plan would not alter this unpleasant fact, but said that the proper response would be to arrange disarmament negotiations.[65] However, he also defended the reputation of Wiesbaden's military forces, saying that they were not conspicuous, and did not constitute a negative presence in the area.

Armed with the report, Exner and Löwenberg traveled to Washington D.C. in late June and July 1987 for discussions with Pentagon officials.[66] Upon returning, they stirred up a new controversy with allegations that for years the Americans had tried to suggest alternatives to WAB to the German government, with no success. Exner received this information from General Carl E. Vuono, the U.S. Army Chief of Staff from 1987 to 1991.[67] The matter continued to confuse when Vuono denied Exner's report that the Americans were ready to give up any deployment of aircraft at WAB. When asked if there was a chance that a Null-Lösung could happen, he claimed that he had answered: "Theoretisch gesehen ist das eine Möglichkeit" (Theoretically it is a possibility).[68]

In November, some action on the state court case finally occurred, when the Bundesverwaltungsgericht in Berlin proposed a compromise agreement between the state and federal government. In the compromise, the federal government would hold hearings in accordance with paragraph 30 of the Air Traffic Law, during which the city, state, and other public bodies would have a chance to comment on the disadvantages of the proposed deployment. Both sides accepted the court's proposal rather than going to trial.[69] It demonstrated the success of the effort by the BI, state and AG, in spite of recent state elections which had put a CDU Minister-President, Walter Wallmann, in power. The federal government, unfortunately, further earned its reputation for double-dealing when it suggested allowing a deployment of thirty-nine aircraft while the hearings went on. The BVM argued that since the hearings were centered on the question of more than one hundred aircraft coming to WAB, an aviation unit with less than one hundred aircraft would not contradict the purpose of the hearings.[70] Not unexpectedly, the city and state forcefully rejected the hair-splitting argument of the BVM.[71]

As ordered by the court, the state government began to collect statements for the hearings. It requested statements from two professional organizations with expertise in air traffic issues – the Bundesanstalt für Flugsicherung and the Flugplankoordinator of Frankfurt Airport (FAG) – as well as groups affected by the stationing – cities, towns, the AG, the BI, environmental and safety groups. Towns, in particular, met and prepared their reports with the participation of interested citizens. In Delkenheim, one of the towns most affected by the plan, an open meeting was so well attended that there was standing room only. The meeting lasted four hours and the consensus fell against the stationing.[72] As a columnist in the *Tagblatt* noted, "Die Jahre der Besatzung und des ‚kalten Krieges' sind vorbei (...)" (the years of the occupation and the "Cold War" are past). Popular support of the opposition movement was overwhelming.

Erbenheim Reactivation as a National Issue

The statements by the affected organizations were intended to provide the Bonn government with input on the proposed stationing and help it determine whether the plan was appropriate. Many residents and activists hoped that the final result would be a Null-Lösung. Diehl, however, scoffed that the entire process was a waste of time, since the Bonn government had already decided on the stationing – the only question was how many aircraft would arrive. Bundestag representative Heidemarie Wieczorek-Zeul, a longtime opponent of the Pershing II plan and increased military spending in general, agreed with him in this case, that "die Bundesregierung die Anhörung der hessischen Landesregierung als reine Farce behandelt" (The federal government is treating the state hearings as pure farce).[74]

Unfortunately, subsequent events proved them correct. In June 1988, the office of the BVM wrote to Wieczorek-Zeul, admitting that the entire plan to station 181 aircraft had not changed. Further, although the stationing of the first of three Apache battalions, envisioned for 1987, had been delayed, it would take place by the end of 1988, thus adding thirty-nine aircraft to the fifty-seven already in Wiesbaden.[75] The BVM assured the AG that it had no intention of circumventing the hearings, but Exner threatened to go to court to stop further deployments.[76] On 29 July the city brought charges against the federal government in two separate cases.

Throughout August, as the date of the proposed deployment drew nearer, the issue heated up. A few days after the city went to court, Exner received information that as early as October 1987, the BVM and General Otis had secretly agreed to deploy up to one hundred aircraft in Wiesbaden.[77] According to news reports, Wörner had urged General Otis to station the aircraft in WAB before the end of the hearings. "Mach mal!" (Go ahead!) the *Kurier* characterized Wörner's letter.[78] Exner was enraged: "Ich frage mich, welche Interessen vertritt die deutsche Bundesregierung und der deutsche Verteidigungsminister!" (I ask myself which interests the German federal government and German defense minister represent.)[79] On August 11, the CDU/FDP state government announced that it had considered statements from the Bundesanstalt für Flugsicherung and the Flugplankoordinator of FAG. Based on information provided by the two organizations, it unanimously rejected the proposed deployment "für die Flugsicherheit und die Menschen" (for flight safety and humanity).[80] Opponents greeted the decision with joy, but it was not legally binding in any way.[81]

Activists hoped that the defense ministry would agree to delay the deployment of the thirty-nine aircraft for the time being. So it was with great distress that the city learned in late August that the BVM decided to allow the battalion to arrive as scheduled.[82] The next day, however, on 25 August, the Verwaltungsgericht Wiesbaden issued a ruling against the stationing, saying that the government had to inform the Americans that a permit process (Genehmigungsverfahren nach § 6, 30 Abs. 3 LuftVG) would have to be held first.[83] New defense minister Prof. Dr. Rupert Scholz criticized the court decision and the increasingly strong rhetoric surrounding the issue, condemning the use of verbal ripostes like "Salami-Taktik" and "Besatzungsrechtsdenken" – used in the court's own press release[84] – as being distracting and unworthy attacks.[85] Scholz said that the deployment of the thirty-nine aircraft could not be stopped at this point, because they were already on a ship being transported from the U.S. to West Germany. Furthermore, he said, it would be a security risk to NATO if the aircraft were not at WAB.[86] In response, the state government joined the city, bringing renewed charges against the federal government in the Bundesverwaltungsgericht.

On 1 September, Judge Dr. Manfred Kögel ruled again in favor of Wiesbaden, that permission to go ahead with the stationing before the hearings were over was against the law.[87] A third court ruling on 8 September confirmed the two earlier rulings against the deployment.[88] By this time, the *Tagblatt* said, the issue was "längst nicht mehr ein lokales oder regionales Thema" (no longer a local or regional issue), but rather part of a national debate over the Atlantic alliance.[89] Ambassador Richard Burt defended the American position against charges of "Besatzungsrecht": "Ich kann mir keine Situation vorstellen, in der die USA gegen den Willen der deutschen Regierung oder der deutschen Bevölkerung Schritte unternimmt." (I can't imagine any situation where the United States would take steps against the will of the German government or German people.) He went on to say, not entirely accurately, that for the past forty years the Americans had been in Germany as invited guests. "Wenn wir nicht mehr willkommen sind, gehen wir nach Hause." (If we are no longer welcome, we'll go home.)[90]

In spite of the growing controversy, American and German officials in Wiesbaden took care that local relations continued along their traditionally cordial lines. Representatives of the local American community assured Exner that the Americans did not want to take any measures that would upset German sensibilities. Exner also noted the curious fact that relations between the Americans and the city "noch nie so eng gewesen seien wie jetzt" (have never been as close as now).[91] Ironically, the national convention of German-American clubs was held in Wiesbaden in 1988, for the first time since 1969. The controversy was mentioned by the president of the club, Hilde Rittelmeyer, who said that some people saw the debate as a "Spielart des Anti-Amerikanismus" (a game of anti-Americanism), but that German-American friendship was as close as ever.[92]

In the beginning of November, Hannelore Rönsch announced that the defense council had reached a compromise position on the aircraft – no more than one hundred helicopters and no fixed-wing Starfighters.[93] The CDU administration of the state agreed to this compromise, but it did not satisfy many opponents – in fact, it enraged them. The following week the BI organized a march to the gates of WAB. About 3,500 people attended, according to the police and the BI. In a meeting of the Stadtparlament the following month, SPD and CDU members nearly came to blows. In February 1989, the city sued the federal government yet again, this time to compel the government to work with the Americans to make sure that flight height limits were being observed. The problem of low-flying aircraft had become sufficiently severe to bring the matter to the courts.[94]

Throughout 1989 the issue lay before the Bundestag. In February, the Ausschuss für Verkehr discussed the matter.[95] In the summer of 1989, the SPD and their coalition partners in opposition, the Greens, proposed in the Bundestag a vote on the WAB crisis. The SPD, led by Wieczorek-Zeul, proposed that Rönsch's compromise arrangement of one hundred aircraft at WAB be rejected. Then, just as debate on the proposal was about to start, the BVM announced that a public hearing would be held in October, and the twenty-four communities and groups which had made statements to the state government would be allowed to submit their materials. While the procedure was a result of the suit brought by the BI and the city, the BVM's timing was suspect: Wieczorek-Zeul observed that the hearing appeared to be an end run around the Bundestag vote.[96]

Throughout the late autumn the Bundestag debated the issue. It put off a final decision on whether to recommend acceptance or rejection of the plan twice in October and then on 16 November as well. In the middle of November, another scandal ensued when Wieczorek-Zeul displayed a telex from the BVM to USAREUR, dated 15 November, giving USAREUR permission to station two units of UH-60 (Blackhawk) helicopters in Wiesbaden. Chief of Public Information for USAREUR

James Boyle said that the letter had merely been written in advance of the vote in the Bundestag, but Wieczorek-Zeul and Exner accused the BVM of an excess of loyalty to the Americans. "[The BVM] hat sich wie ein Frühstücksdirektor der amerikanischen Streitkräfte benommen und nicht wie ein Verteidigungsminister, der dem Parlament und der deutschen Bevölkerung gegenüber verantwortlich ist!" (the BVM has acted as a lapdog of the American forces, and not as a defense minister who is responsible to the legislature and the German people) said Wieczorek-Zeul. Exner said that the defense ministry was being controlled by the Americans.[97] Accusations against the BVM were becoming increasingly strident.

On 14 December the Bundestag voted on the deployment, and the vote was a disappointment for opponents. The CDU and FDP voted together as coalition partners in favor of the stationing of up to one hundred aircraft at WAB. Stoltenberg made much of the compromise, noting that under the new plan a decrease of annual flight hours from 100,000 to 60,000 made the noise problem diminish considerably. Wieczorek-Zeul countered that with the turn toward democracy in the former east bloc, "ein neuer Schritt zur Aufrüstung" (a new step in armament) was not a good idea,[98] and that the CDU was not capable of putting the interests of the people and the nation ahead of those of the Americans.[99] Nevertheless, on 18 December the BVM triumphantly affirmed the Bundestag vote, giving the Americans permission to station three battalions of Apache attack helicopters in Wiesbaden.[100]

As soon as the decision was relayed to the Magistrat, city lawyers went to court to stop the stationing.[101] There was some confusion, however, at the end of the year about whether the BVM would actually allow the plan to continue. On 19 December, Stoltenberg said that the stationing could take place only with the permission of the city, but in January he seemed to change his mind again, calling the stationing necessary, and suggesting that within a week he would allow it to go forward.[102]

In response to Stoltenberg's flip-flop, Exner came up with yet another idea for combating the deployment: suing the American military in the U.S. Court of Appeals, charging that the U.S. forces in Wiesbaden were breaking American environmental laws.[103]

Fortunately, this did not turn out to be necessary. During the last months of 1989, the Berlin Wall fell and with it the communist governments of Eastern Europe. Even as the debate in the Bundestag raged, activists discussed the question of WAB's ultimate use should the Americans go home. In an early statement on the question, Domes made clear that the position of the BI was against any use of the airfield, whether by civilian or military aircraft.[104] Some experts suggested that WAB could become an extension of the overburdened Frankfurt Airport, and Exner at first noted that fixed wing aircraft, which ascended quickly, were preferable to the low-flying, slow helicopters.[105] But he was forced to backtrack quickly, as others involved in the opposition rejected this distinction. He went on record opposing any further use of WAB as an airfield, whether for military or civilian aircraft.[106]

By the late 1980s, opposition to the deployment of aircraft had widened into the larger issue of opposition to increased armament, especially in light of the changes occuring in the Soviet Union.

Already in early 1990, rumors of troop drawdowns circulated through towns and cities hosting U.S. forces. President George Bush proposed a bilateral withdrawal of 195,000 troops, and the first base closings proceeded apace in 1992 and 1993. Due to its location and extensive facilities, Wiesbaden was an unlikely location for a complete withdrawal of American forces, but speculation on the fate of WAB and the other bases in the Wiesbaden area gained intensity nonetheless. City leaders agreed unanimously that WAB should not become a civilian airfield, an adjunct to the enormous FAG.[107] Other options from the early seventies reemerged – housing areas, a technical school, city offices.

The decade ended as it had begun – with uncertainty and questions. Both Germans and Americans, however, found it hard to believe that the American presence in Wiesbaden would ever really end. The decade had seen protests against the reactivation, as well as terrorist threats against Americans. Yet the Lindsey Air Station Festival continued to draw thousands each summer through the gates on Schiersteiner Straße, and on any given day both German and English could be heard in the PX and Commissary at Hainerberg. By the late 1980s, a unique German-American subculture had been in existence for decades – second and even third-generation German-Americans, bilingual and bicultural, but also immersed in the distinct subculture of the U.S. military. The demographic impact of the U.S. forces certainly had a greater long-term influence than the controversy, heated as it was, over the deployment of aircraft. As the Cold War wound down and NATO debated its next steps, Wiesbaden would continue to be a valuable and central location for the U.S. forces in Germany.

---

1   See Daniel J. Nelson, *Defenders or Intruders? The Dilemmas of U.S. Forces in Germany* (Boulder and London: Westview Press, 1987).
2   *WT*, „Künftig noch mehr Sorgfalt", 2 September 1977.
3   *WT*, „Ölverschmutzung des Käsbachs bleibt Thema eins", 27/28 May 1978.
4   *WT*, „Strahlen-Panne in Kastel: 20 Laborfässer falsch beschriftet. 200 000 Reagenzgläser mit Radioaktivproben im Müllcontainer", 24 January 1983.
5   *WT*, „Drei Minuten vor zwölf", 16 November 1981.
6   *WT*, „Manöver-Kritik am US-Manöver", 21 January 1982.
7   *WT*, „Amerikaner üben auf der Platte", 23 February 1982.
8   *WT*, „Überraschungs-Manöver schreckte Bürger auf", 23 June 1982.
9   *WT*, „Gutes Verhältnis nicht belasten", 21 July 1982.

10 *WT*, „General Watson verläßt die Stadt", 10 January 1983.
11 Allan R. Millett and Peter Maslowski, *For the Common Defense: A Military History of the United States of America,* revised and expanded edition (New York: The Free Press, 1994), 612–3.
12 http://www.12bde.wiesbaden.army.mil/History/History.htm, "History of the 12th Aviation Brigade", 19 May 2000.
13 *WT*, „Erbenheim: Keine Kampfhubschrauber", 2/3 October 1982.
14 *WT*, „'Schwarze Habichte' schweben auf die Air Base: Für sechs alte kommen 15 neue Hubschrauber", 9 December 1982.
15 *WK*, „'Keine unzumutbare Belastung für Erbenheim'. Hitzige Debatte um Hubschrauber-Stationierung", 18/19 June 1983.
16 *WT*, „Noch keine Kampfhubschrauber in Sicht", 21 June 1983.
17 *WT*, „Hubschrauber: ‚Erbenheim ist nicht Texas!'", 24 June 1983.
18 Ibid.
19 *WK*, „Hubschrauber als ‚Eingreifreserve' für Krisengebiete?", 24 June 1983.
20 *WK*, „Protest gegen Hubschrauber", 5 May 1983.
21 *WT*, „Börner sieht Vertrauensbruch", 11 November 1983.
22 *WT*, „Börner: Jeder Flugbetrieb sollte unterbleiben", 17 November 1983.
23 Ibid.
24 For a discussion of this issue on the national policy level, see Jeffrey Herf, *War by Other Means: Soviet Power, West German Resistance, and the Battle of the Euromissiles* (New York: The Free Press, 1991).
25 BI spokesman Horst Domes, interview with author, tape recording, Delkenheim, Germany, July 1997.
26 *WK*, „Wörner sicherte Hubschrauber-Gegnern zu: Alle Möglichkeiten werden ausgeschöpft", 28/29 January 1984.
27 *WT*, „Wörner lehnt eine Aktivierung des Flugplatzes Erbenheim ab: Bonn möchte intensiv nach alternativen Standorten suchen", 28–29 January 1984.
28 *WK*, „Flugbetrieb zunächst auf Probe", 21 February 1984.
29 *WT*, „Verwirrspiel um den Flugplatz", 26/27 February 1984.
30 *WK*, „Jentsch bestätigt neue Stationierungszahlen für Erbenheim. OB strebt gemeinsame Entschließung gegen Reaktivierung an", 9 March 1984; *WT*, „Erbenheimer Flugplatz nun doch reaktiviert. Bis 1990 sollen 156 Hubschrauber kommen", 9 March 1984.
31 *WT*, „Resolution gegen Reaktivierung", 30 March 1984; *WT*, „Flugplatz-Reaktivierung bleibt Streitpunkt: Vorgehen nach Mainzer Vorbild nicht in Sicht", 31 March/1 April 1984; *WK*, „CDU und SPD über Flugplatz-Resolution völlig zerstritten. Heftige Debatte ohne Ergebnis im Ältestenausschuß", 31 March/1 April 1984.
32 *WT*, „Der Oberbürgermeister spricht von einem Flop", 30 August 1984.
33 *WT*, „Streit um Reaktivierung will kein Ende nehmen", 22/23 September 1984.
34 *WK*, „Landesregierung will wegen Erbenheim Gericht anrufen", 13 September 1984.
35 *WT*, „Erbenheim wird ausgebaut", 22/23 September 1984.

36 *WT*, „US-General: Es bleibt bei Erbenheim. Bis Ende 1990 rund 180 Flugzeuge!", 5 October 1984.
37 *WK*, „Flugplatz Erbenheim: Börner klagt gegen Wörner", 8 November 1984.
38 *WT*, „Nun weniger Flugzeuge nach Erbenheim? Dr. Jentsch spricht von nur 100 Maschinen", 31 January 1985.
39 *WK*, „Erbenheim-Debatte und nichts Neues: SPD fordert Kampf gegen Reaktivierung, CDU freut sich über Reduzierung", 2/3 February 1985.
40 *WT*, „Hubschrauber in Erbenheim weiter strittig. Bürgerinitiative: Rechtsgrundlagen fehlen!", 23/24 February 1985.
41 The American position on this issue was somewhat more nuanced. American officials welcomed the position that the bases were extraterritorial, but they always tried to avoid controversy and opposition relating to military measures. They had no wish to complicate their mission further by incurring the wrath of their neighbors. However, in terms of the airbase itself, they argued that in fact the landing field had been used for aircraft occasionally, during exercises, so there was no question of deactivation and reactivation.
42 *WT*, „US-Soldaten: ‚Was sollen wir noch hier?'", 23 December 1982.
43 See the very moving account of these events in Jayne Traendly, "The History of the Wiesbaden Medical Center", DoD publication, 1993.
44 *WT*, „Amerikaner sagen Freundschaftsfest ‚Lindsey' ab", 30 March 1982.
45 Hans Josef Horchem, *Die Verlorene Revolution: Terrorismus in Deutschland* (Herford: Busse Seewald, 1988), 150.
46 "Commander's Bulletin" to All Air Force Personnel in the Wiesbaden Area, from George J. Vehrs, Colonel, USAF, 2 Aug 1978, in R.M.A. Hirst, "How to Goldplate an Antique or Ninety Years at Lindsey, A History of Lindsey Air Station, Wiesbaden, Federal Republic of Germany", unpublished mss, 1987.
47 *WT*, „Amerikaner investieren in ihre Einrichtungen", 10 September 1981.
48 *WP*, "Facilities Improved for a Better Life Here", 10 May 1984.
49 *WP*, "Rose Glasses Right Color in Wiesbaden", 5 February 1987.
50 *WK*, „So laut wie Frankfurt: Erbenheimer Lärm gemessen", 13 November 1985.
51 *WT*, „Amerikaner bei Exner: Mehr Dialog!", 29 November 1985.
52 *WT*, „Flug-Simulator in Erbenheim?", 4 December 1985.
53 *WT*, „Lauter als der Hauptverkehr: Der Fluglärm ist unerträglich", 14/15 Dec 1985.
54 See EXNER: Protocols of Arbeitsgemeinschaft Flugplatz WI-Erbenheim, Arbeitsgemeinschaft Flugplatz Erbenheim ab Dezember 1988; also EXNER: Arbeitsgemeinschaft Flugplatz Erbenheim, protocols and correspondence, 1986–88.
55 *WT*, „AG gegen Flugplatz-Reaktivierung", 15/16 March 1986.
56 EXNER: Arbeitsgemeinschaft Flugplatz Erbenheim, Verwaltungsklage Michael Hofferbert and Ulrich Koch, Landeshauptstadt Wiesbaden gegen Bundesrepublik Deutschland, I/4-32/86, 2 June 1986.
57 See for example *WK*, „Weiterer Schritt für Nullösung auf Erbenheimer Flugplatz", 1 August 1986.
58 *WK*, „1987 keine neuen Hubschrauber in Erbenheim", 18 December 1986.

59 EXNER: Arbeitsgemeinschaft Flugplatz Erbenheim, Letter from Wolfgang Kassebohm of Air Traffic Services Consulting to Reinhard Edel, Rechtsamt, 21 October 1986.
60 WT, „Militärische Daten öffentlich ausgebreitet", 15 October 1986.
61 Wolfgang Kassebohm, ATSC, Gutachtliche Stellungnahme über die durch eine Reaktivierung des US-Flugplatzes Wiesbaden-Erbenheim zu erwartenden Auswirkungen für den Bereich des Stadtgebietes Wiesbaden und des Main-Taunus-Kreises, December 1986.
62 EXNER: Arbeitsgemeinschaft Flugplatz Erbenheim, Deutscher Ausschuß zur Verhütung von Vogelschlägen im Luftverkehr e.V., „Biotopgutachten für den Flugplatz Wiesbaden-Erbenheim", 1986, 4.
63 WK, „Reaktivierung oder Deponie", 8 April 1987.
64 Erich Schmidt-Eenboom, *Wiesbaden – Eine Analyse der militärischen Strukturen in der hessischen Landeshauptstadt* (Starnberg, Forschungsinstitut für Friedenspolitik, E.V., Juni 1987), 106.
65 WK, „Für einen Hubschrauber ein ganzes Klinikum", 14 May 1987.
66 WK, „Gespräche im Pentagon sollen Reaktivierung des Flugplatzes Erbenheim verhindern helfen", 3 April 1987.
67 WT, „US-Armee: Bereit, in Erbenheim zu reduzieren. Gab Bonn den Amerikanern keine Antwort?", 6 July 1987.
68 WT, „Amerikaner: Von Null-Lösung nie die Rede. US-General Vuono geht auf deutliche Distanz", 24 July 1987.
69 EXNER: Arbeitsgemeinschaft Flugplatz Erbenheim, Letter from AG to Lt. General John D. Woodmansee, Commander V Corps, 23 November 1987.
70 WK, „Gilt Anhörung nicht für alle Hubschrauber?", 21 January 1988.
71 WT, „Exner: ‚Das kann man mit uns nicht machen!'", 21 January 1988.
72 WK, „Bürgerversammlung über Militärflugplatz: niemand ist dafür", 8 June 1988.
73 WT, „Der Kommentar", Ulrich Zink, 8 June 1988.
74 WT, „Stationierung doch vor Abschluß der Anhörung?", 24 June 1988.
75 EXNER: Flugplatz Erbenheim II, Letter from the Bundesminister der Verteidigung to Heidemarie Wieczorek-Zeul, 21 June 1988.
76 WK, „Klage gegen Stationierung", 26 July 1988.
77 For the correspondence in this matter, see EXNER: Flugplatz Erbenheim III.
78 WK, „Bewirkt Wiesbaden die Wende in der Bonner Erbenheim-Politik?", 6/7 August 1988.
79 WT, „Stationierung ist beschlossene Sache", 4 August 1988.
80 WT, „Land Hessen gegen Erbenheim-Ausbau", 11 August 1988.
81 WT, „Wichtiger Schritt zur Null-Lösung: OB Exner sieht die Position bestätigt", 11 August 1988.
82 WT, „Neuer Zündstoff im Flugplatz-Streit: Bonner Bescheid schlug wie Bombe ein", 25 August 1988. Three days later, on 28 August, Americans and West Germans learned that forty-three people were killed and 500 injured when Italian jets crashed at

the Ramstein air show, in front of over 300,000 people. The shocking tragedy brought a new urgency to questions about air traffic safety.
83 EXNER: Flugplatz Erbenheim IV, Verwaltungsgericht Wiesbaden, VII G 796/88, Landeshauptstadt Wiesbaden gegen Bundesrepublik Deutschland, 25 August 1988.
84 EXNER: Flugplatz Erbenheim IV, Verwaltungsgericht Wiesbaden, Pressemitteilung „Gericht rügt Salamitaktik und Besatzungsrechtsdenken der Bundesregierung", 25 August 1988.
85 WT, „Bonner Hardthöhe bleibt in Sachen Erbenheim hart", 29 August 1988.
86 WT, „Hubschrauber per Schiff unterwegs?", 30 August 1988.
87 EXNER: Flugplatz Erbenheim IV, Verwaltungsgericht Wiesbaden, VII H 944/88, Landeshauptstadt Wiesbaden gegen Bundesrepublik Deutschland, 1 September 1988.
88 EXNER: Flugplatz Erbenheim IV, Verwaltungsgericht Wiesbaden, VII H 944/88, Landeshauptstadt Wiesbaden gegen Bundesrepublik Deutschland, 8 September 1988.
89 WT, „Der Kommentar: Erbenheim-Welle", 5 September 1988.
90 WT, „'Wenn wir nicht willkommen sind, gehen wir nach Hause'", 22 September 1988.
91 WT, „Neues Gutachten zu Erbenheim. Magistrat will Klarheit haben", 20 October 1988.
92 WT, „Deutsche und Amerikaner: Freundschaft ist gefestigt", 24 October 1988.
93 WT, „Hannelore Rönsch: Tragbarer Kompromiß. Rund 100 Hubschrauber – keine Starrflügler", 10 November 1988.
94 EXNER: Flugplatz Erbenheim – Anhörung am 15.2.89, Klage Landeshauptstadt Wiesbaden gegen BRD, 7 February 1989.
95 EXNER: Flugplatz Erbenheim – Anhörung am 15.2.89, Auswertung der öffentlichen Anhörung vor dem Ausschuß für Verkehr des Deutschen Bundestages am 15.2.1989.
96 WT, „Wieczorek: ‚Ein glatter Wortbruch'", 25 August 1989.
97 WT, „Vor Bundestagsentscheidung war Stationierung abgehakt", 18 November 1989.
98 WT, „Amerikaner können jetzt in Erbenheim stationieren", 15 December 1989.
99 WT, „Sie zog sehr viele auf ihre Seite", 15 December 1989.
100 EXNER: Flugplatz Erbenheim V, Entscheidung des Bundesministers der Verteidigung, 18 December 1989.
101 EXNER: Flugplatz Erbenheim V, Klage vor dem Verwaltungsgericht Wiesbaden, VII E 1124/89, 18 December 1989.
102 WT, „Stoltenberg plant Sofortvollzug für Erbenheim", 15 January 1990.
103 WT, „Landeshauptstadt will vor US-Gericht klagen", 25 January 1990.
104 Domes, interview with author, July 1997.
105 WT, „Spekulationen um Erbenheimer Flugplatz", 14 June 1989.
106 WT, „Keine Begeisterung für zivilen Flugplatz", 15 June 1989.
107 WT, „Gegen die zivile Nutzung Erbenheims", 2 February 1990.

AFTER THE COLD WAR

With the dramatic fall of the Berlin Wall in November 1989, and the collapse of the Iron Curtain, the rationale for the American presence suddenly ceased to exist. The events of autumn 1989 took most Americans by surprise; although Germans and Americans had followed Mikhail Gorbachev's reforms through the mass media, almost no one expected the system that had been in existence for fifty-odd years to evaporate in the blink of an eye. Unsure of the future, the Americans in Wiesbaden continued on as if nothing had changed – a reasonable response under the circumstances.

As it became clear that a massive drawdown was likely to occur, the civilian community began to voice hopes for a "peace dividend" – material benefits from a withdrawal of troops. This "dividend" would not be insignificant – in all of Hesse, there were over 200,000 military personnel, family members and civilian employees (German and American), adding up to the heaviest military presence in any state of West Germany.[1]

Wiesbaden, of course, had always hosted a large American military population. Heidemarie Wieczorek-Zeul pointed out that the Americans held almost three percent of the land in the Wiesbaden metropolitan area, and that if they left there would be over 4,000 housing units available, which would go far to solving the fierce housing crunch in Wiesbaden.[2] A *Tagblatt* article on 3 May 1990 noted that if the Americans left the city, as many as 5,000 apartments would be available.[3] Even Defense Minister Wallmann wrote to his party comrade, Helmut Kohl, suggesting that the Americans leave Wiesbaden and Frankfurt because of the dense population.

Another benefit to a withdrawal would be the cessation of longtime irritants, such as maneuver damage and noise from training. Articles in the papers described the unbearable noise of the Rheinblick shooting range, and observed that if it continued to exist, at least it should be opened to German use. And, of course, opponents cheered the diminution of the threat of aircraft noise from the deployment of the 12th Aviation

Brigade, but they cautioned against using WAB as an extension of Frankfurt Airport. Both Frank Beucker and Wieczorek-Zeul came out firmly against using WAB as a civil airbase, and called for concrete plans to be made public. The BI, too, came out strongly against a civilian use of the airfield, noting that it had not fought for years to stop military noise, only to accept noise from civilian aircraft.[4]

Finally, many Germans celebrated the opportunity to reexamine and change the dynamic of the arms race that had absorbed so much money, time and energy throughout the 1980s. A group called Arbeitskreis "Eine Region wehrt sich" demonstrated at the Mauritiusplatz every day between five and seven o'clock in the evening for three months, under the slogan "Entrüstet Wiesbaden". While this group protested aircraft noise, they also objected to the general militarization of the region. More and more people seemed to be agitating for a change in the defense policy of NATO, the United States, and the CDU-led federal government.[5]

After the Cold War, citizens' movements continued to oppose air traffic over Wiesbaden, arguing that the Rhine-Main area was already over-burdened by the huge Frankfurt Airport.

A further surprise occurred when Iraqi forces invaded the Gulf state of Kuwait in August 1990. This development had enormous repercussions for the Americans in Wiesbaden. Most significantly, the aircraft from 12th Aviation Brigade were deployed to Saudi Arabia on 13 August 1990. The one battalion that had been successfully stationed in Wiesbaden left to fly missions over Iraq and Kuwait. They were joined there by the two battalions which concerted opposition in Wiesbaden had prevented from coming to Europe. A large proportion of the active duty personnel stationed in Wiesbaden, from supply specialists to medical personnel, also left for the Gulf.

Through most of 1991 the BVM, which had continued to wrestle with the court cases brought by the city, informed the Verwaltungsgericht Wiesbaden that a proceeding scheduled for 23 October was moot, because the U.S. forces were changing their stationing plan. The city agreed that the proceedings did not need to continue, and on 19 November the court dismissed the case.[6] On 15 June 1992, the entire unit – the 6th Cavalry Regiment – was deactivated as part of the downsizing project.[7] The Magistrat, however, voted to reactivate the court case, because although the Apaches were finally gone, downsizing plans included the transfer of utility helicopters from Frankfurt to Wiesbaden. The number of aircraft – seventy-one to seventy-three – envisioned for WAB was smaller than the 181 of earlier plans, but still unacceptably high. In late 1993 a compromise solution was reached, allowing a total of sixty aircraft to deploy to WAB. The AG accepted this lower figure, though the BI and Wieczorek-Zeul continued to push for a deactivation of WAB.

In Sept 1990, USAREUR created a base consolidation plan, abolishing the old military communities centered around individual base complexes like Wiesbaden, and creating Area Support Groups (ASGs) consisting of larger areas. Wiesbaden joined the 104th ASG in October 1997, along with other surviving installations in the region. Camp Pieri, the first Wiesbaden base to close in the post-Cold War years, shut its doors in October 1992, and was first used as a hostel for ethnic Germans coming from the east. More recently it was converted into a housing area known as "Auf der Heide".[8] Other small installations such as Schierstein, home of the secretive 497th RTG intelligence unit, were dismantled as well.

The Americans returned LAS to the Germans in September 1993. After considerable discussion and uncertainty, the base was renovated under the auspices of a specially-created Stadtentwicklungsgesellschaft, and became an extensive housing area and administrative headquarters known as Europaviertel.[9] Former base buildings were converted for a wide variety of public and private uses. The Rocker Club, for example, became a Syrian Orthodox church, while the former headquarters of USAFE on LAS was taken over by the Bundeskriminalamt. The older

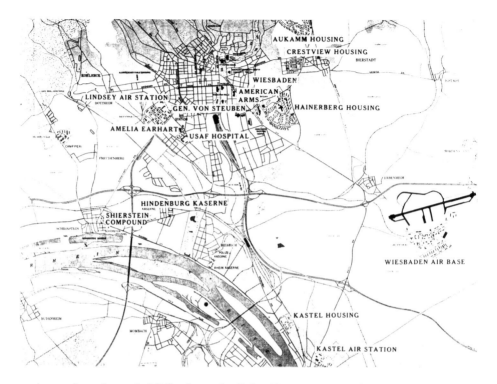

A map from the early 1950s shows the U.S. military presence during the Cold War. Almost all of these installations have been returned to their German owners.

buildings on LAS were protected under Germany's strict preservation laws, but newer buildings were torn down or modified, and condominiums were built on former motor pool areas and other spaces. While many in the community feared that LAS would require extensive environmental cleanup efforts to rid it of petroleum and other chemical waste products before it could be used for residential housing, in fact the damage from pollution was much less extensive than feared. Heinz-Peter Albertsmeier, head of the development efforts, noted that LAS was no more polluted than any civilian gas station might be.[10]

Other smaller pieces of property were returned to the German government, such as the "White House" on Paulinenstraße, formerly the home of the American Community Council and in the 1990s the Public

Affairs Office. The return of the "White House" fostered some controversy over its eventual fate: as an historically valuable protected building, it could not be torn down, but it needed extensive renovation before it could be used – renovation for which the German government did not have the necessary funding. By the late 1990s, however, the Americans returned the building to the Germans.

In the first seven years after the fall of the Berlin Wall, a total of 191 properties in Hesse alone were released to their civilian owners.[11] In spite of this consolidation, however, Wiesbaden remained a central location. By 1993 it was clear to all that WAB would not be given up.[12]

Lindsey Air Station was closed in September 1993.
Several years later construction began on the „Europaviertel".

Throughout the 1990s, as units were deactivated and bases closed, many of the surviving organizations moved to Wiesbaden. Helicopters continued to fly, albeit in smaller numbers – in the late 1990s only sixteen UH-60s were stationed in Wiesbaden. The U.S. Army, in fact, gave WAB a new name – Wiesbaden Army Airfield (WAAF) – to emphasize that it was no longer an Air Force installation.

Although not all the military bases in Wiesbaden were given up to the Germans, and aircraft noise continued to annoy the neighbors of the airfield, in one sense the "peace dividend" did pay off: most Americans no longer lived in housing "on the economy" – in German homes and apartments. The number of Americans in Wiesbaden dropped almost in half – from about 20,000 to about 13,000, and the apartment complexes in Hainerberg, Aukamm, and Crestview could house all the families needing homes. For the first time in fifty years, any American military personnel who wished to could live in military housing. In fact, in the mid-1990s even civilian employees of the military were offered housing in Hainerberg – an offer many accepted, because the exchange rate during most of the 1990s was extremely unfavorable to the Americans, and base housing much less expensive.

Official relations between the German and American communities continued to be as cordial and friendly as they had been during the Cold War. Hildebrand Diehl was elected Oberbürgermeister of Wiesbaden in 1997, and he continued the tradition of close contact with his American counterparts. He had vigorously defended the Americans during the reactivation controversy in the 1980s; moreover, as a member of the postwar generation he had grown up with the American presence. He not only regarded it as integral to western defense, but also remembered the early years of American soldiers and installations in the Occupation era.

The increasing multiculturalism of Wiesbaden and of Germany has also had an impact on the Americans forces in the city. Americans of all races have long since ceased to be exotic or unusual members of German society, and as postunification Germany grapples with the integration of a variety of religious and ethnic minority communities, the Americans appear by contrast to be all the more familiar. While the release of bases and troop drawdowns were at first welcomed by many or most Germans, anecdotal evidence suggests that some began to view their replacements – ethnic Germans from the East Bloc, Bosnian refugees, asylum seekers from around the globe – not as an improvement. The Americans, after all, brought their own security forces, their own sources of income, and their own shopping and housing areas – and an understanding that eventually, they would go home.

By the late 1990s, German-American friendship in Wiesbaden had changed significantly from the early years of fascination and envy. As more Americans moved onto the housing areas, opportunities for contact diminished even further. Many Americans living in the housing areas ventured into the community very rarely, or not at all; more Americans lived in Wiesbaden without learning the German language or gaining even a superficial knowledge of German culture and history. Friendship efforts like the German-American Women's Club continued, but the focus changed from the American military population to a wider circle of international women living in Wiesbaden. Clubs specifically targeting the military, such as the Kontakt Club, have languished in recent years, in spite of the energetic and sustained efforts of a few committed individuals such as Public Affairs Officer Paul Nelson to engage American military personnel in such efforts. German interest has waned as well, but older Germans still remember the American presence with affection, and support contact more than their American counterparts.

The horrific events of 11 September, 2001 changed the face of the American community once more. The residents of Wiesbaden reacted with shock and deep sympathy to the disaster, and expressed their solidarity with the Americans. Immediately after the terrorist attacks in New York and Washington, military installations throughout the world went on high alert. In Wiesbaden, the attacks did what decades of desultory discussions had never achieved: the fencing and barricading of the American housing areas, as well as the American Arms Hotel on Frankfurter Straße, as well as the distribution of new "German-style" license plates for American automobiles. These security measures had been debated and rejected as unnecessary in the mid-1980s, when German left-wing terrorists threatened military installations and personnel.

Extensive security measures had not been implemented in earlier years in part because they would have created enormous traffic difficulties in the heavily-populated city. Streets in Hainerberg and Aukamm Housing Areas were used as thoroughfares by many German commuters, and any change meant delays and detours. In the immediate aftermath of the 11 September tragedy, the citizens of Sonnenberg and Bierstadt bore the inconvenience with sympathy and willingness, but as the months wore on, it became less clear to many citizens why the housing areas remained blocked. Some charged that the Americans had overreacted to the crisis – that terrorists were not likely to choose the tiny Aukamm Housing Area as a target. Others suggested that the measures were a matter of bureaucratic inefficiency that merely caused irritation to German neighbors of the American installations, and threatened to erode good German-American relations. Finally in the summer of 2002, almost a year after the terrorist attacks, the main streets through the Aukamm Housing Area were opened during the day; Hainerberg remains closed and tightly controlled.

It is impossible to know what the future of the American community in Wiesbaden will be. Consolidations continue – recently, the military installation at Bad Kreuznach is being closed and the units from that city moved to Wiesbaden. The BI continues to be active in the fight against aircraft noise, but in an ironic twist, it now often argues for a continued military presence – considered to be much less onerous than a civilian satellite airport would be. In the summer of 2002, yet another controversy erupted over plans to station fifteen aircraft from Heidelberg at WAAF, fixed-wing aircraft which, according to defenders of the plan, would create less noise than the low-flying helicopters. The Americans, however, have promised to decrease dramatically the number of aircraft allowed at WAAF from sixty to twenty-five, and the number of annual flight hours from 30,000 to 10,000 by the year 2005. This would make the skies over Wiesbaden, and in particular the long-suffering communities around WAAF, much quieter. In any case, it is unlikely that the Americans will release the airbase any time soon, but it is impossible to know for sure.

While the future of the American community in Wiesbaden is unclear, the past fifty years have produced colorful memories of German-

American cooperation, friendship, families – as well as disagreement and compromise – on all levels, public and private, institutional and individual. Thousands – maybe millions – of Americans remember Wiesbaden with fondness and gratitude for their time spent in a city rich with beauty and history. The American community is proud to be part of that history.

---

1 *WT*, „200 000 Hessen leben von den Soldaten und ihren Einrichtungen", 18 May 1990.
2 *WT*, „Drei Prozent der Stadtfläche sind von Amerikanern belegt", 28 March 1990.
3 *WT*, „Wenn Amerikaner gehen: 5000 Wohnungen frei", 3 May 1990.
4 *WT*, „Bürgerinitiative für Null-Lösung in Erbenheim", 10 May 1990.
5 *WT*, „Region wehrt sich immer mehr gegen Fluglärm", 6 April 1990.
6 EXNER: Flugplatz Erbenheim VI, Sachstandsbericht: US-Militärflugplatz Wiesbaden-Erbenheim, 1992.
7 http://www.12bde.wiesbaden.army.mil/History/History.htm, "History of the 12th Aviation Brigade", 19 May 2000.
8 http://www.seg-wiesbaden.de/PDF/GB1999.pdf, "Neues Wohngebiet ‚Auf der Heide'", September 2000.
9 Landeshauptstadt Wiesbaden Konversionsprojekt "Camp Lindsey", (two parts) Stadtentwicklungsgesellschaft Wiesbaden mbH, 1998.
10 *Mainzer Rheinzeitung*, „Camp Lindsey besser als sein Ruf", 11 July 1995.
11 Stadtentwicklungsgesellschaft Wiesbaden mbH. Landeshauptstadt Wiesbaden. Konversionsprojekt „Camp Lindsey". Von der Kaserne zum neuen Europaviertel. Wege moderner Stadtteilentwicklung. Teil 2. 4 February 1997, 1.
12 EXNER: US-Truppen-Reduzierungen, Letter to Bundestag representative Norbert Wieczorek from Exner, 17 March 1993.

ILLUSTRATION SOURCES

p. 23: Lt. L.T. Brezan, U.S. Army Signal Corps (From the collection of Ronald M.A. Hirst); **p. 30:** StadtA Wi Best. WI/3 Nr. 19; **p. 41:** StadtA Wi 004248; **pp. 47–48:** National Archives and Records Administration, Maryland; **p. 52:** Harold G. Scholl (From the collection of Ronald M.A. Hirst); **p. 57:** StadtA Wi 004253; **p. 58:** StadtA Wi Best. WI/3 Nr. 22; **p. 64:** From the collection of Ronald M.A. Hirst; **p. 65:** StadtA Wi 004254; **p. 67:** Gisela Mieschel; **p. 69:** Wiesbadener Kurier, 8 June 1946; **pp. 73–75:** From the collection of Ronald M.A. Hirst; **p. 84**: Emil Jörg (By courtesy of Dr. Thomas Brasser); **p. 91:** Center for Air Force History, Washington, D.C., 7101 unit history; **p. 93:** StadtA Wi 003484; **p. 96:** StadtA Wi Best. NL 35; **p. 97:** Wolfgang Eckhardt; **p. 101:** StadtA Wi 000954; **p. 107:** StadtA Wi 003245; **pp. 109–110:** StadtA Wi Best. WI/3 Nr. 19; **p. 114:** By courtesy of Dr. Thomas Brasser; **p. 121:** Wiesbadener Tagblatt, 6/7 February 1971; **p. 133:** Wiesbaden Post, 16 January 1970; **p. 138:** Wiesbadener Kurier, 7 July 1972; **p. 141:** StadtA Wi Best. NL 75 Nr. 1191; **p. 144:** Wolfgang Eckhardt; **p. 147:** StadtA Wi Best. NL 35; **pp. 159, 160, 165:** Wolfgang Eckhardt; **p. 180:** StadtA Wi 003255; **p. 182:** 1. Lt. A.T. Gilroy (From the collection of Ronald M.A. Hirst); **p. 184, 185, 193:** StadtA Wi Best. NL 76; **p. 200:** BI-info N° 45, January 1999; **p. 202:** From the collection of Ronald M.A. Hirst; **p. 203:** Wolfgang Eckhardt.

ACRONYMS

4ATAF	4th Allied Tactical Air Force
ABW	Air Base Wing
ACC	American Community Center
ADA	Air Defense Artillery
AG	Arbeitsgemeinschaft
ARC	American Red Cross
ASG	Area Support Group
ATC	Air Transport Command
ATSC	Air Traffic Services Consulting
AVF	All-Volunteer Force
AWOL	Absent Without Leave
BBU	Bundesverband der Bürgerinitiativen Umweltschutz
BI	Bürgerinitiative
BVM	Bundesverteidigungsministerium
CCC	Central Collection Center
CDU	Christlich Demokratische Union
CPO	Civilian Personnel Office
CRP	Cost Reduction Program
DM	Deutsche Mark
DoD	Department of Defense
DoDDS	Department of Defense Dependent Schools
DP	Displaced Person
EATS	European Air Transport Service
EES	European Exchange Service
EUCOM	European Command
FAG	Frankfurt Airport
FDP	Freie Demokratische Partei
FRG	Federal Republic of Germany
GYA	German Youth Activities
HICOG	[U.S.] High Commander of Germany
I&E	[Troop] Information and Education

LAS	Lindsey Air Station
MG	Military Government
MVOB	Motor Vehicle Operations Branch
NATO	North Atlantic Treaty Organization
NTS	NATO Troop Statute
OIS/OI	Office of Information Services/Office of Information
OMG(G)H	Office of Military Government, (Greater) Hesse
OMGUS	Office of Military Government, United States
PAO	Public Affairs Office
PIO	Public Information Office
PW	Prisoner of War
PWOC	Protestant Women of the Chapel
PX/BX	Post Exchange/Base Exchange
RB	Regierungsbezirk
REDCOSTE	Reduction of Cost and Forces in Europe
SK	Stadtkreis
SPD	Sozialdemokratische Partei Deutschlands
UN	United Nations
UNRRA	United Nations Relief and Rehabilitation Administration
USAFE	United States Air Forces, Europe
USAREUR	U.S. Army Europe
USFET	United States Forces, European Theater
VD	Venereal Disease
WAAF	Wiesbaden Army Airfield
WAB	Wiesbaden Air Base
WAC	Women's Army Corps
WAF	Women in the Air Force
WARCOM	Wiesbaden Armed Forces Community
WCC	War Crimes Commission
WMP	Wiesbaden Military Post
ZI	Zone of the Interior

Citation Abbreviations

National Archives at College Park, College Park, MD

AGO: War Department, The Adjutant General's Office, Washington, War Department Records Branch, A.G.O. Historical Records Section; 80th Infantry Division; RG 94 (The Adjutant General's Office: WWII Operations Reports, 1940–1948).

ETOUSA: General Correspondence 1944—46; HQ Command Wiesbaden Detachment, European Theater, U.S. Army; RG338 (Records of United States Army Commands 1942 –).

HESS1: Hesse Historical Report (October 45 – June 46) Vol. I Sections 4–14; The Control Office: Historical Reports of OMG, Hesse 1945–49; Records of the Executive Office; RG 260 (OMGUS).

HESS2: Hesse Historical Report (July 46 – December 46) The Control Office: Historical Reports of OMG, Hesse 1945–49; Records of the Executive Office; RG 260 (OMGUS).

HESS3: Hesse Historical Report (January 47 – March 47) The Control Office: Historical Reports of OMG, Hesse 1945–49; Records of the Executive Office; RG 260 (OMGUS).

HESS4: Hesse Historical Report (April 47 – June 47) The Control Office: Historical Reports of OMG, Hesse 1945–49; Records of the Executive Office; RG 260 (OMGUS).

HESS5: Hesse Historical Report (1 July 47 – 30 September 47) The Control Office: Historical Reports of OMG, Hesse 1945–49; Records of the Executive Office; RG 260 (OMGUS).

HESS6: Hesse Historical Report (1 January 47 – 31 March 47) The Control Office: Historical Reports of OMG, Hesse 1945–49; Records of the Executive Office; RG 260 (OMGUS).

IOT: Inspections and Organizations and Troops General Correspondence 1944–1946; HQ Command, Wiesbaden Detachment, European Theater, U.S. Army; RG338 (Records of United States Army Commands 1942–).

PIR 1: Political Intelligence Reports – Wiesbaden 6 June 45 – 15 March 47; Political Intelligence Reports Wiesbaden June 45 through Political Intelligence Reports – Bad Nauheim November 46; The Intelligence Division: Correspondence and Other Records, 1945–49; Records of Office of Military Government, Hesse; RG 260.

United Nations Archives, New York, NY

UNRRA1: Team 615 – Wiesbaden; Box 49; "Unorganized Series"; Germany Mission: Unites States Zone, Area Teams; UNRRA.

UNRRA 2: District 2: Monthly Reports to Zone Director UNRRA Headquarters; Box 9; District Files; Germany Mission: United States Zone District Operation and Administration; UNRRA.

Stadtarchiv Wiesbaden

USAFE: Unit Histories of Headquarters Command, USAFE, 1946–58.

WK: *Wiesbadener Kurier.*

WT: *Wiesbadener Tagblatt.*

EXNER: Papers of Oberbürgermeister Achim Exner (Best. NL 76).

Public Affairs Office, Wiesbaden Military Community

WP: *Wiesbaden Post* – weekly base newspaper published for American forces.

Bibliography

Abelshauser, Werner. *Wirtschaft in Westdeutschland 1945–1946: Rekonstruktion und Wachstumsbedingungen in der amerikanischen und britischen Zone*. Stuttgart: Deutsche Verlags-Anstalt, 1975.

Archey, Walter J., Jr. *A Brief History of the Black Officer in the United States Air Force (1947–1975)*. Research Study for Air Command and Staff College, Air University, Maxwell AFB, Alabama, May 1976.

Backer, John H. *Winds of History: The German Years of Lucius DuBignon Clay*. New York: Van Nostrand Reinhold Company, 1983.

Beier, Gerhard. *SPD Hessen: Chronik 1945 bis 1988*. Bonn: Dietz, 1989.

Bembenek, Lothar and Axel Ulrich. *Widerstand und Verfolgung in Wiesbaden 1933–1945: Eine Dokumentation*. Gießen: Anabas-Verlag, 1990.

Benz, Wolfgang, ed. *Die Bundesrepublik Deutschland*. 3 vols. Frankfurt am Main: Fischer Taschenbuch Verlag, 1983.

Benz, Wolfgang. *Potsdam 1945: Besatzungsherrschaft und Neuaufbau im Vier-Zonen-Deutschland*. München: Deutscher Taschenbuch Verlag, 1986.

------. *Zwischen Hitler und Adenauer: Studien zur deutschen Nachkriegsgesellschaft*. Frankfurt am Main: Fischer Taschenbuch, 1991.

Beusse, William E. "Perceptions of equal opportunity and race relations among military personnel." Brooks AFB, Tex: Department of Defense, Dept of the AF, AF System Command, AF Human Resources Laboratory, 1976.

------. "Factors related to the incidence of disciplinary actions among enlisted personnel." Brooks AFB, Tex: Department of Defense, Dept of the AF, AF System Command, AF Human Resources Laboratory, 1977.

Botting, Douglas. *From the Ruins of the Reich: Germany, 1945–1949*. New York: Crown Publishers Inc., 1985.

Botzenhart-Viehe, Verena. *The German Reaction to the American Occupation, 1944–1947*. USC Santa Barbara, 1980.

Bower, Tom. *The Pledge Betrayed: America and Britain and the Denazification of Postwar Germany*. Garden City, N.Y.: Doubleday, 1982, c1981.

Bracher, Karl Dietrich, et al. *Republik im Wandel, 1969–1974, Die Ära Brandt*. Vol. 5/1 of *Geschichte der Bundesrepublik Deutschland*. Stuttgart: Deutsche Verlags-Anstalt; Wiesbaden; Brockhaus, 1986.

Braun, Hans-Joachim. *The German Economy in the Twentieth Century: The German Reich and the Federal Republic*. London and New York: Routledge, 1990.

Burns, Rob and Wilfried van der Will. *Protest and Democracy in West Germany: Extra-Parliamentary Opposition and the Democratic Agenda*. New York: St. Martin's Press, 1988.

Clay, Lucius D. *Decision in Germany*. Garden City, NY: Doubleday, 1950.

Cleveland, Harlan. *NATO: The Transatlantic Bargain*. New York: Harper and Row Publishers, 1970.

Coates, Charles and Roland Pellegrin. *Military Sociology*. University Park, MD: Social Science Press, 1965.

Connolly, John M. *The U.S. Air Force Information Officer Overseas: A Need for Special Applications of Information Technology*. M.S. Thesis, Boston University, 1964.

Cortright, David. *Soldiers in Revolt*. New York: Doubleday, 1975.

Cottrell, Alvin J. and Thomas H. Moorer. *U.S. Overseas Bases: Problems of Projecting American Military Power Abroad*. Beverly Hills, CA: Sage Publications, 1977.

Davis, Franklin M. Jr. *Come as a Conqueror: The United States Army's Occupation of Germany, 1945–1949*. New York: Macmillan Co., 1967.

Dollinger, Hans, *Deutschland unter den Besatzungsmächten, 1945–1949: Seine Geschichte in Texten, Bildern und Dokumenten*. München: K. Desch, 1967.

Duke, Simon. *United States Military Forces and Installations in Europe*. New York: Oxford University Press, 1989.

------. *U.S. Military Forces in Europe: The Early Years, 1945–1970*. Boulder: Westview Press, 1993.

Düwell, Kurt. *Entstehung und Entwicklung der Bundesrepublik Deutschland 1945-1961*. Köln: Böhlau, 1981.

Emig, Erik. *Georg Buch: Leben und Wirken eines Sozialdemokraten*. Bonn: Courir, 1983.

Eschenburg, Theodor, ed. *Geschichte der Bundesrepublik Deutschland*. Stuttgart: Deutsche Verlags-Anstalt, 1983.

Gatzke, Hans Wilhelm. *Germany and the United States, A "Special Relationship?"*. Cambridge, Mass: Harvard University Press, 1980.

Gerson, Joseph and Bruce Birchard. *The Sun Never Sets: Confronting the Network of U.S. Foreign Military Bases*. Boston: South End Press, 1991.

Gimbel, John. *The American Occupation of Germany: Politics and the Military, 1945-1949*. Stanford, CA: Stanford University Press, 1968.

------. *A German Community Under American Occupation: Marburg, 1945-52*. Stanford, CA: Stanford University Press, 1961.

------. *The Origins of the Marshall Plan*. Stanford, CA: Stanford University Press, 1976.

Glaeßner, Gert-Joachim et al. *Die Bundesrepublik in den siebziger Jahren. Versuch einer Bilanz*. Opladen: Leske & Biedrich, 1998.

Glaser, Heike. *Demokratischer Neubeginn in Wiesbaden: Aspekte des sozialen, wirtschaftlichen und politischen Wiederaufbaus nach 1945*. Wiesbaden: Magistrat der Landeshauptstadt Wiesbaden – Stadtarchiv, 1995.

Glatzer, Wolfgang et al. *Recent Social Trends in West Germany 1960-1990*. Frankfurt am Main: Campus Verlag; Montreal and Kingston, London, Buffalo: McGill-Queen's University Press, 1992.

Goedde, Petra. *GIs and Germans: Culture, Gender and Foreign Relations, 1945-1949*. New Haven, CT: Yale University Press, 2002.

Gravois, Martha. *Hot Dogs, Apple Pie and Wiener Schnitzel: Army Families in Germany (1946-1986)*. (n.p.), 1986.

Grube, Frank and Gerhard Richter. *Die Schwarzmarktzeit: Deutschland zwischen 1945 und 1948*. Hamburg: Hoffmann und Campe, 1979.

Hanrieder, Wolfram F. *Germany, America, Europe: Forty Years of German Foreign Policy*. New Haven: Yale University Press, 1989.

------. *The Stable Crisis: Two Decades of German Foreign Policy*. New York: Harper & Row, 1970.

------. *West German Foreign Policy, 1949–1979*. Boulder, CO: Westview Press, 1980.

Harkavy, Robert E. *Bases Abroad: The Global Foreign Military Presence*. New York: 1989.

Hauser, William L. *America's Army in Crisis: A Study in Civil-Military Relations*. Baltimore: Johns Hopkins University Press, 1973.

Hildebrand, Klaus et al. *Von Erhard zur Großen Koalition 1963–1969*. Stuttgart: Deutsche Verlags-Anstalt, 1995.

Hirst, R.M.A. *Ninety Years at Lindsey or How to Goldplate an Antique*. 3 vol. Unpublished mss. 1987.

Hoffmann, Daniel. *Truppenstationierung in der Bundesrepublik Deutschland. Die Vertragsverhandlungen mit den Westmächten 1951–1959*. München: R. Oldenbourg Verlag, 1997.

Höhn, Maria. *GIs, Veronikas and Lucky Strikes: German Reactions to the American Presence in the Rhineland-Palatinate during the 1950s*. Doctoral dissertation, University of Pennsylvania, 1995.

Ingraham, Larry. *The Boys in the Barracks: Observations on Military Life*. Philadelphia: Institute for the Study of Human Issues, 1984.

Krieger, Wolfgang, *General Lucius D. Clay und die amerikanische Deutschlandpolitik, 1945–1949*. Stuttgart: Klett-Cotta, 1987.

Kröller, Wilhelm. *Chronik der Stadt Wiesbaden: Über das Schicksalsjahr 1945*. 2 vol. Wiesbaden: mss, 1945/46.

Kropat, Wolf-Arno. *Hessen in der Stunde Null 1945–1947. Politik, Wirtschaft und Bildungswesen in Dokumenten*. Wiesbaden: Selbstverlag der Historischen Kommission für Nassau, 1979.

Latour, Conrad F. and Thilo Vogelsang. *Okkupation und Wiederaufbau: Die Tätigkeit der Militärregierung in der amerikanischen Besatzungszone Deutschlands, 1944–1947*. Stuttgart: Deutsche Verlags-Anstalt, 1973.

Lenz, Walter. *An Analysis of the USAF System for Recruiting Enlisted Personnel*. Maxwell AFB; US Air University, Air War College, 1975.

Leuerer, Thomas. *Die Stationierung amerikanischer Streitkräfte in Deutschland. Militärgemeinden der U.S. Army in Deutschland seit 1945 als ziviles Element der Stationierungspolitik der Vereinigten Staaten*. Ergon Verlag, 1997.

Madison, John Harvey. *United States Military Presence in Germany: Past Commitments and Present Outlook*. M.S. Thesis, George Washington University, 1970.

Malzahn, Manfred. *Germany 1945-1949: A Sourcebook*. London and New York: Routledge, 1991.

Mendershausen, Horst. *Troop Stationing in Germany: Value and Cost*. Santa Monica, CA: Rand Corporation for the USAF, December, 1968.

Merritt, Anna. *Public Opinion in Occupied Germany: the OMGUS Surveys, 1945-1949*. Urbana: University of Illinois Press, 1970.

------. *Public Opinion in Semisovereign Germany: the HICOG Surveys, 1949-1955*. Urbana: University of Illinois Press, 1979.

Morgan, Roger. *The United States and West Germany, 1945-1973*. New York: Oxford University Press, 1974.

Moskos, Charles. *The American Enlisted Man: The Rank and File in Today's Military*. New York: Russell Sage Foundation, 1970.

Müller-Werth, Herbert. *Geschichte und Kommunalpolitik der Stadt Wiesbaden. Unter besonderer Berücksichtigung der letzten 150 Jahre*. Wiesbaden: Franz Steiner Verlag, 1963.

NATO Handbook. Brussels: NATO Information Service, 1980.

Nelson, Daniel J. *A History of U.S. Military Forces in Germany*. Boulder and London: Westview Press, 1987.

------. *Defenders or Intruders? The Dilemmas of U.S. Forces in Germany*. Boulder and London: Westview Press, 1987.

Newhouse, John. *U.S. Troops in Europe: Issues, Costs and Choices*. Washington, DC: The Brookings Institution, 1971.

Noelle, Elisabeth and Erich Peter Neumann, eds. *The Germans: Public Opinion Polls 1947–1966*. Bonn: Verlag für Demoskopie, Allensbach, 1967.

Owen-Smith, Eric. *The West German Economy*. New York: St. Martin's Press, 1983.

Peterson, Edward. *The American Occupation of Germany: Retreat to Victory*. Detroit: Wayne State University Press, 1977.

Pollock, J.K. and H. H. Meisel. *Germany Under Occupation: Illustrative Materials and Documents*. Ann Arbor: University of Michigan Press, 1947.

Rupieper, Hermann-Josef. *Die Wurzeln der westdeutschen Nachkriegsdemokratie: Der amerikanische Beitrag 1945–1952*. Opladen: Westdeutscher Verlag, 1993.

Schlange-Schöningen, Hans, ed. *Im Schatten des Hungers. Dokumentarisches zur Ernährungspolitik und Ernährungswirtschaft in den Jahren 1945–1949*. Hamburg: P. Parey, 1955.

Schmidt-Eenboom, Erich and Barbara Dietrich. *Die militärischen Strukturen in der Hessischen Landeshauptstadt*. FF Kurzstudie, Weilheim: Staricha, 1987.

Schmidt-Eenboom, Erich and Jo Angerer, et al. *Amerikanische Freunde: die Politik der US-Streitkräfte in der Bundesrepublik*. Frankfurt am Main: Luchterhand, 1990.

Schmitt, Hans A. (ed.). *U.S. Occupation in Europe After World War II*: papers and reminiscences from the April 23–24, 1976, conference held at the George C. Marshall Research Foundation, Lexington, Virginia. Lawrence: Regents Press of Kansas, 1978.

Schott, Herbert. *Die Amerikaner als Besatzungsmacht in Würzburg (1945–1949)*. Würzburg: Freunde Mainfränkischer Kunst und Geschichte; 1985.

Seile, Signe. *Die GIs: Amerikanische Soldaten in Deutschland*. Reinbek bei Hamburg: Rowohlt, 1985.

Shea, Nancy. *What Every AF Wife Should Know*. 3rd edition. Harrisburg, PA: Stackpole Books, 1966.

Smith, Jean Edward, ed. *The Papers of General Lucius D, Clay: Germany 1945-1949*, vol. 1 and 2. Bloomington and London: Indiana University Press. 1974.

Spoo, Eckert. *Die Amerikaner in der Bundesrepublik: Besatzungsmacht oder Bündnispartner?* Köln: Kiepenheuer & Witsch, 1989.

Stambuck, George. *American Military Forces Abroad*. Columbus: Ohio State University Press, 1963.

Tent, James F. *Mission on the Rhine: "Reeducation" and Denazification in American-Occupied Germany*. Chicago: University of Chicago Press, 1982.

Traendly, Jayne E. *The History of Wiesbaden Medical Center*. Wiesbaden: The Medical Center, 1993.

Treverton, G.F. *The 'Dollar Drain' and American Forces in Germany*. Athens: Ohio University Press, 1978.

Trittel, Guenter J. *Hunger und Politik: Die Ernährungskrise in der Bizone (1945-1949)*. Frankfurt: Campus Verlag, 1990.

Truitt, Wesley Byron. *The Troops to Europe Decision: The Process, Politics, and Diplomacy of a Strategic Commitment*. Doctoral dissertation, Columbia University, 1968.

United States Department of State Historical Office. *Documents on Germany, 1944-1961*. Committee on Foreign Relations, United States Senate. New York: Greenwood Press, 1968.

United States GPO. *Military Damage Claims in Germany – A Growing Burden: Report to the Chairman, Committee on Appropriations, House of Representatives*. Washington, DC: U.S. GPO, 1980.

Weichel, Thomas. *"Wenn dann der Kaiser nicht mehr kommt...". Kommunalpolitik und Arbeiterbewegung in Wiesbaden 1890-1914*. Wiesbaden: Stadtarchiv, 1991.

Wertsch, Mary Edwards. *Military Brats: Legacies of Childhood inside the Fortress*. New York: Fawcett Columbine, 1991.

Willett, Ralph. *The Americanization of Germany, 1945-1949*. London, New York: Routledge, 1989.

Wolf, Charlotte. *Garrison Community: A Study of an Overseas American Military Colony*. Westport, CT: Greenwood, 1969.

WPU-Geschichte, Elly-Heuss-Schule o.O. "'Chewing-gum, cigarettes and no fraternisation:' Wiesbadener über den Nachkriegsalltag." Wiesbaden: Selbstverlag, 1987.

Ziemke, Earl. *The US Army in the Occupation of Germany*. Washington, DC: Office of Military History, 1975.

Zink, Harold. *The United States in Germany 1944–1955*. New York: Van Nostrand, 1957.